The Bible in Literature Courses

Biblical Images in Literature

Edited by Roland Bartel
with James S. Ackerman
and Thayer S. Warshaw

NASHVILLE ABINGDON PRESS NEW YORK

BIBLICAL IMAGES IN LITERATURE

Copyright © 1975 by Abingdon Press

Library of Congress Cataloging in Publication Data

Main entry under title:
Biblical images in literature.
  (The Bible in literature courses)
  Includes index.
  1. Bible in literature—Addresses, essays, lectures. I. Bartel,
Roland. II. Series: Bible in literature courses.

PN 56.B5B5   820'.9'31   75-14171

ISBN 0-687-03439-6

Biblical quotations in Part 1, Chs. 8, 9, and 16, and Part 3, Chs. 1 and 9, unless otherwise noted, are from the Revised Standard Version of the Bible, copyrighted 1946, 1952, and 1971, by the Division of Christian Education, National Council of Churches, and are used by permission.

Acknowledgment is made to the following for permission to reprint copyrighted material quoted within the various chapters:

Mark E. Cassidy for the dialogue quoted on pp. 368-70.

The Christian Century Foundation for three poems which originally appeared in *The Christian Century:* "Simon the Cyrenian Speaks" by Glen Baker (July 20, 1938 issue), copyright 1938 Christian Century Foundation, reprinted by permission; "Simon of Cyrene" by Georgia Harkness (April 12, 1933 issue), copyright 1933 Christian Century Foundation, reprinted by permission of The Christian Century Foundation and the Executors of the Estate of Georgia Harkness; "Men Follow Simon" by Raymond Kresensky (April 14, 1927 issue), copyright 1927 Christian Century Foundation, reprinted by permission of The Christian Century Foundation and Mildred Kresensky Allen.

Delacorte Press / Seymour Lawrence for material excerpted from *Slaughterhouse-Five,* by Kurt Vonnegut, Jr., copyright © 1969 by Kurt Vonnegut, Jr. Reprinted by arrangement with Delacorte Press / Seymour Lawrence and Jonathan Cape Ltd.

Harcourt Brace Jovanovich, Inc., and Faber and Faber Ltd. for "Journey of the Magi," from *Complete Poems 1909–1962* by T. S. Eliot, copyright, 1936, by Harcourt Brace Jovanovich, Inc.; copyright, 1963, 1964, by T. S. Eliot. Reprinted by permission of the publishers.

MANUFACTURED BY THE PARTHENON PRESS AT NASHVILLE, TENNESSEE, UNITED STATES OF AMERICA

Contents

Preface by James S. Ackerman and Thayer S. Warshaw   9

Introduction by Roland Bartel   13

Part One: The Bible in Fiction

    I. HAWTHORNE'S USE OF THE BIBLE IN *THE SCARLET LETTER* by Roland Bartel   19

    II. ALLEGORY IN "RAPPACCINI'S DAUGHTER" by Oliver Evans   23

    III. MELVILLE'S USE OF THE BIBLE IN *BILLY BUDD* by Roland Bartel   30

    IV. MELVILLE'S USE OF THE BIBLE IN *MOBY-DICK* by Nathalia Wright   36

    V. PATON'S USE OF THE BIBLE IN *CRY, THE BELOVED COUNTRY* by Roland Bartel   65

    VI. *THE MAYOR OF CASTERBRIDGE* AND THE OLD TESTAMENT'S FIRST BOOK OF SAMUEL: A STUDY OF SOME LITERARY RELATIONSHIPS by Julian Moynahan   71

    VII. THE BIBLICAL LAYER IN FRANZ KAFKA'S SHORT STORY "A COUNTRY DOCTOR" by Hillel Barzel   89

    VIII. THE THEME OF THE FALL IN ALBERT CAMUS' *THE FALL* by William R. Mueller   103

    IX. THE FUNCTION OF CHRISTIAN IMAGERY IN *THE FALL* by Sandy Petrey   109

    X. THE HUMOR OF THE ABSURD: MARK TWAIN'S ADAMIC DIARIES by Stanley Brodwin   118

    XI. BIBLICAL INTERPRETATION IN *HUCKLEBERRY FINN*, CHAPTER 14 by Stuart Lewis   134

    XII. *OF MICE AND MEN:* JOHN STEINBECK'S PARABLE OF THE CURSE OF CAIN by William Goldhurst   137

XIII. THE BRAND OF CAIN IN "THE SECRET SHARER"
by Porter Williams, Jr.   148

XIV. THE RENDING OF THE VEIL IN W. E. B. DU
BOIS'S *THE SOULS OF BLACK FOLK*
by Jerold J. Savory   154

XV. HEMINGWAY'S ANCIENT MARINER
by Carlos Baker   158

XVI. THE IRONIC CHRIST FIGURE IN
SLAUGHTERHOUSE-FIVE
by Dolores K. Gros Louis   161

XVII. CHRIST FIGURES IN MODERN LITERATURE: AN
ANNOTATED BIBLIOGRAPHY
by Dolores K. Gros Louis   176

XVIII. BRIEF COMMENTS ON OTHER WORKS OF FIC-
TION WITH BIBLICAL ALLUSIONS
by Roland Bartel   179

A. "Flowering Judas," Katherine Anne Porter   179
B. "Judas," Frank O'Connor   183
C. "Judas," John Brunner   184
D. *A Separate Peace*, John Knowles   185
E. *The Pearl*, John Steinbeck   187
F. "By the Waters of Babylon,"
Stephen Vincent Benet   188
G. "Exodus," James Baldwin   190

Part Two: The Bible in Poetry

INTRODUCTION by Roland Bartel   195

I. WILFRED OWEN
TEACHING WILFRED OWEN'S WAR POEMS AND
THE BIBLE by Roland Bartel   198

II. COUNTEE CULLEN
(with Commentary by Roland Bartel)   210

III. A. E. HOUSMAN
(with Commentary by Roland Bartel)   222

IV. ARNA BONTEMPS
(with Commentary by Roland Bartel)   228

V. T. S. ELIOT
A BRIEF INTERPRETATION OF "JOURNEY OF
THE MAGI" by Elizabeth Drew   235

VI. KARL SHAPIRO
KARL SHAPIRO'S "ADAM AND EVE"
by Frederick Eckman   239

VII. HENRY WADSWORTH LONGFELLOW   249

VIII. VACHEL LINDSAY   257

IX. EDGAR LEE MASTERS   260

X. EDWIN MUIR   265

XI. D. H. LAWRENCE   272

XII. THE BIBLE IN NEGRO SPIRITUALS
by Roland Bartel   279

XIII. TWO BIBLICAL PASSAGES THAT HAVE AP-
PEALED TO POETS
(with Commentary by Roland Bartel)   284

     A. SIMON THE CYRENIAN   284
     B. PETER'S DENIAL OF JESUS   286

Part Three: The Bible in Drama

I. BIBLICAL ANGELS AND ENGLISH SHEPHERDS:
THE GOSPEL TRADITION IN *THE SECOND
SHEPHERDS' PLAY*
by C. Clifford Flanigan   297

II. SHAKESPEARE'S USE OF SCRIPTURE
by Edna Moore Robinson   308

III. CHRISTOPHER FRY'S USE OF THE BIBLE IN *A
SLEEP OF PRISONERS*
by John H. Hafner   320

IV. BIBLICAL PERVERSIONS IN *DESIRE UNDER
THE ELMS* by Peter L. Hays   327

V. HOW GENUINE IS *THE GREEN PASTURES?*
by Nick Aaron Ford   335

VI. *THE GREEN PASTURES* AGAIN
by Doris B. Garey   340

VII. MACLEISH'S *J.B.* by Murray Roston   344

VIII. MACLEISH'S *J.B.*—IS IT A MODERN *JOB?*
by W. D. White   353

IX. TEACHING *JOB* AND *J.B.*
by Ruth D. Hallman   364

X. ABOUT A TRESPASS ON A MONUMENT
by Archibald MacLeish   373

INDEX TO BIBLICAL TEXTS
ALLUDED TO OR DISCUSSED   379

Preface

Reading literature, no less than writing it, is a creative act. The author counts on the creative participation of his reader, expecting him to read actively, consciously or subliminally—especially when metaphors and allusions are encountered. The reader enhances this creative experience by bringing to the literature his own knowledge of the world and of its cultural achievements. Among the most important achievements of Western culture is the Bible, and it is not surprising that it finds its way so often into our literature.

Surveys are regularly conducted among college literature departments, asking what books students should have assimilated as background for literature. Each time the Bible comes out at the top of the list. Until ten years ago, not much was done in secondary schools to fill this need; even in colleges many English departments had let their Bible courses languish. Among the agents of change was, peculiarly, the United States Supreme Court. Its decisions of the 1960s forbade prayers and devotional Bible reading in public schools; its opinions, however, encouraged study of the Bible as a secular subject.

There has been of late an increasing awareness of the Bible's importance to any study of literature. The Bible itself is literature, and much of it is carefully crafted writing; but it is also a pervasive influence upon writers. Secondary school literature courses (and anthologies for these courses) increasingly include biblical selections, both as examples of literature and as sources whose reverberations abound in other literature. Elective courses proliferate, focusing on the Bible *as* literature and the Bible *in* literature.

This book is the second volume in the series The Bible in Literature Courses, which has grown out of five years of our summer institute program at Indiana University for teachers of secondary school English. Initiated by the university's Department of Religious Studies and generously funded by the Lilly Endowment, Inc., the institute has included on its staff several literary scholars and educational consultants, to serve and to learn from over three hundred teachers from every part of the country.

The first volume, *Literary Interpretations of Biblical Narratives*, examined the Bible *as* literature. The present book deals with the Bible *in* literature. Roland Bartel has had a long-standing interest in the relationship between the Bible and Western literature. His position as chairman of the Department of English at the University of Oregon, his association with the university's secondary school teacher education program, and his visit to our institute as a lecturer make him a most fortunate choice as editor of this book. In addition to his own contributions he has drawn together critical essays from many sources, covering a wide variety of literature, always with an eye to the secondary school classroom.

Through his introductory essay and the articles he has chosen, Mr. Bartel has made a major contribution toward giving specific definition to the scope of the amorphous "Bible in literature" field. To have included literature that does not use biblical imagery centrally but is related to the Bible only in theme would have been to broaden the field too much at one end (e.g., tying *Candide* to the book of Job because both works consider unmerited suffering). Nearly every human theme appears somewhere in the Bible, so that such a broadening of scope would have justified relating nearly all of literature to the Bible. At the other end, it was thought appropriate to exclude literature in which the biblical imagery is not central or thematic but appears only as a passing, footnotable allusion, as in most of Shakespeare.

Mr. Bartel takes the area between these extremes,

where the connection is both clearly biblical and clearly thematic. The area is wide enough for considerable range. In some cases the setting and characters are biblical, as with Twain's Adamic diaries. In other instances the biblical layer is a subtle undertone in an otherwise completely modern story, as in *Slaughterhouse-Five*. *The Second Shepherds' Play* lies somewhere in between.

This book makes other attempts at variety apart from the number of ways in which authors use biblical imagery. Our selection of what is currently taught in secondary schools leans heavily toward American literature, but it does include some modern European literature and some from earlier periods. We have also tried to provide a range, both in genre and in levels of ability and maturity demanded of students.

Since the book is an innovative venture, we are quite aware that we have made only a start. Far more than is the usual case with anthologies or collections of essays, we regret the omissions—analyses of the Bible's influence upon many other pieces of Western literature appropriate for secondary school courses. We hope that teachers and other readers will be inspired to branch out from this book on their own. We also hope that literary scholars will continue to produce critical analyses of thematic biblical imagery in literature useful for the classroom.

We wish to thank Jo Ann Carlton and Nancy Loker, administrative assistants in our institute, for efficiently following through on the many and varied tasks involved in preparing this volume. And once more we express our appreciation to our respective wives, Alexandra and Bernice, for their support—far beyond the legal or moral obligations of their marriage vows.

James S. Ackerman
Thayer S. Warshaw

Introduction

This book has been prepared for students and teachers of literature who would like some help when they come across biblical allusions in a literary work. All the articles included here—those written specifically for this book and those first published elsewhere—have the same purpose: they examine the effect of the Bible on selected works of literature. They are not studies of the general influence of the Bible, but close analyses of the ways authors have used specific parts of the Bible in developing the theme and form of their novels, short stories, poems, and plays.

In selecting the material for this book, I was guided by several considerations. The articles had to deal with literature that can be taught in English classes. The biblical element in the literary work had to be significant enough to warrant extended discussion rather than footnotes. The articles had to appeal to teachers and general students of literature who are interested in getting as much as possible out of a work of literature. Finally, both the articles and the works of literature had to deal with identifiable parts of the Bible rather than with general biblical themes and concepts. Thus one might argue that all literature dealing with the creation or the fall of man is ultimately related to the Bible. I have included discussions of such literature only if it contained unmistakable references to the book of Genesis.

As I explored the many ways in which the Bible has entered into our literature, I soon concluded that it has made its greatest impact in the form of allusions. This is not to say that novels, plays, and poems that retell, expand, or paraphrase parts of the Bible are without interest. By comparing such literary works with the Bible—Thomas Mann's novels about Joseph, Zora Hurston's novels about Moses and Jonah, Sholem Asch's novels about Paul and Jesus, Lord Byron's poems about the Old Testament in *Hebrew Melodies*—we can learn a great deal about both the Bible and literature. The number of such works is seemingly endless, and they constitute a major tribute to the literary influence of the Bible. Yet I find a greater significance in effective biblical allusions. The fact that authors dealing with secular materials rely on the Bible to drive home a thematic point or a character trait suggests how indispensable the Bible has become to the formation and understanding of our literature. These allusions also test the author's ability to integrate and harmonize diverse materials. With very few exceptions, the literary works analyzed in this book utilize the Bible by means of allusions rather than by retelling or adaptation.

Each of the articles in this book demonstrates that studying biblical allusions is an effective way of opening up a work of literature. A successful allusion operates like a metaphor. It is, in fact, an implied comparison in that it invites the reader to use his knowledge of the Bible to interpret the material before him. When Thoreau concludes one of his paragraphs in "Spring," the second last chapter of *Walden,* with the words "All things must live in such a light. O Death, where was thy sting: O Grave, where was thy victory, then?" we realize what the melting of the ice and the greening of the vegetation means to him. He culminates his effort to describe his thoughts and feelings about the coming of spring by borrowing the magnificent words that Paul used to describe his confidence in the resurrection (I Cor. 15:55). When Wallace Stevens says in his short poem "The Death of a Soldier" that the slain soldier "does not become a three-days personage," he also alludes to the resurrection, but his purpose is quite different from that of Thoreau. He does not borrow stately words from the Bible, nor does he allude to a memorable event in the Bible to exalt his own material. He refers to the resurrection of Christ for purposes of contrast: the soldier is no Christ figure; he will not rise from the dead and his death will not receive much notice. This allusion is effective because it is handled with restraint and is integrated into the idiom of the poem. Thoreau's allusion also fits into the style of its context. Having described his fascination with the coming of spring through several lyrical paragraphs, Thoreau appropriately concludes his description with the eloquent words and concept of Paul.

These examples illustrate the importance of examining the function of an allusion. Is it used in the same way as it is used in the Bible (Thoreau), or is it adapted to serve quite a different purpose (Stevens)? Once this question has been answered, the allusion can then be studied like any other literary device. What is its function? Does it apply only to its immediate context, or does it reverberate throughout the literary work? What, if anything, would be missed if it were not recognized? Has it been handled with enough subtlety to stimulate the imagination, or is it a routine embellishment? What are the similarities and differences between the biblical context and the new context in which the allusion appears? Is it so conspicuous that it detracts from the new context, or does it fit smoothly into its new surroundings?

In essay number 421, which Joseph Addison published in the *Spectator* on July 3, 1712, he discusses the contribution of allusions to the pleasures of the imagination. He says that the art of a writer shows itself in the successful use of an allusion, which, like a metaphor, "casts a kind of glory round it, and darts a lustre through a whole sentence." He recommends that since the purpose of an allusion is "to illustrate and explain the passages of an author, it should be always borrowed from what is more known and common than the passages which are to be explained." Unfortunately, Addison's advice no longer applies to the Bible; it is not so well known that allusions to it are self-explanatory.

I am deeply indebted to James S. Ackerman, Associate Professor of Religious Studies at Indiana University, and

Thayer S. Warshaw, English teacher in Newton High School, Newtonville, Massachusetts. They corrected my errors and suggested new insights in more places than I care to admit. I am also grateful to my wife, Betty, who supported this venture in every way she could.

Roland Bartel

Part One:
The Bible in Fiction

I Hawthorne's Use of the Bible in *The Scarlet Letter*

Roland Bartel

Department of English,
University of Oregon

Direct allusions to the Bible in *The Scarlet Letter* are actually not very numerous, yet no one would question the pervasive influence of the Bible on the novel. This influence is felt primarily in the language. The pronouns "thee," "thou," "thy," and "ye" give the novel a biblical tone, as do such phrases as "and it came to pass," "stood in their midst," "take no thought," "daily bread," "unto me," "fallen among thieves," "application of the rod, enjoined by Scriptural authority," and many others. Since the story takes place in colonial America soon after the publication of the King James translation of the Bible, the biblical echoes in the novel are not surprising. However, more than historical appropriateness is involved. The biblical tone often serves an ironic function: it magnifies the hypocrisy and self-righteousness of those who profess to safeguard the morals of the community.

Some of the allusions to the Bible help to clarify and intensify the material in the novel through implied similarities. Referring to Hester's badge as a brand of Cain (2, 3, 5, cf. Gen. 4)[1] relates her suffering for adultery to the suffering of the world's first murderer, an outcast who said, "My punishment is greater than I can bear." When we are told that the tapestry in Dimmesdale's library represents the story of David, Bathsheba, and Nathan (9, cf. II Sam. 11), we feel more strongly the gravity of Dimmesdale's secret sin. We assume that whenever Dimmesdale works on his sermons in the library, the tapestry will remind him of his own adultery and will thus intensify his suffering. We also assume that his secret sin will eventually have to be

[1] The numbers in parentheses refer to chapters in the novel and the chapters of the books of the Bible.

revealed, as David's was. We assume, finally, that although Chillingworth is no prophet, his effect on Dimmesdale will be similar to Nathan's effect on David. When the townsman tells Chillingworth that the details of Hester's sin are still unknown because no Daniel has arrived to explain the mystery (3, cf. Dan. 5), we see that in the eyes of Hester's neighbors her offense is as ominous as the handwriting on the wall. When we are told that Dimmesdale preaches with a tongue of flames (10, cf. Acts 2), we get a better understanding of his unusual eloquence—a pentecostal type of inspiration that the stolid older clergymen do not have.

Some allusions clarify and intensify through contrast rather than through similarity. The striking beauty of Hester and her baby is suggested by comparing them to the many paintings of the Madonna and Child, "but only by contrast, of that sacred image of sinless motherhood, whose infant was to redeem the world" (2, cf. Luke 1 and 2). In delivering his election day sermon Dimmesdale is as inspired as the prophets of Israel, but whereas the prophets concentrated on the coming judgment for Israel, Dimmesdale forecasts a glorious future for God's new settlement in America (23). This forecast of a New Jerusalem in America has an irony of its own. Chillingworth twice tells his patient Dimmesdale that saintly men belong in the New Jerusalem (9, 20, cf. Rev. 21). Such reminders aggravate the spiritual torture of Dimmesdale, for he knows that while he is describing the Puritan colony as the New Jerusalem, he is actually a secret blemish on the community.

Calling Hester's daughter a pearl of great price (6, cf. Matt. 13) is an allusion that suggests both contrast and similarity. The merchant in the parable exemplifies the value of the kingdom of heaven when he sacrifices all his lesser pearls for the one pearl of great price. Hester does not exemplify her society's concept of the kingdom of heaven when she commits her sin, yet she, like the merchant, sacrifices everything for a single possession. When the allusion is used a second time, it sharpens still further the contrast between Hester and the Puritans.

Preacher Wilson admonishes Pearl to learn the catechism and to consider it as a pearl of great price to be worn in her bosom. To mother and daughter, both of society's requirements for salvation, wearing the scarlet A and learning the catechism, are oppressive rather than redemptive.

Another example of emphasis through contrast occurs in the final platform scene. Dimmesdale tells the crowd that Hester's badge has always "cast a lurid gleam of awe and horrible repugnance round about her" (23). "Round about" is a common biblical phrase, but it is best known in connection with the Christmas story when "the glory of the Lord shone round about" the shepherds, announcing the birth of the Redeemer (Luke 2). What is gained by associating the gleam of repugnance round about Hester with the gleam of hope round about the shepherds? Quite a bit, if we are willing to go back through the novel and consider the possibility that to some extent Hester and Pearl serve a redemptive function in the story.

The complexity of Hester's role in the novel is suggested in part by several other biblical allusions associated with her. When we are told that she "forbore to pray for her enemies" (5, cf. Matt. 5) lest her prayers turn into a curse, we respect both her self-knowledge and her self-control. We also respect her self-knowledge when she recognizes that "her deed had been evil" and could not produce good results (6, cf. Matt. 7:18). When we are told that her daughter represents to her the pearl of great price, we cannot help associating her, sympathetically to a large extent, with the parable of Jesus; and when in the next paragraph we are told that Pearl is so beautiful that she is "worthy to have been brought forth in Eden; worthy to have been left there, to be the plaything of the angels" (6, cf. Gen. 2), we begin to wonder whether Hester and Pearl may have some sort of corrective function among these stern Puritans. This possibility is strengthened if we accept one of her final thoughts as an allusion to the Bible. When Hester joins the festive crowd and contemplates her possible escape to Europe, she says to herself that in "yet a little while" she will be free from her oppressive surroundings (21). The expression "yet a little while" is used four times by Jesus in discussing his imminent departure from earth (John 7:33, 12:35, 13:33, and 14:19). If we accept the allusion, then we see that Hester, while hardly a Christ figure, sees herself as a possible catalyst in this society. She has not changed anyone, but she can justify her actions, and her existence, with the thought that she has shown these people an alternative to the severity and sternness of their inhibited and diminished lives.

The title of the novel may be another indication of the inadequacy of the Puritan attitude toward Hester. To her neighbors her scarlet letter suggests "a scarlet woman, and a worthy type of her of Babylon" (8, cf. Rev. 17) and serves as a symbol that "was not mere scarlet cloth, tinged in an earthly dye-pot, but was red-hot with infernal fire" (5, cf. Rev. 9). However, the reader familiar with the Bible will recall a well-known context for the word "scarlet" that is ignored by the Puritans: "though your sins be as scarlet, they shall be as white as snow" (Isa. 1:18). Is Hawthorne again using the Bible to point up the hypocrisy of the unforgiving Puritans and at the same time reminding the reader that Hester is atoning for her sins and deserves a better fate in her community? If so, then the earlier comparison of Hester and Pearl to the paintings of the Madonna and Child which was presented "only by contrast" (2) takes on additional meanings in the context of the novel as a whole. Finally, what Porter Williams says about the brand of Cain in his article on "The Secret Sharer," reprinted in this book, seems to be applicable here: the references to Hester's badge as the brand of Cain may actually suggest that Hester enjoyed divine protection and compassion in dealing with the heartless Puritan society.

[This discussion has been limited to explicit biblical allusions and parallels. It has not dealt with such biblical themes as sin, penance, and penitence, which are obviously central to the novel.—Ed.]

II Allegory in "Rappaccini's Daughter"*

Oliver Evans

Department of English,
California State College, San Fernando

Randall Stewart says "The marked interest in Hawthorne is one of the most striking phenomena of our time."[1] Some evidence of this may be seen in the fact that in the eight-year interval between 1949 and 1957 five books containing fairly detailed analyses of "Rappaccini's Daughter" were published in this country,[2] so that this story, like James's *The Turn of the Screw*, bids fair to become a testing ground for future critical ingenuity.

All of these studies are interesting, but there is little agreement among their authors concerning the final meaning of the story and the consistency of its allegory. Since the main source of this disagreement is the allegorical identities of the main characters, it becomes necessary, in order to understand Hawthorne's intention, to establish these identities as firmly as possible.

From the reference to Eden in "Rappaccini's Daughter," it is clear that Hawthorne intended some sort of analogy with the Biblical story. Of these references, the first is the

---

*From "Allegory and Incest in 'Rappaccini's Daughter'" (pp. 185-195), © 1964 by The Regents of the University of California. Reprinted from *Nineteenth-Century Fiction*, Vol. 19, No. 2, pp. 185-190, by permission of the Regents.

[1] "The Golden Age of Hawthorne Criticism," *University of Kansas City Review*, XXII (1955), 44-46.

[2] Ray B. West and R. W. Stallman, *The Art of Modern Fiction* (New York, 1949); Richard Harter Fogle, *Hawthorne's Fiction: the Light and the Dark* (Norman, 1952); William Bysshe Stein, *Hawthorne's Faust* (Gainesville, 1953); Hyatt H. Waggoner, *Hawthorne* (Cambridge, Mass., 1955); Roy R. Male, *Hawthorne's Tragic Vision* (Austin, 1957).

23

most explicit. When Giovanni sees Rappaccini avoiding contact with the flowers of his own cultivation, Hawthorne comments: "It was strangely frightful to the young man's imagination, to see this air of insecurity in a person cultivating a garden, that most simple and innocent of human toils, and which had been alike the joy and labor of the unfallen parents of the race. Was this garden, then, the Eden of the present world?—and was this man, with such a perception of harm in what his own hands caused to grow, was he the Adam?" It will be seen that the possibility that Rappaccini is to be identified in some way with Adam has been suggested by Hawthorne himself. West and Stallman, however, see difficulties in this: "Who is the Eve?," they ask. "And who are the other characters in the allegorized Eden?" (p. 30)

Before attempting to answer these questions and to construct a case for Rappaccini-as-Adam, I should like to consider the two remaining alternatives—that he is God, and that he is Satan. It is difficult to reconcile Rappaccini's fear of the flowers with the omnipotence of a true deity; furthermore, the malevolent influence he exerts throughout the story and the author's own description of him as "afflicted with inward disease" would tend to rule out this assumption. It is more tempting to think of him as Satan, and indeed the story, thus viewed, has an architecture that is inversely analogous to that of the story in *Genesis* and could perhaps be considered a kind of parody thereof: the garden, instead of being a place of joy and innocence, is a place of melancholy and evil; Beatrice is Adam, created evil, or at least partly so, instead of good; Giovanni is Eve, created by Satan so that she will have a companion in her evil (just as God created Eve for a purpose at once similar and opposite); Baglioni is the serpent who instead of suggesting to Giovanni (Eve) that he do evil, suggests that he do good (by means of the antidote); and the antidote is the apple which, being partaken of by Adam rather than Eve—and a good rather than an evil substance—causes the tragedy. This interpretation has considerable symmetry;

there is an almost point-by-point correspondence with the original story, even down to the reversal of the sexes and the function of the serpent,[3] but it reduces the story to a mere exercise in ingenuity: as a parable it is meaningless, and the terms in which Hawthorne refers to the "Eden of the present world" suggest that he intends a parable, or at least an allegory[4] of his own rather than a parody of Holy Writ. As allegory, the only moral comfort offered by this interpretation of the story is that Satan's plans for Adam and Eve are thwarted—but this, when we remember God's original plan for the Biblical pair, is perhaps a dubious comfort. The theory that Rappaccini is Satan, Giovanni Adam, and Beatrice Eve is less tenable still, and has been refuted by West and Stallman: "Why is she the daughter of Rappaccini—of Satan? And why is Satan so much more vulnerable to the poison than Beatrice (Eve)?" (p. 30).

West and Stallman, unable to identify Rappaccini in the Eden myth, concluded that he had no allegorical identity, and that the story was not an allegory at all, a conclusion in which they were joined six years later by Waggoner, who prefers instead to call it a "symbolic structure" (p. 105). The problem of classification, however, is less interesting than the problem of meaning: unless Rappaccini be positively identified as Adam, no satisfactory meaning emerges from the story, and we are forced to conclude that Hawthorne erred in suggesting the analogy with Eden. This, of course, is possible, but in the case of a writer of Hawthorne's stature the critic does not do him justice if, before arriving at this conclusion, he does not carefully examine the situation.

In answer to the question "Who is Eve?" (where Rappaccini is Adam), it should be remembered that in the account of Creation in the second chapter of *Genesis*, the one containing the story of Eden, it is stated that God

---

[3] This interpretation, it will be noted, accounts for the allegorical identity of Baglioni, who, according to Waggoner, "has so far proved resistant to any attempt to place him in an allegorical scheme" (p. 116).

[4] See Hawthorne's introduction to "Rappaccini's Daughter."

created Eve *from one of Adam's ribs,* and that in this sense it is possible to consider her as Adam's offspring as well as his companion and future mate. This would explain the fact that in Hawthorne's story Beatrice is Rappaccini's daughter, and it could explain also certain suggestions of incest which appear in the story but which are never fully developed and of which Hawthorne himself may not have been entirely conscious. . . . If we think of Rappaccini as a man guilty of intellectual pride (for Hawthorne the Unpardonable Sin) who attempts to rival God, it will be apparent that *he has two identities:* the true one (as Adam) and the false one which he creates for himself (as God). It is in this latter role that, in imitation of the God of *Genesis*, he selects a companion for his offspring, and in this sense Giovanni also is Adam—but a false one, since Rappaccini is a false God. The true Adam in Hawthorne's parable is Rappaccini, and both Beatrice and Giovanni may be regarded as his creations, for the latter, though not the offspring of his loins, is, at the end of the story, the monstrous offspring of his science. It is perhaps a partial awareness of this that causes Male (to date the most thorough explicator of the story) to say that Giovanni feels toward Beatrice "more like a brother than a lover" (p. 64). There is thus yet another potential element of incest in the story, that which characterizes the romance of Beatrice and Giovanni.

The only variation from the Scriptural story is that Hawthorne causes Adam to infect Eve rather than vice versa, and here Male's comment may be enlightening: "Hawthorne, writing 'Rappaccini's Daughter' during his idyllic married life at the Old Manse, could not fully accept Milton's version of Eve in the Fall. With characteristic chivalry he transferred minor bits of Eve's original role to Adam, as he playfully did in 'The New Adam and Eve'" (p. 68).

Rappaccini, the man whose intellect has been cultivated at the expense of his heart, is too obviously the typical Transcendental villain—by way of Gothic romance, with which Hawthorne was well acquainted[5]—for us to ignore the implication that he is the erring Adam of the "Eden of the present world," and that his error consists, as did that of the original pair, in wanting to *know too much*—to have access to a world of knowledge that is forbidden to man. The Biblical story furnished Hawthorne with a convenient analogy for showing what must happen to man when, in the pride of his intellectual achievements, he attempts to usurp the function of God. It is not for nothing that Hawthorne has made his false god a scientist—like Aylmer in "The Birthmark" and Ethan Brand in the story of that name, who also committed the unpardonable sin of performing experiments on other human beings. Hawthorne's suspicion of science is of course a part of his Romantic heritage,[6] and the concern that moral science would not keep pace with technology is found in American literature as early as the eighteenth century: Franklin expressed it, so did Jefferson, and it may be said to have reached a sort of climax with Emerson and Thoreau. When Hawthorne causes Baglioni to observe that Rappaccini has produced "new varieties of poison, more horribly deleterious than Nature, without the assistance of this learned person, would ever have plagued the world with," it is fairly obvious that he is referring to scientism, and to the evils that he feared would result from the rapidly increasing mechanization of life in the nineteenth century. The "Eden of the present world," Hawthorne is saying in his parable, is a place of false values, a place dominated by the false god of scientific materialism (Baglioni calls Rappaccini a "vile empiric"), and as such is doomed. Beatrice and Giovanni, the progeny of this erring Adam, though themselves innocent, have inherited his sin, as is apparent in the pathetic scene where Beatrice asks Rappaccini, "My father, wherefore didst thou inflict this miserable doom upon thy child?"

[5] See Jane Lundblad, *Nathaniel Hawthorne and European Literary Tradition*, Essays and Studies on American Language and Literature, No. 6 (Uppsala, 1947), pp. 81-149.

[6] See Rudolph von Abele, *The Death of the Artist* (The Hague, 1955), pp. 12-13; also Stein, p. 93.

Two circumstances remain to be explained: Rappaccini's fear of the evil he has created, and the fact—which may seem to contradict it—that he apparently cannot recognize it as evil, since he tells Beatrice, when she reproaches him, that she ought to be grateful to him for the exceptional power he has given her. But there is no real contradiction: it is traditional for a creator to fear his own invention and to recognize a threat in it (as in the golem legends and Mrs. Shelley's *Frankenstein*), and a parent who would systematically expose his daughter to poison would certainly not hesitate to feign a moral blindness for the purpose of causing her to feel an illusion of superiority. Beatrice's essential virtue, however, will not allow her thus easily to be deceived: "I would fain be loved, not feared." It is but further proof of Rappaccini's villainy that, after exposing her to perils that he himself fears, he will not acknowledge that they are perils.

It is unnecessary to give allegorical identity to the characters of Baglioni and Lisabetta in Hawthorne's version of the Eden story, since these characters exist outside of that story: they never once enter the garden, nor do they participate in any of the action which takes place there. (Even Baglioni's final speech is delivered from a window.) I do not mean that these characters have no function in the story as a whole, but that they are not important to the Eden allegory, where they serve merely as props to facilitate the action of the principals.

That at least one of Hawthorne's intentions in "Rappaccini's Daughter" is to allegorize the second Fall of Man in the "Eden of the present world," thus dramatizing what he regarded as the dilemma of the nineteenth century—the choice between scientific materialism and moral idealism—I think is a fairly safe assumption, and I have shown how it is possible, by casting Rappaccini in the role of Adam, so to read the story. This is not to say that the chief interest in "Rappaccini's Daughter" lies in Adam and his Fall, or in the moral to which the allegory points: Hawthorne may very possibly have intended this to be so, but in that case I believe that (as he observes in the *Italian Notebooks* concerning Guido Reni's portrait of Beatrice Cenci) the author "painted better than he knew,"[7] and that the artistic purpose triumphed over the didactic—which often happens in the best of Hawthorne. At any rate, I tend to agree with Fogle and Waggoner that the focus of the story is on Beatrice rather than Rappaccini, and that she is the most interesting character in it.

[We should not overlook the fact that Hawthorne mentions Dante at the beginning of the story. It would be instructive to compare the Beatrice of this story with the angelic Beatrice whom Dante meets in Paradise, in the third book of the *Divine Comedy*. In fact, a three-way comparison might well be undertaken: Rappaccini's Garden, the Garden of Eden, and Paradise.—Ed.]

[7]*The French and Italian Notebooks of Nathaniel Hawthorne*, ed. George Parsons Lathrop (Cambridge, Mass., 1890), p. 90.

III Melville's Use of the Bible in *Billy Budd*

Roland Bartel

Melville uses the conflict between natural innocence (Billy Budd) and natural depravity (Claggart) to raise some questions about the nature of evil and the nature of man. The references to the Bible help to establish the importance and complexity of these questions.

The nature of Billy Budd's innocence is revealed through a series of allusions to the Bible. Three of these allusions associate Billy Budd with Jesus. In the first chapter Captain Graveling, commander of the merchant ship *Rights of Man*, says that Budd's presence on his ship eliminated quarreling among the mates because a "virtue went out of him, sugaring the sour ones." In Mark 5:30, Luke 6:19, and Luke 8:46, we are told that a virtue went out of Jesus when he healed his followers. In the twentieth chapter Melville says that Claggart's false charges stunned Billy Budd so much that his face was "a crucifixion to behold," and in the final chapter we learn that pieces of the spar on which Billy Budd was hanged came to be regarded by other sailors as chips from the cross. Four other references associate Billy Budd with Adam prior to the fall. He is described as one who had not yet been "proffered the questionable apple of knowledge" (2);[1] as "a sort of upright barbarian, much such perhaps as Adam presumably might have been ere the urbane Serpent wriggled himself into his company" (2); as one who had never experienced the bite of the serpent of malice (13); and as one who "might have posed for a statue of young Adam before the Fall" (19). Another reference relates his innocence not to Christ or Adam but to the

[1] The numbers in parentheses are chapter numbers in *Billy Budd and the Critics*, ed. William T. Stafford (Belmont, Calif.: Wadsworth Publishing Co., 1961). Some editions number the chapters in a different way.

"period prior to Cain's city and citified man" (2, cf. Gen. 4:17). He is an upright barbarian or noble savage who has not been corrupted by the evils of civilization represented by Cain's city and the urbane serpent. He is, in fact, illiterate and unsuspecting of evil in others.

But Billy Budd is more than an allegorical character representing the innocence of Adam and Jesus. He is an individual trying to survive in a world that does not accept his basic purity. Since his character is similar to that of Adam before the fall, he is not prepared to deal with the evil that came into the world after the fall. However, Melville is not merely reenacting the fall by juxtaposing the innocence of Billy Budd with the depravity of Claggart. He is rather dramatizing some of the basic paradoxes of our existence that emerge from the conflict between certain principles embodied in certain kinds of individuals.

Billy Budd's inability to accommodate himself to the world of reality is suggested through several biblical allusions that support the nonbiblical episodes and state-ments about his character. Of special significance in this connection is the statement in the second chapter that Billy Budd was without "any trace of the wisdom of the serpent" and yet he was not quite a dove. When Jesus commissioned his twelve disciples to take the gospel to a hostile world, he warned them that they would be "as sheep in the midst of wolves" and that they would have to be "wise as serpents, and harmless as doves." Billy Budd's lack of the sophistica-tion needed to endure a hostile environment could hardly be expressed more emphatically than by this allusion to Matthew 10:16. There are other flaws in his innocence. He cannot control his impetuosity; he gives Red Whiskers a much bigger drubbing than necessary (1), and he kills Claggart impulsively (20). If Billy Budd's being found in a basket (2) is a reference to Moses' being found in a basket, (Exod. 2), the parallel would have a twofold significance. Moses was also impetuous and killed an Egyptian (Exod. 2), and, like Billy Budd, he had a speech defect (Exod. 4). Are we to assume that Billy Budd could have become a Moses, whose handicaps he shared, if he had had the wisdom of a serpent? Not an unreasonable possibility, since it helps to emphasize the strength of the hostile forces that destroyed him.

As we turn from the flawed innocence of Billy Budd to the depravity of Claggart, we approach the central mystery of the novel. What is the nature of evil and why is it so dominant in human affairs? Melville's puzzlement over this question is suggested first of all by a number of paradoxes. Billy Budd is referred to as a fighting peacemaker (1), an upright barbarian (2), and an angel who must hang (20). The chaplain is a prince of peace serving the god of war (25). The French revolutionists who set out to correct the wrongs of others became wrongdoers themselves (Preface). The British mutineers of 1797 later won great glory for Nelson and for England (3). The culminating paradox is Melville's observation that the roles of the leading characters have been reversed: "In the jugglery of circumstances . . . innocence and guilt personified in Claggart and Budd in effect changed places" (22). Small wonder that Melville twice referred to the "mystery of iniquity" (12 and 22), a phrase that the apostle Paul used in II Thessalonians 2:7 to describe the evil force that was impeding the spread of Christianity.

The mystery of Claggart's iniquity leads Melville to wonder who really is the best interpreter of human nature. In chapter 12 he speculates briefly that because of man's natural depravity it would seem that clergymen would be better witnesses in criminal cases than lawyers or physicians. Because of their training and insight clergymen can assess the moral responsibility associated with the "mysteries of iniquity." In the preceding chapter he reached a similar conclusion. He noted that knowledge of the world blunts man's capacity to understand human nature. The best authorities on human nature, the ones best qualified to shed "light into obscure spiritual places," are the Hebrew prophets; and paradoxically most of them were not men of the world but recluses (11). The fact that the Bible is so helpful in dealing with the mystery of iniquity makes Melville regret that it is no longer a familiar book (11).

Claggart's depravity is a major enigma that cannot be oversimplified any more than Billy Budd's innocence can be oversimplified in allegorical terms. Billy Budd's stuttering was evidence enough of the encroachment of "the arch interferer, the envious marplot of Eden" (2); and Claggart, though depraved, still had a conscience (14), albeit a diabolical one, as Melville makes clear with his reference to the devils who pretend to believe but actually tremble in fear because of their evil nature:

> For though consciences are as unlike as foreheads every intelligence, not excluding the Scriptural devils who "believe and tremble," has one. (Chapter 14)

> Thou believest that there is one God; thou doest well: the devils also believe, and tremble. (James 2:19)

In fact, there are times when Claggart, like Milton's Satan, can appear to be repentant. When he enviously watches Billy Budd happily performing his duties, he resembles the man of sorrows, a reference to the famous passage on the suffering servant in Isaiah 53:3. Claggart's hypocrisy magnifies the mystery of his depravity. When one of the members of the drumhead court asks why Claggart invented his false accusations, Billy Budd cannot answer him, and Captain Vere interrupts to say that the question is unanswerable.

Melville's other allusions to the Bible, though not directly related to his central theme, have the effect of enhancing the tone of high seriousness in the novel. His seemingly casual references to seven dramatic moments in the Bible help to universalize and dignify his story. He says that Claggart's envy of Billy Budd was much deeper than Saul's envy of David (13, cf. I Sam. 18); that when Claggart lied to Captain Vere, Claggart's look was similar to "that of the spokesman of the envious children of Jacob deceptively imposing upon the troubled patriarch the blood-dyed coat of young Joseph" (19, cf. Gen. 37); and that his death was comparable to the death of Ananias, another notorious liar (20, cf. Acts 5). Captain Vere's argument to the drumhead court that sailors, even though they move and have their being on the ocean, must still obey their king, echoes the famous oration of the apostle Paul on Mars Hill in which he argues for the supremacy of God in whom "we live and move and have our being" (22, cf. Acts 17). When Captain Vere is faced with the dreadful necessity of urging the death sentence on the handsome sailor whom he has come to regard as his own son, his moral dilemma is made unusually poignant by being compared to Abraham's probable feelings when told to sacrifice his only son (23, cf. Gen. 22). When the morning of Billy Budd's execution approaches, we are told that the night transferred its pale robe to the coming dawn the way Elijah disappeared into heaven and dropped his mantle on Elisha (26, cf. II Kings 2). The necessity for firm discipline on board the ship, resulting finally in the execution of Billy Budd, is justified by implication when the recent excesses of the French Revolution are equated with the Apocalypse (8, cf. Rev.). Through all these allusions Melville enhances the gravity of his story by linking it to the Bible at critical points.

In a story as rich in biblical allusions as this one, the reader is justified in considering parallel situations that are not supported by verbal borrowings—provided, of course, that these parallels add meaning to the story and do not encourage digressive speculation. There are, for example, several similarities between the life of Billy Budd and the life of Jesus. Both were reluctantly condemned by superiors—Captain Vere and Pontius Pilate—who believed they had to enforce the law to prevent public uprisings. The death of both is accompanied by disturbances in nature. As a matter of fact, the death of Billy Budd is almost certainly linked to the ascension of Jesus rather than to the crucifixion. When Jesus ascended to heaven "a cloud received him out of their sight" (Acts 1:9), and when Billy Budd was executed "the vapory fleece hanging low in the

East, was shot through with a soft glory as of the fleece of the Lamb of God seen in mystical vision and simultaneously therewith, watched by the wedged mass of upturned faces, Billy ascended; and, ascending, took the full rose of the dawn" (26). Finally, there are hints that Claggart represented the evil principle found both in Satan and in Judas and the other adversaries of Jesus. In the role of Satan he destroyed Billy Budd's Adam-like innocence, and in the role of Judas he destroyed his Christlike goodness. When Claggart suborned a seaman to try to bribe Billy Budd with two guineas we are reminded of Judas and the thirty pieces of silver, and when he brought his false accusations to Captain Vere we are reminded of the false charges brought to Pontius Pilate by the chief priests and elders.

In *Billy Budd* and in the Bible the reader is confronted with the same basic archetypal questions about the nature of evil and its relation to goodness and innocence. It is hardly surprising, then, that Melville's references to the Bible are extensive and detailed and that they are thoroughly woven into the fabric of his narrative.

[For additional interpretations of this novel, see *Melville's Billy Budd and the Critics*, ed. William T. Stafford. See especially the eight excerpts in section 4, "Christian and Classical Parallels."—Ed.]

IV Melville's Use of the Bible in *Moby-Dick**

Nathalia Wright

Department of English,
University of Tennessee

Melville's dramatic sense, animating all his imagery, is not the sort, however, which creates objectivity in character. His people lead an interior existence. The details of their outward appearance are scanty, and the little inconsequential habits of action by which they might be made visible are missing. Types rather than individuals, they are "characters" in the seventeenth-century sense, embodying the most general states of mind: aspiration, utilitarianism, innocence. Simple rather than complex, they are variations of relatively few patterns. Compared with the infinite variety of Melville's images and of his style, the number of his character types and his themes is small indeed. Half a dozen at the most served him, as they served Hawthorne.

For about half these patterns the Bible provided prototypes: the type of Ishmael, of Ahab, and of Jesus. . . . The Biblical Ishmael is banished to "the wilderness of Beer-sheba" and grows up in the "wilderness of Paran," a phrase underscored in Melville's Bible. It is the solitary wastes of the sea, rather, in which the narrator of *Moby-Dick* wanders; or, in his own words, the "wilderness of waters." Periodically he flees the society of men, even though it offers him safety and joy. Like his shipmate Bulkington, he is impelled by some strange predestination to reject the lee shore for the "howling infinite,"[1] and

*The following excerpts are taken from Nathalia Wright, *Melville's Use of the Bible* (Duke University Press, 1969). Reprinted by permission of the Publisher. Copyright 1969, Duke University Press, Durham, North Carolina. The book is organized thematically rather than by the stories in which Melville used the Bible, hence the necessity of selecting the material from various parts of the book and renumbering the footnotes.

[1] *Moby-Dick*, I, 133. All references to Melville's works are to the Constable edition.

thereby symbolically casts off all impediments in the pursuit of truth.

This brings Melville, in fact, to the very heart of the Ishmael story: the divine revelation to Hagar as she and her son languished in the desert. Before his birth Hagar was visited by an angel who instructed her to call the child *Yishma'el*, meaning "God shall hear." The name was a prophecy, fulfilled a few years later when, perishing of thirst in the desert, he was saved by the miraculous appearance of a well of water. On this occasion an angel spoke again to Hagar.

Except for the element of deliverance, which he associated with illusion rather than reality, this is Melville's allegory. Truth is to be sought in the solitary wilderness. In his imagination the waste place and the green landscape are symbols—in *Mardi, Moby-Dick, Pierre, Clarel*. The illusory haunt of truth, or superficial truth, is the oasis, the verdant isle, the secure land, the fertile field, the sweetness of society and domesticity. These are safe and felicitous; these are attainable. But reality itself, the abstract and the ultimate, resides in the wilderness, whether of land or of sea;[2] in the unhuman, indefinite, perilous waste.

That is, it is to be found here if it is to be found anywhere. The going is lonely and rough, but, harshest fact of all, the end may never be reached. For Melville's heroes, like the knights of medieval romance, are engaged in a quest rather than an achievement. In the wilderness through which they pass no divine voice speaks, as it spoke to Hagar. But here the unanswerable question is asked. It is a place of revelation. And if nothing more is revealed than that the nature of reality is like the nature of the desert—vast, voiceless, and fearful—that is itself a mature, a profound, and a positive discovery. . . .

But in the Bible the desert or wilderness is a common

---

[2] In his copy of the New Testament Melville wrote beside Matt. 13:2 the words "The Sea." The verse describes Jesus teaching from a boat on the lake of Galilee, an association of the truth with a body of water which Melville himself was so fond of making.

setting for a vision of one kind or another. The Exodus itself in the history of the Hebrews represents the closest communion they ever had with Jehovah. Surely mindful of that fact, Melville marked in his Bible several verses referring to the wilderness in which they sojourned,[3] and also marked similar descriptive passages in Stanley's *Sinai and Palestine*. He knew, too, of the connection established by both Testaments between a life in the wilderness and the ability to prophesy: John the Baptist emerged from the desert to preach, and Jesus retired into it for spiritual enlightenment. It was a phenomenon to which he referred more than once: in *Clarel*, in *Billy Budd*. He underscored in Matthew 3:3 the words: "The voice of one crying in the wilderness," and concluded in his speculations "Of Deserts":

> But to pure hearts it yields no fear;
> And John, he found wild honey here.[4]

In his Journal he shuddered at the Judean landscape which, he thought, "must have suggested to the Jewish prophets, their ghastly theology," but he added: "Is the desolation of the land the result of the fatal embrace of the Deity? Hapless are the favorites of Heaven."[5]

In the Old Testament, moreover, the idea of revelation is sometimes associated with particular places, and repeatedly with the vicinity of Beer-sheba, whither Hagar and Ishmael were banished. It was an important holy place in Hebrew history, where theophanies were frequently vouchsafed. Here Jehovah spoke to Hagar, Isaac, Jacob, and Elijah. In the stories of Hagar and of Elijah, favorites of Melville's, the scene is specifically "the wilderness" outside the town.

This episode of Ishmael's deliverance at Beer-sheba is the basis for one more analogy between his story and that of *Moby-Dick's* narrator. Both seem to lead charmed lives, though among Melville's heroes Ishmael is unusual in this

[3] Exod. 3:1; 13:18, 20; Jer. 2:2, 6.
[4] *Clarel*, I, 217.
[5] *Journal up the Straits*, pp. 88, 92.

respect. As Hagar's son was saved by a miracle from a death in the desert, so with the wreck of the *Pequod* only the sailor Ishmael escapes, and that by a margin so narrow as to seem miraculous. This is a parallel unacknowledged by Melville's actual text. But the survival of Ishmael the sailor is linked with that of another Biblical character, Job's servant, whose words are affixed to the Epilogue: "And I only am escaped to tell thee." Again two Biblical types seem to have been interchangeable in Melville's mind, as Jonah and Ishmael were in *White Jacket*. . . .

In addition to furnishing Melville with the original Ishmael the Old Testament gave him also a model for his most celebrated character: Captain Ahab, who is named for King Ahab, seventh king of Israel after the division of the tribes.[6] In fact, King Ahab's story and that of his predecessor, King Jeroboam, account for an entire group of persons in *Moby-Dick:* Ahab, Fedallah, Starbuck, Elijah, Gabriel, Macey, and the *Jeroboam* and the *Rachel*.

The *Pequod's* Captain Ahab is associated with his Biblical namesake at the outset of the narrative. Acquainting Ishmael with his history, Peleg reminds the young sailor that "'Ahab of old, thou knowest, was a crowned king!'" To this the Presbyterian Ishmael replies: "'And a very vile one. When that wicked king was slain, the dogs, did they not lick his blood?'"[7] Whereupon, begging him never to repeat this remark, Peleg relates the circumstances of Ahab's being so named and the predictions which have followed him:

"Captain Ahab did not name himself. 'Twas a foolish, ignorant whim of his crazy, widowed mother, who died when he was only a twelvemonth old. And yet the old squaw Tistig, at Gay Head, said that the name would somehow prove prophetic. And, perhaps,

[6] This, of course, does not preclude the possibility that Melville got the name of Ahab from another source and then developed the Biblical analogy, as he did in *Israel Potter*. In J. Ross Browne's *Etchings of a Whaling Cruise* "Captain A_____" of the *Styx* bears a distinct resemblance to Captain Ahab of the *Pequod* (Charles R. Anderson, *Melville in the South Seas* (New York: Columbia University Press, 1939), p. 43).

[7] *Moby-Dick*, I, 99.

other fools like her may tell thee the same. I wish to warn thee. It's a lie."[8]

Despite Peleg's valiant protest, the prophecy about Captain Ahab does not prove to be a lie. Not only the tragic end of his life but the essential duality of his character also is foreshadowed in the Old Testament story. For the picture of King Ahab which emerges in I Kings is a composite of two points of view: that of the sources, according to which he was an able and energetic ruler, and that of the didactic compiler, who saw him also as a dangerous innovator and a patron of foreign gods.[9]

King Ahab's political shrewdness is evident in the series of alliances he made with surrounding kingdoms, his accruing wealth in the ivory palace he built. He married the princess Jezebel of Phoenicia, made peace with Jehoshaphat of Judah, and, according to Assyrian inscriptions, furnished Ben-hadad of Damascus with troops against Assyria. Being in his turn attacked by Ben-hadad, he concluded his victory by sparing his enemy's life and arranging for each kingdom to have bazaars in the capital of the other. The alliance was thus one of trade and commerce, and as such was violently opposed by the prophetic party of Israel. It lasted, according to the Biblical record, only three years. When hostilities with Damascus were renewed, Ahab was slain in battle, defending his kingdom. It was then that the dogs, as Ishmael ghoulishly remembered, licked his blood.

Like the king of Israel, the captain of the *Pequod* is shrewd in his secular associations. As a captain he is able and courageous; as a whaleman he is successful, for forty years temporizing with the great dangers of the deep for the wealth which it yields. The very evidence of this success is fantastically like that in King Ahab's story: Captain Ahab, too, lives in an ivory house, "the ivory *Pequod* " as it is often called, tricked out in trophies of whale bones and teeth from profitable voyages. Yet in the end trade is no less treacherous to the captain than to the king. Perhaps it

[8]*Ibid.*, I, 207.
[9]Many biblical scholars question this reading of the text.—Ed.

could not be otherwise. For as Ishmael's account testifies, its nature is to be now a friend and now an enemy, and the best merchants are, like Bildad and Starbuck, strictly utilitarian. To this category Ahab apparently belonged until his last voyage, which, incidentally, was to have taken three years, just the length of time which King Ahab's bazaars in Damascus lasted. But the *Pequod's* last voyage, unlike its others, is not entirely commercial, and the blame for its disaster must be divided. From the morning on which Captain Ahab nails up the golden doubloon as a prize for Moby-Dick, it becomes a pursuit through invisible waters of an immortal spirit. And a duel is begun between the prudent Starbuck and the haunted Ahab. For Ahab cannot compromise. In the realm in which he hunts the white whale there are no alliances with the enemy. His voyage is disastrous when, in the midst of a profitable whale hunt, he becomes involved in the unequivocal pursuit of supernatural truth.

All this recalls the second nature of King Ahab, an able politician but in the religious sphere a patron of foreign gods. It is on this account that Ishmael remembers him as "vile" and "wicked." In the Biblical narrative Ahab offended Jehovah by introducing the Phoenician Baal as one of the gods of Israel at the time he married Jezebel of Phoenicia, whose father, according to Josephus, was a priest of Astarte. It appears that Ahab never intended thus to displace but only to supplement Jehovah. But Jehovah, who claimed the exclusive right to Israel's worship, tolerated no alliances with neighboring gods, or even with neighboring kings. He never forgave Ahab for sparing Ben-hadad's life. With Jehovah an enemy was always an enemy. And so he contrived with false prophets to bring King Ahab to destruction. Like the captain of the *Pequod*, King Ahab attempted to compromise in an uncompromising realm.

Indeed, Peleg's epithet for Captain Ahab is perhaps a better description of King Ahab than any in the Book of Kings: "'a grand, ungodly, god-like man.'"[10] Like King

[10]*Moby-Dick*, I, 99.

Ahab, he worships pagan gods. His particular deity is the spirit of fire, and he adores other objects of this cult: the light, the sun, the stars. His harpooner is a fire-worshiping Zoroastrian, Fedallah, the Parsee. In the midst of the typhoon Ahab invokes the fire already burning at the mast-ends, whereupon it leaps thrice its height—a feat itself which is a match for Elijah's calling down the fire on Mount Carmel to confound King Ahab's Baalite prophets. Finally, as though all this were not "ungodly" enough, Captain Ahab tempers the whale barbs not in water but in the heathen blood of Tashtego, Queequeg, and Daggoo. His voice is lifted defiantly to heaven, in what Melville told Hawthorne was the very motto of the book: "'Ego non baptizo te in nomine patris, sed in nomine diaboli!'"[11]

Of course, Ahab's death, is not an instance of divine retribution in the orthodox sense. A romantic paganism is part of his nature, and not the least element of which he is compounded is Milton's Satan himself. The epithets applied to him by Ishmael and Starbuck—"infidel," "impious," "diabolic," "blasphemous"—describe a towering rebel who is akin to all other rebels in history, King Ahab among them.

Yet when in this character Captain Ahab does meet death, it is through hearkening, like King Ahab, to false prophecy. In the case of King Ahab it was the jealous Jehovah who betrayed him. Before trying to recover Ramoth-Gilead, which was in the hands of his old enemy, the King of Damascus, Ahab consulted his four hundred prophets. They promised him victory. But Micaiah, "a prophet of the Lord," who was summoned at the request of Ahab's ally, Jehoshaphat, said he would be slain. To explain this discrepancy in the two prophecies, Micaiah then related a vision he had, in which Ahab's prophets were revealed to be divinely inspired liars. On this occasion he saw Jehovah enthroned and surrounded by angels, and heard him call for someone who would persuade Ahab to engage in the fatal

[11]*Ibid.*, II, 261.

battle. For Ahab's death had apparently already been determined, and to the divine inquiry a spirit appeared who said: "I will go forth, and I will be a lying spirit in the mouth of all his prophets."[12] But in spite of Micaiah's story, Ahab believed the words of the false prophets, and thus deluded went to his death.

A false prophet contributes also to Captain Ahab's death. He is Fedallah, who appears increasingly in this role in the last of *Moby-Dick*. His actual prophecy, however, sounds less like an echo of the Bible than of *Macbeth*, with Birnam Wood moving to Dunsinane. Cryptically Fedallah predicts that before Ahab dies he must see two hearses on the sea—the first not made by mortal hands, the second made of American wood. He promises even then to precede his captain as pilot, and concludes by assuring Ahab that only hemp can kill him. All this is an accurate forecast of the tragic end, but it fatally deceives Ahab, who sees in it an assurance of victory.

On the other hand, there is no end to the honest prophecies that are made to Captain Ahab. The balance of influence is reversed in the two stories. King Ahab had four hundred false prophets and one who was true, but Melville sees to it, with characteristic irony, that Captain Ahab defies all creation in order to believe his single malevolent angel. The pleadings of Starbuck, the ravings of the mad Gabriel, the testimony of ships which have met the whale, the whisperings of his own heart, and a host of omens in nature—all these he ignores, heeding only Fedallah.

Starbuck, in the intimate relation he bears to his captain, also has an antecedent in the original Ahab story. With his frenzied attempts to conciliate the powers which Ahab is determined to alienate he suggests the God-fearing Obadiah, governor of King Ahab's house, who, when Jezebel persecuted the Israelite prophets, concealed a hundred of them in a cave and sustained them there until the danger was past. He was on good terms, too, with the prophet Elijah.

[12] I Kings 22:22.

This prophet, the great Tishbite who denounced King Ahab and Queen Jezebel, provided Melville with the name for the pock-marked lunatic whom Ishmael and Queequeg encounter twice before sailing. As the two avidly listen, he enumerates the strange tales which have been told about Captain Ahab and insinuates that not only he but the entire crew of the *Pequod* will never return from the voyage. The significance of his name can hardly have escaped the Biblically astute Ishmael, who calls him a "prophet" and exclaims portentously as they leave the creature, "Elijah!"

Possibly Ishmael remembered that the actual words of the prophet Elijah to King Ahab include a curse, which in the Books of Kings is habitually pronounced upon the wicked kings of Israel: "[I] will make thine house like the house of Jeroboam the son of Nebat."[13] Its meaning is devastatingly clear. Jeroboam, the first king of Israel after the tribal division, though actually a courageous opponent of the tyrant Solomon, is charged in the Old Testament with fostering sacrilegious rituals and sacrifices in the new kingdom. For his offense Jehovah allowed his son to die and vowed to destroy his dynasty. And so the wicked successors of Jeroboam were described as walking "in all the way of Jeroboam the son of Nebat, and in his sin wherewith he made Israel to sin,"[14] and were promised the same punishment. Jeroboam is thus not only a forerunner, but his fate is a forecast of the fates of all the kings who followed him, including King Ahab.

And for this predecessor of King Ahab the *Jeroboam* in *Moby-Dick*, a predecessor of the *Pequod*, is named. Of the four vessels met by the *Pequod* which have already encountered Ahab's quarry, the *Jeroboam* is the first. Her fate is prophetic. It is a message of warning to all who follow, articulated by Gabriel and vindicated by the *Samuel Enderby*, the *Rachel*, the *Delight*, and at last the *Pequod*. The *Jeroboam's* pursuit of Moby-Dick has resulted in the loss of her mate and may in some mysterious way be

[13]*Ibid.*, 21:22, *et passim.*
[14]*Ibid.*, 16:26, *et passim.*

44

responsible for the epidemic among her crew, but the whale has escaped. And so the other four vessels, pursuing the same course, meet similar misfortunes, without slaying Moby-Dick.

The "utter wreck" of the *Pequod*, in its turn, was probably made inevitable by Melville's own flair for spectacle, but the corroboration for it is complete in the stories of King Jeroboam and King Ahab. Compared with the partial losses of the *Jeroboam*, the *Enderby*, the *Rachel*, and the *Delight*, the destruction of the *Pequod* is appalling indeed. But it is a fitting end for the monomania of Ahab, which none of the other captains shared. So in the case of King Ahab the account of his death is elaborated by more details of violence than are to be found in that of any of the Israelite kings before him. The reason is not far to seek. He vexed Jehovah more than all the rest: ". . . and Ahab did more to provoke the Lord God of Israel to anger than all the kings of Israel that were before him."[15]. . .

Now the history of King Jeroboam, part of the background history of King Ahab, is memorialized in *Moby-Dick* by more than the name of a vessel. In the crew of the *Jeroboam* there are two characters who correspond to members of King Jeroboam's household: Macey and Gabriel. The mate Macey, who is dexterously lifted from the boat by the whale and cast to his death in the sea, takes the place of King Jeroboam's son, Abijah. When Abijah fell ill his parents appealed in vain to Jehovah's prophet; the child died for the father's sins.

The role of this prophet, Ahijah, is matched aboard the *Jeroboam* by Gabriel. At first assuring King Jeroboam of success, Ahijah was compelled by the king's idolatry to condemn not only his son but his whole house to death. Gabriel of the *Jeroboam* was also a prophet, so called among the Neskyeuna Shakers, and his predictions to Macey and to Ahab are fulfilled. His argument with Macey, whom he tries to dissuade from lowering for Moby-Dick, is similar to Ahijah's quarrel with the idolatrous King Jeroboam: Macey

[15]*Ibid., 16:33.*

45

is committing sacrilege in hunting Moby-Dick, since the whale is an incarnation of the Shaker deity.

But of course, unlike Ahijah, Gabriel is mad. And to emphasize the fact Melville associated him thoroughly with apocalyptic lore, almost obliterating his connection with the Jeroboam story. In calling himself the Archangel Gabriel, this character assumes the name of the being sent to reveal to Daniel the meaning of his vision, though not identified as an archangel until the New Testament. Otherwise, however, Melville's Gabriel is more imbued with the vision of John; he carries in his vest pocket the seventh vial of God's wrath—the earthquake—and announces himself deliverer and vicar-general of the isles of the sea. In this scheme the fate of Macey has an explanation quite different from its meaning in relation to the story of King Jeroboam. His death is the result of the wrath of God being poured out of one of the vials, as Gabriel says. And the ensuing epidemic on board the *Jeroboam* may be attributed to the same cause. For the angels with the vials are, in the Evangelist's vision, the same angels who have the seven last plagues, and the plagues seem to be visited on the earth by means of the vials' being broken.

But there is an important limitation to this dire program in Revelation. The vials and the plagues are to destroy only the heathen world, or those who worship the beast with seven heads. This suggests the analogous fact that in *Moby-Dick* only those who pursue the white whale are doomed. It suggests, further, that Melville had identified in his imagination the whale and the beast which "[did] rise up out of the sea"[16] to overcome its virtuous opponent and even to curse God. Such an identification is never expressed, but it would account for the name which he gave his Neskyeuna Shaker. For although this name is not part of the story of the seven vials at all, there is a connection between the two. The beast in Revelation, with its leopard, bear, and lion members and its ten horns, is a combination of the four beasts which rise from the sea in Daniel's vision,

[16] Rev. 13:1; see also Dan. 7:3.

to be explained by the angelic Gabriel. Thus linked by the beast or beasts of the sea, the name and the message of the *Jeroboam's* "prophet" are naturally, even inevitably, related.

It is true that in Melville's mind, as in the mind of Coleridge, many associations existed whose links are not visible in what he wrote. The name of Gabriel points to one of these associations. The names of the ships in *Moby-Dick* indicate another. Though two Israelite kings—Ahab and Jeroboam—are the only ones whose names appear prominently in the novel, others were in Melville's thought. His imagery attests the fact. It seems even possible that his recollection of the entire succession determined the number of ships in the novel. Beginning with the *Pequod*, excluding the *Moss* with its short run from New Bedford to Nantucket, and ending with the *Delight* there are ten vessels which sail the open sea. The number is equal to the number of kings of Israel from Saul, the first, to Ahab. In this series the *Jeroboam* comes fourth, corresponding to the place of King Jeroboam I.

Nor were Jeroboam and Ahab the only wicked ones among them. A long line of wicked rulers at last drew Jehovah's wrath upon the entire kingdom, and the Babylonian captivity ensued. This sequel to the Ahab story is briefly touched upon at the conclusion of *Moby-Dick* in the name of the whaler *Rachel*. Cruising deviously over the waters in search of the captain's son, who was lost in pursuit of the white whale, this vessel is pictured as a mother inconsolable in the loss of her children: "But by her still halting course and winding, woeful way, you plainly saw that this ship that so wept with spray still remained without comfort. She was Rachel, weeping for her children, because they were not."[17]

She personifies Jacob's wife, the spiritual mother of all Israel, whom Jeremiah imagines weeping over the captivity of the remnants of her nation, as on their way to Babylon they pass near her tomb. This is the ship which in the end

[17]*Moby-Dick*, II, 315.

rescues Ishmael, the *Pequod's* sole survivor. So in Jeremiah's prophecy Rachel is comforted by the assurance of Jehovah that, despite the sins of their sovereigns for which they have had to suffer, the tribes will be returned from captivity.

There is, in any case, a decided association in Melville's mind between the ships in *Moby-Dick* and characters in the Bible, evidence again of his fondness for personification. There is the *Jeroboam*, the *Pequod* captained by Ahab, the *Rachel*, and the *Jungfrau*. Unlike the other three, however, this last ship is not a piece of Israelite history. It represents the Five Foolish Virgins of Jesus's parable, who, going to meet the Bridegroom without oil in their lamps, tried to borrow from their five wise sisters. For Master Derick de Deer of the *Jungfrau*, or *Virgin* as Ishmael obligingly translates, eagerly boards the *Pequod* to obtain oil from Ahab for his empty lamp-feeder.

There is one more character in *Moby-Dick* who seems to be named for a character in the Bible. He is the Quaker Captain Bildad, half-owner of the *Pequod*. In contrast to his profane partner, Captain Peleg—whose name is also Biblical—he is pious, poring over the Scriptures and interspersing his nautical vernacular with quotations from them. But he also has a reputation for being a hard master and has devoted his life to the spilling of whale blood. His name is appropriate to his type, for it is the name of Bildad the Shuhite, the "traditionalist" of Job's three friends. Actually, the speeches of the three are scarcely individualized in the poem, and a wisdom philosophy is common to all: only the wicked are punished and the righteous shall surely prosper. This thesis, strenuously denied by Job and by the author of *Moby-Dick*, underlies Captain Bildad's prudent advice to the sailors: "'Don't whale it too much a Lord's days, men; but don't miss a fair chance either, that's rejecting Heaven's good gifts.'"[18]

Bildad the proprietor, like Bildad the Shuhite, has perhaps not divorced religion and business, as Ishmael

[18]*Ibid.*, I, 130.

thought, but united them. He seems to practice piety and to aim at the conversion of all his sailors in order to insure a prosperous voyage for the *Pequod*. The verse of Scripture in which he is engrossed when Ishmael meets him affords Melville singular opportunity for punning upon Ishmael's "lay" in the ship's profits, but at the same time it is one of the few New Testament maxims which matches the utilitarianism of Job's friends, with its cunning advice about spiritual dividends: "*'Lay* not up for yourselves treasures upon earth, where moth—'"[19] . . .

The prophet Elijah is properly a part of the history of King Ahab, but in *Moby-Dick* the captain of the *Pequod* and the stammering soothsayer never meet. Pierre is a combination of two unrelated Biblical characters, but he represents neither completely. Though he is an incarnation of the gentle Jesus, Billy Budd strikes a man down to his death.

Nor are the lives of Melville's characters in any significant way influenced by the lives of their Biblical prototypes. Personalities are carried over, but not always corresponding events. So little interest did he have in reconstructing a second Ishmael in the sailor of the *Pequod* that Melville allowed the character virtually to disappear the moment Ahab entered the scene. And as for Ahab, he is destroyed through his own imprudent action, not because his character resembles in some remarkable particulars that of King Ahab. For a moment he is a counterpart of the Israelite monarch, but in that moment his fate is merely exalted, not explained.

In fact, Peleg's boast about Ahab may be applied to the whole host of Melville's characters. Affected as they are by Scriptural patterns, by literary and historical types, constituting, indeed, types themselves, each nonetheless achieves a life of his own. The impressionable Ishmael, about to sail the boundless seas under a strange captain, hears one of his proprietors say of him: "'Oh! he ain't Captain Bildad; no, and he ain't Captain Peleg; *he's Ahab,*

[19]*Ibid.*, I, 96.

boy. . . .'"[20] So many parallels are necessary to describe Ahab because he matches none completely but is a spirit moving free and uncapturable through the world. . . .

The great motif that appears in *Moby-Dick* is prophecy. Innumerable prophetic patterns ornament the tale—the tablets in the Whalemen's Chapel, the name of Peter Coffin, Ahab's loss of his comforting pipe, the dropping of the trumpet from the hands of the *Albatross's* captain as he prepared to answer Ahab's query about Moby-Dick, the fish swimming away from Ahab and toward the *Albatross*, the *Pequod's* encounter with the mysterious squid, the fates of the *Jeroboam*, the *Samuel Enderby*, the *Rachel*, and the *Delight*, Fedallah's standing in Ahab's shadow, Ahab's construction of another log and line, and his regulation of the thunderstruck compass. But in addition to these omens and implications there are articulate prophets in the book: the squaw Tistig, Father Mapple, Elijah, Gabriel, and Fedallah. And the entire story may be said to be the account of the fulfillment of their prophecies.

Now these prophets belong to a particular school of prophecy: the Hebrew. All but Fedallah are verbally connected with some Old Testament prophet or prophecy, and Father Mapple has even caught the idiom of that speech. In fact, Melville seems to have associated the whole prophetic profession with the Hebrews. With his penchant for the particular rather than the general, he referred to "'the Hebrew prophets'" and a "prophet of Israel"[21] when his context called for only the common noun.

He seems to have distinguished, too, among these prophets of Israel. For the prophets in *Moby-Dick*, who are by no means of equal stature—some are eloquent, some are mere sound and fury—correspond to certain definite types among the Hebrews. It is the emergence of these types, in fact, which constitutes the chief development of their prophecy. Usually said to have three stages, it begins with

---

[20]*Ibid.*, I, 99.
[21]*Billy Budd and Other Prose Pieces*, p. 45; *Poems*, p. 188.

the simple soothsayer, or foreteller, like the Witch of Endor. Such prophets are the Gay Head Indian Tistig and Elijah. Both, in general but unmistakable terms, foretell Ahab's death; and Elijah includes in his fate all who are associated with him. This kind of prophecy may be followed out by succeeding events in history, which, in *Moby-Dick*, thoroughly vindicate these crude seers.

As it became more sophisticated, Hebrew prophecy reached its culmination in the person of the interpreter or spokesman of Jehovah, such as Amos, Hosea, and Isaiah. Father Mapple is this type of prophet. In his sermon to the whalemen he endeavors as no other person in all Melville's novels to illuminate and rationalize the workings of an apparently blind fate. Even the text of his discourse is in keeping with his character: the story of the prophet Jonah.

Declining at last into an apocalyptic type of foretelling, Hebrew prophecy in its later phase is best represented by the last part of the Book of Daniel. Unlike the soothsayer, the apocalyptic foreteller cannot be vindicated by history; he speaks of things which do not happen in time. To this class of prophets Gabriel belongs. He not only narrates events which may be verified, such as the death of Macey, but he claims knowledge of facts which are beyond proof: he insists upon his own archangelic identity and recognizes in Moby-Dick the incarnation of his Shaker God.

Besides individuals such as these, who are all true prophets, there appeared among the Hebrews equivocal or false prophets. The subject is an obscure one, complicated by the fact that such prophets might be deliberately misled by Jehovah, as were those of Ahab's court. Even the fulfillment of the prophecy was not always adduced as a test, though it remained the popular one. Actually, the main distinction between the true and false prophets seems to have been a moral or spiritual one, founded upon the individual's intent, and thus not immediately perceptible. So Fedallah may be said to belong to this class of prophets. For although his predictions to Ahab are verified by events in the last chapter of *Moby-Dick*, he plays a false role with

51

his captain, luring him to his death with apparent promises of success.

The oracular nature of Fedallah's speech, it is true, is somewhat reminiscent of Greek prophecy, a school to which Melville occasionally referred figuratively but which he came no nearer imitating than this. Had he been less saturated with the tradition of the Bible he might have associated the insanity which he occasionally bestowed on his prophets with Greek rather than Hebrew thought. Unlike Jehovah's spokesmen, the oracles of the Olympian gods were often as enigmatical to themselves as to their hearers. But between the mad priestesses of Delphi and Dodona and Melville's cracked Elijah and Gabriel there is no connection. His conception of the unseen world was not Greek. If the gods choose to speak, Starbuck observes, "'they will honourably speak outright; not shake their heads, and give an old wives' darkling hint.'"[22]

It is largely the presence of these prophetic characters which creates in *Moby-Dick* its mood of fate—a mood pervading so many of Melville's books. For like the Hebrew prophets, hopelessly entangled in their national destiny, these individuals are defeatists, first to last, prophesying ill fortune for a mischosen course. . . .

One of the great Hebrew messages of doom, on the other hand, reverberates throughout *Moby-Dick*. It is the prophecy that the commercial states of Phoenicia, Tyre and Sidon, would be destroyed[23]—a prediction the more remarkable because history had not thus far pointed to the precarious nature of a mercantile economy or to its possible downfall. Melville later marked Stanley's discussion of this subject in his copy of *Sinai and Palestine*, and in his own Bible he underscored the word "merchants" in Job 41:6: ". . . shall they part him [leviathan] among the merchants?"

The story of King Ahab itself is illustrative of this theme, since the prophets of his court opposed his trade with the

[22]*Moby-Dick*, II, 341.
[23]Isa. 23:1, 15; Ezek. 26-28.

heathen Ben-hadad. It is a detail of the narrative which in *Moby-Dick* undergoes a characteristic metamorphosis. Actually the catastrophe overwhelming the *Pequod* is the result not of the commercial purpose of her voyage but of that purpose's being abandoned. Yet so quickly and so far behind are the claims of trade left that they are in effect totally irrelevant. The whaling enterprise is of no more genuine consequence than King Ahab's bazaars or Phoenicia's ships, while Captain Ahab's "fiery hunt" goes eternally on, in a realm in which Father Mapple and the Old Testament seers are equally at home.

For if most of Melville's pessimistic prophets in *Moby-Dick* dwell exclusively upon the horror of the forthcoming catastrophe, ignoring its significance and its original cause, one does not. Father Mapple has a conception of the law itself which underlies the whole narrative. He thus embodies the true purpose of Hebrew prophecy, which is revelation, not mystery-mongering. From his seaworthy pulpit in the Whalemen's Chapel he not only issues a warning of destruction, but he defines the fundamental statute which, once broken, precipitates that destruction.

For his text on this occasion the resourceful Mapple turns to the one book in the Bible written for an audience of whalemen. The choice is nothing less than inspired. But the appropriateness of its selection and the arresting nautical idiom in which it is retold cannot hide the fact that between this tale and the theme of Father Mapple's discourse there is the greatest discrepancy. Far from illustrating his philosophy, it is the best example in all the Old Testament to support the opposite point of view.

As Mapple pictures him, Jonah himself is a kind of Ishmael, called to set himself against the city of Nineveh by warning the populace that for their sins they are about to be destroyed. Being unwilling to obey, he takes ship to escape from Jehovah. Thus far Mapple follows the Biblical story. But in assigning a motive for Jonah's flight he diverges from it. In the last chapter of the Book of Jonah the prophet makes a clear defense of himself when he professes to have known that Jehovah's heart was soft and to have suspected that the divine decree for their destruction would be revoked if the wicked Ninevites were moved by his preaching to repentance. Therefore, in order to avoid seeing his prophecy so controverted, he embarked for Tarshish. His suspicions have been vindicated; he has threatened Nineveh with destruction, the people have repented, and Jehovah, touched by their renewed allegiance to him, has pardoned them. The prophet appears to himself vain and even ridiculous. But more than that, he can but appear sadly primitive by the side of this compassionate Jehovah. . . .

It is an entirely different motive which is ascribed to Jonah's flight by Father Mapple. His Jonah has none of the vindictive spirit of the fire-eating Biblical prophet; on the contrary, he shrinks from preaching a doctrine of destruction because of the enemies he will create. Realizing how unwelcome the truth of the Lord will be to the wicked city, he is appalled to think of the hostility he will raise there. And for this reason he flees from the very land, hoping to escape his duty. But even in his flight he becomes the thing he wishes to escape becoming: an outcast among his fellows, bringing hatred upon himself in their midst. Even nature conspires against him, brewing up such a gale that the crew is forced to sacrifice him for its own safety. His only recourse now being to accept the will of Jehovah, Jonah repents of his disobedience and sets out for Nineveh.

Like Josephus, Father Mapple omits the last of Jonah's story. There is nothing in his sermon about Jehovah's compassion for the repentant city, his pardon, and his gentle remonstrance with his harsh prophet. This final chapter of the book, as the most casual reader will agree, is its heart and its beauty. To it Melville cannot have been insensitive or, like the Pharisaic Josephus, opposed. But the structure of *Moby-Dick* calls for the sermon and the narrative to agree, and in the tragic voyage of the *Pequod* there is no divine interference.

Father Mapple's story of Jonah, then, is not the one

related by the Biblical scribe. But it is substantially the story of another Old Testament prophet: Jeremiah. Among the four great prophets his name appears least often in Melville's pages—less than half a dozen times in all. Yet in itself this fact may signify little. Melville was often at pains to disguise and even to disavow his sources, as he claimed, for example, never to have seen a copy of Porter's *Cruise*, upon which he drew for *Typee*. That he read Jeremiah is attested by the well-marked pages of this book in his Bible, where he also marked the prophecies of Isaiah, Ezekiel, Daniel, Joel, Jonah, and Habakkuk. The details of Jeremiah's life, however, would seem to have had a peculiar appeal for him.

It is, in some respects, the noblest life in the Old Testament. The divine call to prophecy found Jeremiah a diffident and reluctant young man, unlike Ezekiel, for instance, shrinking from Jehovah's harsh role for him, which was to be "a defenced city, and an iron pillar, and brasen walls against the whole land, against the kings of Judah, against the princes thereof, against the priests thereof, and against the people of the land."[24] For something like twenty years his sensitive nature, even while obeying, struggled against this divine plan, and his contest with kings and princes was accompanied by an interior battle. Such, in fact, is the character ascribed by Father Mapple to the quite dissimilar prophet Jonah.

Indeed, the times in which Jeremiah lived are more aptly described as divinely "brewed . . . into a gale," as Mapple puts it, than Jonah's eighth century. It was, in the southern kingdom, the time of the first Babylonian captivity. Forced into silence during a temporary period of national prosperity, Jeremiah emerged to prophesy that Jehovah would destroy the Temple at Jerusalem. For this inflammatory speech he nearly lost his life, being first put in the stocks by the priests and later imprisoned by the princes.

His soliloquy on the first occasion marked the climax of his long mental conflict, and in it he acknowledged the

[24]Jer. 1:18.

bitter truth which is also Father Mapple's discovery: that peace with the world is unattainable by the man with a divinely appointed task. When he follows Jehovah's command he is maltreated, yet forsake it he cannot. He has tried. And he is constrained not by any external action of Jehovah's, as in the case of Jonah, but by some inner necessity—like that of Ahab:

> O LORD, thou hast deceived me, and I was deceived: thou art stronger than I, and hast prevailed: I am in derision daily, every one mocketh me.
>
> For since I spake, I cried out, I cried violence and spoil; because the word of the LORD was made a reproach unto me, and a derision daily.
>
> Then I said, I will not make mention of him, nor speak any more in his name. But his word was in mine heart as a burning fire shut up in my bones, and I was weary with forbearing and I could not stay.[25]

Not the least element in Jeremiah's painful renunciation of the world is Jehovah's demand, not made on Hosea, for example, for his celibacy. His imagination is haunted, like Ahab's, by the thought of his home, and often the image of the bridegroom's voice stilled by Jehovah appears on his pages. Melville marked one of the passages in his own Bible: "Then will I cause to cease from the cities of Judah, and from the streets of Jerusalem, the voice of mirth, and the voice of gladness, the voice of the bridegroom, and the voice of the bride: for the land shall be desolate."[26]. . . Even the family of the unwilling Starbuck is bereft in the final wreck of the *Pequod*, whose captain had observed: ". . . even the highest earthly felicities ever have a certain unsignifying pettiness lurking in them. . . ."[27]

Unmistakably Jeremiah was no ordinary prophet of gloom, and his sermon regarding the fall of the Temple, for which he was apprehended, was no ordinary prophecy of disaster. It was his contention that Jehovah purposed to

[25] Jer. 20:7-9.
[26] *Ibid.*, 7:34.
[27] *Moby-Dick*, II, 230.

destroy the structure not as a punishment but in the interest of true religion—at first glance a blasphemous and a traitorous idea. But the Deuteronomic reform of King Josiah, by making the Temple the one legitimate center of worship, had formalized and nationalized religion, and it was Jeremiah's purpose to disembody it. As the sanctuary at Shiloh had been destroyed, said he, so it was necessary for Jerusalem to be devastated before the true spiritual nature of religion could be realized. Transferring his theory to politics, Jeremiah assumed the role also of traitor by recognizing Babylon, against which Josiah's court constantly rebelled, as nothing less than a benevolent agent of Jehovah, by means of which his plan for Judah was to be accomplished.

This plan, it must be emphasized, was by no means narrowly retributive. In connection with Father Mapple's sermon, and with Melville's thought in general, it was most significantly a plan of salvation. Despite the melancholy associations which cluster round Jeremiah's name—Melville himself referred to "Jeremiads"—he had the valorous confidence which only a prophet of the spirit can have. Writing to the exiles in Babylon, he urged them to cease all efforts to return to Jerusalem, since by reducing them to dependence upon him there Jehovah purposed to reveal himself to them: "Thus saith the LORD, The people which were left of the sword found grace in the wilderness; even Israel, when I went to cause him to rest."[28] In fact, the salvation of Israel through captivity in Babylon was to follow an earlier pattern: Jehovah's revelation of himself to the tribes in the Exodus. This episode of his national history is the source of Jeremiah's figure of speech, for he quoted Jehovah as saying:

I remember thee, the kindness of thy youth, the love of thine espousals, when thou wentest after me in the wilderness, in a land that was not sown. . . .

Neither said they, Where is the LORD that brought us up out of

[28]Jer. 31:2.

the land of Egypt, that led us through the wilderness, through a land of deserts and of pits, through a land of drought, and of the shadow of death, through a land that no man passed through, and where no man dwelt?[29]

Both verses are marked in Melville's Bible.

The religion envisaged by Jeremiah thus promised on the one hand freedom of the individual spirit and on the other the gravest personal peril. Unfettered by ecclesiastical or political institutions, it was, in the widest sense of the word, spiritual, as unbounded as Melville's sea, as bodiless as his air. The old law of "the sins of the fathers" is superseded by a "new covenant" with each individual. It is the beginning of the New Testament doctrine of personal salvation, quoted by Jesus himself. The law is now written in the heart of a man:

> After those days, saith the LORD, I will put my law in their inward parts, and write it in their hearts; and will be their God, and they shall be my people.
> And they shall teach no more every man his neighbour, and every man his brother, saying, Know the LORD: for they shall all know me, from the least of them unto the greatest of them, saith the LORD. . . .[30]

The verses call to mind not only the self-determining Ahab in *Moby-Dick*, but also Pierre and Billy Budd, whose inner law Melville so passionately contrasted with that without. Old Bardianna even echoes the words of Jeremiah when he says: "'. . . we need not be told what righteousness is; we were born with the whole Law in our hearts.'"[31]

At the same time, the tragic circumstances of his age led Jeremiah more than any other Old Testament prophet to associate also an element of peril with any plan of redemption. And so it is with Melville. The way of truth is uneasy, lonely, and fraught with mortal danger. Even the

[29]*Ibid.*, 2:2, 6.
[30]*Ibid.*, 31:33, 34.
[31]*Mardi*, II, 303.

whale, as Ishmael observes, is best comprehended in his own frightful element:

> How vain and foolish, then, thought I, for timid untravelled man to try to comprehend aright this wondrous whale, by merely poring over his dead attenuated skeleton, stretched in this peaceful wood. No. Only in the heart of quickest perils; only when within the eddyings of his angry flukes; only on the profound unbounded sea, can the fully invested whale be truly and livingly found out.[32]

Without doubt an excursion into the life of Jeremiah illuminates the theme of Father Mapple's sermon as the story of Jonah does not. But neither can the *tour de force* of introducing *Moby-Dick* with the greatest of all whale yarns be improved upon. The loss in literary accuracy is a spectacular artistic gain, and it is with singular dexterity that the lives of the two prophets are entwined.

As Father Mapple tells them, Jonah's adventures illustrate the operation of a destiny which, once set in motion, the individual cannot control or escape. The determination of Jehovah to send Jonah to Nineveh was not to be disputed; even the physical universe plotted to bring about the accomplishment of that purpose. And since Father Mapple is himself a prophet of sorts, the same inexorable fate may be seen operating in the lives of the characters who people *Moby-Dick*—and, for that matter, of all Melville's characters.

But, unlike Jonah, none of them is interfered with by an external force. There is nothing in all Melville's narratives comparable in function to the whale. His notion of tragedy as interior is in the Renaissance rather than the classical tradition, for the force which moves all his major characters is their own. They are like Jeremiah, impelled from within, resolving for his own health not to speak Jehovah's word, yet finding it impossible to be silent. Its fire consumed his bones, as the Persian fire of Ahab's desire burned in him.

Again, returning to Jonah, Melville found there an element of his theme which is not in Jeremiah. It is the

[32] *Moby-Dick*, II, 218.

notion that this inexorable fate is amoral. It is neither controlled by wisdom nor tempered to innocence. The crew of Jonah's vessel would have been destroyed with him had they not separated their lots from his. So the crew of the *Pequod*, ignoring the example, perish with their captain. For though Starbuck perceives the whole terrible scheme of affairs, how in Ahab's precipitate flight to destruction the entire crew is drawn along, he is powerless to alter the situation. Like Pierre, with whom both Lucy and Isabel are sacrificed and whose catastrophe is described in the same figure of speech, he sees that "in tremendous extremities human souls are like drowning men; well enough they know they are in peril; well enough they know the causes of that peril; nevertheless, the sea is the sea, and these drowning men do drown." [33]

Nor is this destiny, as both Jonah and Jeremiah knew, in any way colored by the emotions of men. It is neither tragic nor happy. It does not matter that Jonah was called to be a prophet with an unwelcome message; that Jeremiah was called to bring upon himself derision, calumny, hatred, imprisonment. It does not matter that some persons are called to be Ishmaels against the world. Indeed, there is no happiness except in submission to this will and no misfortune except in the attempt to escape it. As Father Mapple cries:

"Woe to him whom this world charms from Gospel duty! Woe to him who seeks to pour oil upon the waters when God has brewed them into a gale! Woe to him who seeks to please rather than to appal! Woe to him whose good name is more to him than goodness! Woe to him who, in this world, courts not dishonour! Woe to him who would not be true, even though to be false were salvation! Yea, woe to him who, as the great Pilot Paul has it, while preaching to others is himself a castaway! [34]

In this overpowering denunciation Mapple turns for example to the storm which overtook Jonah. He could have

33 *Pierre*, p. 423.
34 *Moby-Dick*, I, 58-59.

found an equally awesome one in Jeremiah's prophecy of the seventy years of captivity, a passage Melville penciled in his Bible.

But now the sermon in the Whalemen's Chapel passes from negation and concludes on a note of wild exultation. And now, finally, it is Jeremiah, with his prophecy that the captives will at length return, who provides the parallel; Melville marked the famous consolation of Chapter 30 as he read it. If one fully acquiesces in this will of the universe, then all the apparent misfortunes of life become transformed into the most exquisite delights. They are, as the man in Stubb's dream remarks, kicks with an ivory leg instead of a common pitch-pine one, and so to be considered honorable.

This is no ordinary happiness. But for characters such as Ahab, Pierre, Taji, Budd, even Media and Nathan common joy does not exist. In its place is a higher, more poignant sense of satisfaction in fulfilling their separate destinies. Each of them could be described by the words which Melville copied on a fly leaf of his New Testament:

In Life he appears as a true Philosopher—as a wise man in the highest sense. He stands firm to his point; he goes on his way inflexibly; and while he exalts the lower to himself, while he makes the ignorant, the poor, the sick, partakers of his wisdom, of his riches, of his strength, he, on the other hand, in no wise conceals his divine origin; he dares to equal himself with God; nay, to declare that he himself is God.

Each testifies to the truth of Father Mapple's eloquent conclusion:

"Delight is to him—a far, far, upward, and inward delight—who against the proud gods and commodores of this earth, even stands forth his own inexorable self. Delight is to him whose strong arms yet support him, when the ship of this base treacherous world has gone down beneath him. Delight is to him, who gives no quarter in the truth, and kills, burns, and destroys all sin though he pluck it out from under the robes of Senators and Judges. Delight,—topgallant delight is to him, who acknowledges no law or lord, but the Lord his God, and is only a patriot to heaven. Delight is to him, whom all the waves of the billows of the seas of the boisterous mob can never shake from this sure Keel of the Ages. And eternal delight and deliciousness will be his, who coming to lay him down, can say with his final breath—O Father!—chiefly known to me by Thy rod—mortal or immortal, here I die. I have striven to be Thine, more than to be this world's, or mine own. Yet this is nothing; I leave eternity to Thee; for what is man that he should live out the lifetime of his God?"[35]

Father Mapple's sermon, then, not merely contributes to the prophetic atmosphere at the beginning of *Moby-Dick*, but it constitutes in itself a prophecy, of which the ensuing narrative is a fulfilment. If there is any doubt about the matter, the last vessel seen by the *Pequod* dispels it. She is the *Delight*, her stove boats and splintered sides mocking her name and publishing to all whalers what an encounter with the white whale means. Surely the name she bears is significant. It is an echo from the conclusion of Father Mapple's sermon in distant New Bedford. The same word ends the prophecy and ends its fulfilment. And far more dramatically than even he could have told, this sorry ship represents the paradox of that word as he used it. For the delight which the uncompromising follower of the truth will have is a delight not of this world, but invisible, in the heart.

Yet the *Delight* is not the last ship of all in *Moby-Dick;* there is, finally, the *Rachel.* And her name, if not an echo of Mapple's sermon, is an echo from Jeremiah. For the verse which is paraphrased in the concluding sentence of the book comes from the prophet's great oracle of consolation, the promise that the exiles will return:

Thus saith the LORD; A voice was heard in Ramah, lamentation, and bitter weeping; Rachel weeping for her children refused to be comforted for her children, because they were not.

Thus saith the Lord; Refrain thy voice from weeping, and thine eyes from tears: for thy work shall be rewarded, saith the LORD; and they shall come again from the land of the enemy.[36]

[35]*Ibid.*, I, 59.
[36]Jer. 31:15-16.

This is the ship which, rescuing the sailor Ishmael, keeps the fate of the *Pequod* from being quite the final word.

This spiritual consolation, this interior delight is the reward of all Melville's prophets and heroes. Yet all the while they advance boldly into the wasteland, they look back with tenderness and longing to the green, companionable glades. So the Israelites in the Exodus looked to Egypt. The hymn which rightfully accompanies Father Mapple's sermon is separated from it by several chapters and belongs to a different occasion, but its mixed mood is the same. . . .

Had Melville's inspiration been any less inclusive or had this achievement been any more definitive, the irregularities of his thought and his style would be intolerable. As it is, these irregularities are nothing else than the "careful disorderliness" [37] which he declared to be for some enterprises the true method. Not definition is its aim, but suggestion; not keen analysis but bold juxtaposition, contrasts and paradoxes, catalogues and citations, reflections, reminiscences, and reverberations. The sea burns, the sands of the desert "Impart the oceanic sense," [38] the great cities of the world are wildernesses. Far from being the definitive book on whaling, *Moby-Dick* is prefaced by extracts from seventy-eight other books and contains allusions to scores more in the text. The subject is inexhaustible.

To this desire to extend the scope of his work, to this fear of appearing final, all Melville's rhetorical devices and all his voluminous sources are subservient. So indiscriminately are they introduced and associated that they tend at last to lose their separate identities. They are but fragments of a boundless creation, undistinguished otherwise in the hands of its creator. Of them all, however, no single one so far extends the bounds of what Melville wrote as the Bible. However he alluded to it he was assured of a contrast with his immediate material: between the common and the great,

[37] *Moby-Dick*, II, 101.
[38] *Clarel*, I, 216.

63

the present and the past, the natural and the supernatural. And though each is a contrast achieved by many other means as well, only this one enabled him to make them all simultaneously, at once magnifying his characters and their affairs, establishing for the briefest moment a background of antiquity, and suggesting the presence of yet another, unseen world beyond the vast scene which meets the eye.

V Paton's Use of the Bible in *Cry, the Beloved Country*
Roland Bartel

The influence of the Bible on *Cry, the Beloved Country* can be seen both in specific passages and in the pattern through which the theme is developed. The most important biblical passage in this connection is David's lament for Absalom in II Samuel 18:33: "And the king was much moved, and went up to the chamber over the gate, and wept: and as he went, thus he said, O my son Absalom, my son, my son Absalom! would God I had died for thee, O Absalom, my son, my son!"

This is one of the most penetrating expressions of grief in all literature, and it is woven into the novel in several ways. There is, first of all, the grief of Stephen Kumalo for his son Absalom, who has deserted his family and tribe and become a criminal in the city. Kumalo's sadness casts a shadow over everything he says and does, and on two occasions it expresses itself in words similar to those of David. His first words when he finds his son in prison, after a long and frustrating search, are "My child, my child" (14);[1] when he climbs the mountain to keep a vigil during the hours preceding his son's execution, the words of David again burst from his lips: "My son, my son, my son" (36).

These passages invite us to observe several other parallels between the novel and the story of David and Absalom. Kumalo's son has broken his family and tribe by deserting his community much as David's son broke up his father's family and government through subversion and conspiracy. The mourning on the part of the inconsolable King David corresponds to the general lament of Stephen Kumalo and others for their native land, a lament contained

[1] The numbers in parentheses refer to chapters in the novel and the chapters of the books of the Bible.

in the title of the novel. The references to the heart-rending cry of David for his son seem to magnify the elegiac tone of all the cries that arise in this novel: Stephen Kumalo crying for his son Absalom, his sister Gertrude, and his brother John; James Jarvis and all his friends crying for his murdered son, Arthur; Stephen Kumalo and his fellow clergyman Theophilus Msimangu crying for the disintegration of tribal life; the lyrical voices in the choral interludes crying for the land itself as well as for the people.

A second biblical passage that is woven into many chapters of the novel is I John 4:18: "There is no fear in love; but perfect love casteth out fear." Just as David's lament for Absalom sets the tone for the main part of the novel referred to in the title, this passage from the New Testament sets the tone for that part of the novel referred to in the subtitle, "A Story of Comfort in Desolation." The subtitle applies primarily to the last part of the novel, where most of the words of hope and acts of restoration occur. This change in emphasis begins when things seem to be at their darkest, the death of the idealistic white reformer Arthur Jarvis at the hands of the black delinquent Absalom Kumalo. The bishop who conducts the service eulogizes the deceased as having lived a life "of intelligence and courage, of love that cast out fear" (21). When Stephen Kumalo returns to his parish he is full of fear because of the disgrace he has suffered from his sister, his brother, and his son. However, the greetings he receives from his parishioners are so warm that he is able to cast out his fear and conclude that "kindness and love pay for pain and suffering" (30). At the conclusion of the novel when he is on the mountaintop awaiting his son's execution, he thinks about the future of Africa and concludes that only love can cast out fear—in this instance the fear in the hearts of those who do not want to see Africa restored.

Closely allied to the concept of casting out fear with love in the rebuilding of Africa is a biblical story that parallels some parts of book three of the novel. When Kumalo returns to his native valley, he finds the country stricken with drought; as he prays for rain the reader is reminded of the drought in Samaria that was broken by Elijah's prayer for rain. Considering the two episodes together helps to deepen, for the reader, Kumalo's concern for the survival of his community and emphasizes his importance in its final restoration.

In a story dealing with the disappearance of a son who falls into disgrace, it is to be expected that the biblical story of the prodigal son (Luke 15) will enter in. The author very wisely keeps this powerful story at a distance so that it does not detract from his own story, but he refers to it often enough to remind the reader of several parallels. When Stephen Kumalo discusses his search for Absalom with his brother John, John asks facetiously whether the prodigal has been found. Stephen replies sadly that the son has been found—in prison (14). When the two meet again after their sons have been apprehended for murder, John proposes to kill the fatted calf when their troubles are over (29); Stephen is so put off by his brother's insincerity that he as much as tells him that he will not cast his pearls before swine (Matt. 7:6). That John may for a moment see himself cast in the role of the prodigal son is suggested in the same scene when he says, "You are my older brother. Speak what you wish." There are other places in the novel where phrases from the story of the prodigal son seem significant. When Kumalo recovers from his brief quarrel with his wife (2), we are told that "he came to himself," the phrase used to describe the prodigal son's recovery of his senses. The allusion suggests the seriousness of Kumalo's brief lapse from sanity. The same phrase occurs in happier circumstances near the end of the story when Kumalo realizes with a start how much his life has been changed by his journey to the big city. Kumalo uses another phrase from the story of the prodigal son when he tells his host and guests in Johannesburg of "that far country" from which he has come (5), probably a subconscious admission that if he does not return to his homeland he will also become a prodigal—like his sister, his brother, and his son.

When the clergymen in the story converse with each other or reveal their thoughts, it is only natural that they should use biblical language. Some of these examples will be noted briefly, for they help us appreciate these men and their problems more fully. When Kumalo gets discouraged in his search for his son, he expresses his despair by quoting Jesus' words on the cross and then reassures himself with the words of the Twenty-third Psalm (10). When he tries to convince a suspicious woman that he will keep in confidence any information she gives him about Absalom, he says that his yea has always been yea and his nay, nay (8, cf. Matt. 5:37), but, interestingly enough, when he offers to swear an oath he ignores the admonition against the swearing of oaths that immediately precedes the biblical passage that he quotes. When he talks with Absalom in prison, his reprimand takes on a sharper edge by being couched in biblical language: "you stole and broke in" (14, cf. Matt. 6:19). When he is depressed by Absalom's disgrace, Father Vincent reassures him with a saying from the Zulu tongue, "When the storm threatens, a man is afraid of his house." Kumalo replies by referring to the house built on sand (Matt. 7:26), an allusion that makes his depression all the more poignant—an old man at the end of his career asking himself whether the defection of his son proves that he, the father, built his house on sand. When Father Vincent reminds him that there may be hope for his son since a thief repented on the cross, Kumalo thinks of the children his son has orphaned and recalls Jesus' words about the gravity of offenses against children (15, cf. Matt. 18:6 and Luke 23:39-43). When Kumalo returns to Ndotsheni and sees the drought, he reveals the depth of his concern for his homeland by twice paraphrasing the words from the cross, "Into thy hands, O God, I commend Ndotsheni" (31, cf. Luke 23:46). Later in the story when the rains have fallen and the restoration has begun, the extent of his relief and joy is suggested by the voice he hears in his imagination, "Comfort ye, comfort ye, my people" (34, cf. Isa. 40). At the end of the story the narrator describes Kumalo's activities in a way that suggests several parallels to the Bible. Climbing the mountain to keep a vigil prior to his son's execution relates his suffering to that of Jesus on the Mount of Olives and in Gethsemane (36, cf. Matt. 26:30-46). When we are told that the next morning he took out his food "gave thanks, and broke the cakes and ate them, and drank the tea," the language echoes the words of the Last Supper (Matt. 26:26-29) and suggests that he is experiencing a mystical communion with his son, who is at that moment being executed in Johannesburg. The darkness that follows the crucifixion in the New Testament has a meaningful contrast in the novel. When Kumalo finishes his communion meal and the time for Absalom's execution has passed, he looks to the east and sees the dawning of a new day. We are told in the last paragraph of the novel that the light will come to the regions that are still in darkness, an echo of another great passage of hope, "The people that walked in darkness have seen a great light" (Isa. 9:2).

The faith of the clergymen is expressed through biblical allusions in several other places. When Father Vincent tells Kumalo that the ways of God are secret (15), an expression used in the last sentence of the novel and in many other places, he is sharing the apostle Paul's firm faith in the eventual triumph of right over wrong (Rom. 11:33-36). When Msimangu preaches his optimistic sermon at the asylum for the blind (13), he appropriately reads from two famous passages of hope, Isaiah 40 and 42. We are told that Msimangu has learned to keep his poise in the midst of discouragement because for him the world of suffering is no continuing city (13, cf. Heb. 13:14).

Four additional biblical allusions may be noted for their contribution to the substance of the story. "Stand unshod upon it, for the ground is holy" (1) acquires a spiritual quality because of its obvious similarity to the words describing the experience of Moses when he saw God in the burning bush (Exod. 3:1-6). The spellbinding effect of John Kumalo's oratory is enhanced by the reference to Pentecost (27, cf. Acts 2:2), and the strength of his talents is suggested by the reference to the parable of the talents (27, cf. Matt. 25:14-30). The statement in the choral interlude in chapter 12 that the light of life may have to be preserved under a bushel for a while, acquires a hopeful connotation because it alludes to the positive statement about the light under a bushel in Matthew 5:14-16.

One of the outstanding features of Alan Paton's use of biblical allusions is the manner in which he keeps them at a distance. He does not permit them to become so prominent that they detract from his story. He creates approximately parallel situations rather than exactly parallel ones, and his verbal allusions are usually rephrased so that the attention remains fixed on his text rather than on the biblical passage alluded to. A classic example of this device is Kumalo's vigil on the mountain in the last chapter. The references to Gethsemane and the Last Supper are clear, but they are so subdued that we never take our minds off Kumalo. The same point must be made about the style. It is tempting to conclude from the repetitions and the cadences in the lyrical passages that the style is essentially biblical, but that would be a mistake. There are many styles in the book. Note, for example, that there is nothing biblical in the language of the Harrisons or the Jarvises. The language of the natives seems closer to their own dialects than to the Bible, yet some biblical qualities are there; however, the biblical style, like the biblical allusions, is unobtrusive and subordinated to the style of the context. As Lewis Gannet has said in his introduction to the 1948 edition of the novel (p. xix), the music of the novel is "a strangely blended folksong, with elements of Zulu and Xosa speech, and echoes of the rhythm of that Jewish-Christian Bible which speaks with such peculiar intimacy to black men in both America and South Africa. . . . It sings with a new-old beauty to the whole world."

[For a series of lesson plans based on this novel, see "A Text-Centered Unit on *Cry, the Beloved Country*," by Thayer S. Warshaw (65¢), Indiana University Institute on Teaching the Bible in Secondary English, Sycamore 203, Bloomington, Indiana 47401.—Ed.]

VI *The Mayor of Casterbridge* and The Old Testament's First Book of Samuel: A Study of Some Literary Relationships*

Julian Moynahan

*Department of English,
Rutgers University*

I

From one standpoint, the major theme of Thomas Hardy's *The Mayor of Casterbridge*[1] is not "character is fate" or "man against himself,"[2] but rather it is the conflict between generations. This is a very ancient subject matter, one of the archetypal themes noted by the Jungian literary psychologist Maud Bodkin, who traces it in classical Greek drama and in Shakespeare's *Hamlet* and *King Lear*.[3] In Hardy's novel the conflicting generations are represented by Michael Henchard, the middle-aged corn factor and mayor, and Donald Farfrae, the energetic young Scotchman whose two-fold abilities, "the commercial and the romantic" (p. 162), while exercised with the best of intentions, prove deadly to his patron. Because of the ineluctability of this theme, it is necessary that the affection between the two men should turn to hate and that Henchard, as the older, should go under. The special bitterness of Henchard's inevitable failure is perhaps

*Reprinted by permission of the Modern Language Association of America from *Publications of the Modern Language Association*, 71 (March, 1956): 118-30.

[1] All page references to *The Mayor of Casterbridge* are to the text ed. published in the series called "Rinehart Editions" by Rinehart & Co. (New York, 1948).

[2] See A. J. Guerard, *Thomas Hardy: The Novels and Stories* (Cambridge, Mass.: Harvard Univ. Press, 1949), pp. 146-153, for a psychiatrically oriented discussion of Henchard's self-destructive and masochistic traits.

[3] *Archetypal Patterns in Poetry* (London, 1934), pp. 23-24.

Hardy's characteristically pessimistic contribution. But we might also relate this quality of bitterness to the lack—increasingly in Hardy's time and almost totally in ours—of a generally accepted religious outlook which could transform Henchard's sufferings into a mitigating ritual and his death into a sacrificial symbol. Whereas Lear dies in the bosom of his family, as it were, surrounded by both his living and dead relatives, in full view of an awed and edified audience, Henchard's death is hidden from the eyes of all men except the faithful "fool" Whittle, whose report is necessarily limited to a few concrete particulars. Under the circumstances, Elizabeth-Jane's "what bitterness lies there!" (p. 337) is, at least on one level of the narrative, a final comment which every reader must echo.

Nevertheless, there is another level of significance in the novel, a level on which Henchard assumes the august dimensions of a legendary king, while his opponent, Farfrae, undergoes a similar enlarging transformation. How does this happen? Through a strategy of association Henchard's career is connected with the career of Saul, the melancholy king of Old Testament narrative; Henchard's shift from affection and trust to suspicion and finally hatred for Farfrae is connected to a corresponding shift in the relations between Saul and David; Farfrae, whose character combines the ingredients of shrewdness, musical sensitivity, and a strong capacity for romantic attachment, is connected to David, the brilliant, poetic, yet politic young Bethlehemite outlander who began his public career as Saul's armour bearer and beloved companion, later became his hated rival, and ended as king of all Israel.

Extended parallels between the Henchard-Farfrae conflict and the Saul-David conflict have never been noted before, so far as I am aware, although every careful reader of the novel notices Hardy's general indebtedness to biblical narrative for allusions and metaphors.[4] The novel's one

[4] Arthur McDowall in his *Thomas Hardy* (London, 1931), p. 74, describes Farfrae as "the David to Henchard's Saul" but does not go on to develop the point.

direct statement of comparison between Henchard and Saul is "Henchard felt like Saul at his reception by Samuel" (p. 189) and is from the episode of the visit to the weather prophet. This disarmingly casual sentence does not encourage the reader to develop the stated resemblance beyond the narrowly circumscribed context in which it occurs. But the resemblance can be developed to a striking degree by anyone who attempts a close reading of those chapters in I Samuel which deal with the relationship of Saul and David along with an attentive rereading of *The Mayor of Casterbridge*.

The identification of characters and incidents with their biblical counterparts does not extend beyond the central dramatic situation of the novel, which I take to be the aggressive rivalry of the two men in their careers and in their personal affairs. Within this area the parallels are both detailed and illuminating. In fact, I would argue that the full meaning of certain scenes can be grasped only by having the reader make the appropriate connections between corresponding features of the Henchard *vs*. Farfrae action and its archaic prototype. But this is a critical question which can be settled only after the existence and scope of the extended parallelism have been established.

II

In *The Mayor of Casterbridge* the hazards of grain speculation seem roughly to correspond with the constant threat of Philistine invasion which haunts the reign of King Saul. When Farfrae arrives in Casterbridge, Henchard is at the height of his power as leading merchant and civil magistrate. But for the moment he is seriously embarrassed from having been forced to sell spoiled corn to the townspeople. Farfrae, appearing from out of the blue, saves Henchard from embarrassment and financial loss by showing him a method for restoring the corn. He asks no payment and wishes to continue his journey to the New

World. But Henchard, with characteristic generosity and impulsiveness, offers Farfrae a position as general manager of his enterprises and is willing to give him a third share in the ownership if he will only stay in Casterbridge. It is immediately clear that on Henchard's side there is a good deal of personal attachment involved and that these personal elements in the relationship are bound up with Henchard's great loneliness and with his sensitivity to music. When the mayor overhears Farfrae's singing at the Three Mariners inn, he pauses in the street and after listening attentively comments "to be sure, to be sure, how that fellow does draw me! . . . I suppose 'tis because I'm lonely" (p. 58).

The part played by music in *The Mayor of Casterbridge* is extremely important and will be discussed in some detail below. Here it is sufficient that we recall the young David's musical accomplishments and the strong sensitivity to music shown by King Saul on many occasions in his career. David recommended himself to Saul by slaying Goliath and by his skill at music. Farfrae recommended himself to Henchard by his saving of the damaged corn and by his musical talent. Both David and Farfrae are not only strangers when they make their first appearances upon the public scene, but they are also "foreigners": Farfrae a Scot among Wessex men; David a member of the tribe of Judah at the court of a Benjamite king. Both make contact with their temporarily inaccessible future patrons when they proclaim confidently that they can settle the problem at hand. Word reaches Saul when the servants carry David's boast by word of mouth; Farfrae quietly sends in his own note.

As though to underline the parallelism which is being established, the language describing Farfrae when he makes his first appearance in the novel is taken, in large part, directly from the only two verses in the entire Bible which give a physical description of David: "He was ruddy and of a fair countenance, bright-eyed and slight in build" (*The Mayor of Casterbridge*, p. 39). "Now he was ruddy, and withal of a beautiful countenance, and goodly to look to" (I Samuel 16.12).[5] "And when the Philistine looked about, and saw David, he disdained him: for he was but a youth, and ruddy, and of a fair countenance" (I Samuel 17.42). The slight build is also traditionally ascribed to David on the grounds that Saul's failure to perform God's commands had convinced Him that the standard of enormous physical strength and great height by which Saul had been selected as first king of the Hebrews was no longer appropriate. Henceforth, the Lord will judge by other criteria and He advises the prophet Samuel to do likewise: "Look not on his countenance, or on the height of his stature; . . . for the Lord seeth not as man seeth; for man looketh on the outward appearance, but the Lord looketh on the heart" (I Samuel 16.7).

Henchard's personal qualities, as they are exposed in the early action of the novel, are entirely congruous with those we usually attribute to Saul. Emphasis is placed on his strength, generosity, moodiness, and an impulsiveness which is intensified at times to an almost suicidal rashness. This last quality is particularly notable in Saul, who is perhaps one of the most famous examples in world literature of the depressive temperament. When we read that Henchard "threw himself back so that his elbow rested on the table, his forehead being shaded by his hand, which, however, did not hide the marks of introspective inflexibility on his features" (p. 79), it is not difficult to connect such an image of brooding with the Saul who was troubled by "an evil spirit from the Lord" (I Samuel 16.14). When Henchard tries to explain to Farfrae how he became involved with Lucetta on the Isle of Jersey he says, "I fell quite ill, and in my illness I sank into one of those gloomy fits I sometimes suffer from, on account 'o the loneliness of my domestic life, when the world seems to have the blackness of hell, and, like Job, I could curse the day that gave me birth" (p. 80). Henchard's gloom is traceable to the rash act which doomed

[5] I make use of the Authorized Version of the Bible for all scriptural citations and references in this essay.

him to loneliness, the sale of wife and child to the sailor, Newson. Saul's gloom is similarly traceable to a rash act which cost him God's favor, his disobedience to God's commands during his military campaign against the Amalekites. At the same time, gloom seems to be constitutional for both these figures. We are seldom privileged to see them in any other state of feeling.

The friendship between Henchard and Farfrae turns sour only gradually. Their relationship is spoiled by Henchard's jealousy of Farfrae's phenomenal popularity with the local farmers and townspeople. From the innocent mouth of a child the older man hears the answer to his query as to why people always want his manager instead of him: "'And he's better-tempered, and Henchard's a fool to him,' they say. And when some of the women were a-walking home they said, 'He's a diment—he's a chap 'o wax—he's the best—he's the horse for my money,' says they. And they said, 'He's the most understanding man 'o them two by long chalks. I wish he was the master instead of Henchard,' they said" (p. 102). In very much the same way Saul grew envious of David, because the younger man's popularity as a military leader against the Philistines exceeded his own. And, as in the novel, the problem is dramatized in terms of the praise of women. When David returned from an expedition he was met by female musicians who improvised songs in praise of his exploits, "and the women answered one another as they played, and said, Saul hath slain his thousands and David his ten thousands" (I Samuel 18.7).

In each case jealousy is accompanied by a growth of gloomy suspicion. Saul suspects that David wants to usurp his throne. Henchard fears that he has put himself in Farfrae's power by telling him too many personal secrets. At the same time, Henchard does not actually dismiss Farfrae from his employment. His suspicions come in waves and "when his jealous temper had passed away, his heart sank within him at what he had said and done" (p. 110). His affection returns—until some new success of his young assistant sets him off again. Eventually, Farfrae must withdraw from Henchard's employment of his own decision, just as David must eventually flee Saul's court after enduring the monarch's murderous rages as long as he can. We sense in both cases that the older men are victims of their emotions rather than masters of them. They are trapped in a cyclic pattern of ambivalent feeling, oscillating between love and hate.

When Henchard has finally maneuvered Farfrae into a position where he can destroy him, when he has him down during the fight in the hayloft, he discovers that he cannot go through with it. He has tied one arm behind his back so that Farfrae may have a fair chance. But is not the tied arm also construable as a symbol of the conflict of feeling which partially paralyzes Henchard during this scene?: "God is my witness that no man ever loved another as I did thee at one time. . . . And now—though I came here to kill 'ee, I cannot hurt thee!" (p. 277). He is overwhelmed with shame and self-hate as he recalls with piercing intensity "that time when the curious mixture of romance and thrift in the young man's composition so commanded his heart that Farfrae could play upon him as on an instrument" (p. 277). As Farfrae departs, Henchard remains in a state of acute depression, huddled in a corner of the loft on a pile of sacks.

The appropriate scene from the biblical narrative to place with this incident is the highly dramatic encounter of David and Saul in the wilderness at En-Gedi. David has been a hunted man for some time when he comes upon his persecutor lying sound asleep. Instead of killing him, he respects the sacrosanct person of the monarch and merely cuts off the border of Saul's robe as a sign of his opportunity and forbearance. When Saul awakes and realizes what has happened he has a poignant moment of intense regret; the old love for David comes flooding back and with it the bitterness of shame. He hears David, who is in hiding near by, cry out for the Lord to judge the cause that is between Saul and himself: "And it came to pass, when David had made an end of speaking these words unto Saul, that Saul said, Is this thy voice, my son David? And Saul lifted up his voice, and wept. And he said to David, Thou art more righteous than I: for thou hast rewarded me good, whereas I have rewarded thee evil" (I Samuel 24:16-17).

In I Samuel the king falls into David's hands twice, and twice is permitted to go on his way unharmed. There are, of course, no regular parallels to these incidents in *The Mayor of Casterbridge*. Instead, it is Henchard who twice is on the verge of murdering Farfrae and who both times lets him go unharmed. On an earlier occasion in the same hayloft which supplied the setting for the fight, Henchard had raised his hand behind Farfrae's back as the latter stood dangerously close to the open loft door. But after an inward struggle, his better impulses had conquered, and he had lowered his arm to his side. We may choose to see in this pair of incidents a sort of transposed or inverted parallelism in which events taken over from the older narrative are remade in order to fit them into the dramatic structure of the novel.

The biblical place-name Adullam undergoes a curious shift as it is taken over into the novel. In I Samuel Adullam is the great cave where David hid from Saul's searching parties. It was apparently an inaccessible hideout in which thieves and smugglers, as well as political refugees like David, might avoid the authorities. In *The Mayor of Casterbridge* Mixen Lane, the thieves' quarter of Casterbridge, is called "the Adullam of all the surrounding villages" (p. 257). This is an appropriate metaphor, but the name plays no part in any system of correspondences between the locations of events in the biblical narrative and locations of similar events in the novel. Farfrae, after all, has no connection with Mixen Lane.

III The motif of music

The Saul-David parallels may serve as a key to an understanding of the extraordinary, even magical, role played by music generally and by Farfrae's musical talents in particular in the action of the novel. Here David's great skill as singer, harpist, psalmist, and, as it happens, dancer should be kept in mind.

Farfrae begins his career in Casterbridge by enchanting the topers at the Three Mariners with his Scotch songs. The lonely mayor is drawn by this music into a feeling of loving kinship with the younger man. The townspeople admire Farfrae for his commercial abilities, but they are attracted to him, at least equally, on account of his singing ability. A turning point in the fortunes of both men is reached when they compete at providing entertainment for the citizenry on the public holiday. Henchard's spread is rained out—throughout the novel Henchard is victimized by inclement weather—while Farfrae's entertainment of music and dance is a success. As the disappointed mayor watches the people flock to Farfrae's ingeniously constructed tent where the Scot is dancing briskly in the costume of a Highlander, he is struck by envy. And when he perceives "the immense admiration for the Scotchman that revealed itself in the women's faces" (p. 108), he is so stung that his surly remarks provoke Farfrae to break openly with him, once and for all.

So intimately is Farfrae's charm bound up with the theme of music that even Lucetta, when she has had no contact with him in his role as a singer, succumbs to his "hyperborean crispness, stringency, and charm, as of a well-braced musical instrument" (p. 159). Here it is not a matter of specific abilities; rather, it is Farfrae's very nature that is being defined metaphorically in musical terms. Another form of this definition in musical terms is given by some expressions already quoted in another connection: Henchard's heart is so "commanded" by Farfrae that the latter could "play upon him as on an instrument." It may be appropriate to recall here that at the beginning of the scene in which these expressions occur—the scene of the hayloft fight—Farfrae had entered the loft building humming the same tune of friendship ("And here's a hand, my trusty fiere, / And gie's a hand 'o thine") which he had sung at the Three Mariners several years previous, upon first arriving in Casterbridge. Henchard's reaction revealed once again the power of Farfrae's music over him: "Nothing moved Henchard like an old melody. He sank back. 'No; I can't do it!' he gasped. 'Why does the infernal fool begin that now!'" (p. 274).

Near the end of the novel, when Henchard has sunk into a fixed despair, we learn that "if he could have summoned music to his aid his existence might even now have been borne; for with Henchard music was of regal power. The merest trumpet or organ tone was enough to move him, and high harmonies transubstantiated him. But hard fate had ordained that he should be unable to call up this Divine spirit in his need" (p. 299). There is a complicated irony here which extends into both sides of our parallelism. Music has power over Saul and over Henchard. Both these inwardly tormented figures are able to escape their melancholy through music. But in both cases the power of music is in the control of their young rivals. In driving away David, Saul drove away the "divine spirit" of music itself. And Henchard in alienating Farfrae has done the same: in the literal sense he has lost Farfrae, the singer of old melodies; and in the sense of the music metaphor he has lost the beloved young friend whose benign control over his feelings was comparable to mastery of a musical instrument.

An even more penetrating irony (or series of ironies) is developed in the superb scene in which the drunken Henchard forces the Casterbridge church choir, who had retired to the Three Mariners for their regular Sunday morning ale, to sing the bloody and vindictive verses 10-15 of the Davidic Psalm CIX, as Farfrae and Lucetta pass by on their way from the church. These verses constitute an elaborate cursing prophecy and in the Tate and Brady metrical version used by Hardy end with these lines:

> A swift destruction soon shall seize
> On his unhappy race;
> And the next age his hated name
> Shall utterly deface. (p. 235)

Henchard intends the curse for Farfrae. He is, from one point of view, attempting to steal Farfrae's magic, the magic of the power of music, and turn it against its owner. He feels that he is only paying Farfrae off in kind, for "it was partly by his songs that he got over me, and heaved me out" (p. 237). The psalm lends itself beautifully to such a purpose, because it is an extremely primitive production, and whoever composed it doubtless assumed that this cursing poem would, of itself, magically confound the enemy upon recitation.

But there are two ironies here. First, as nearly every reader notices, the verses, instead of prescribing a terrible end for Farfrae, do, in fact, describe Henchard's own fate. The final provision of Henchard's bleakly worded will— "and that no man remember me" (p. 336)—echoes the last two lines of the quatrain I have just quoted. Henchard dies alone, and no child or other relative survives him. His line is at an end. The curse which he invoked against Farfrae comes to be enacted on his own miserable head.

A second irony emerges when we refer to the Saul-David parallelism. There is a certain grim humor, of the sort that we have learned to term Hardyesque, in the fact that Henchard should choose a Davidic hymn with which to insult the person who is, after all, the triumphant David of his own personal history. There is also a tremendous pathos as we sense the total blindness and confusion which afflict Henchard. When he points out Farfrae as the man at whom the singing of the psalm was aimed, and the shocked choristers gasp indignantly, we recognize how entirely and pitiably wrong Henchard is. For Farfrae is the "next age" in relation to Henchard, even as David was the next age for King Saul. "Don't you blame David. He knew what he was about when he wrote that" (p. 236), says Henchard to the choir members. It is Henchard's tragedy that he does not know, either in this scene or in the novel as a whole, what he is about.

IV Encountering the supernatural

Let us turn to another scene in *The Mayor of Caster-bridge* where we can trace some detailed parallels to one of the most striking incidents in the career of King Saul. I am referring to the scene in which Henchard visits the weather prophet Fall (pp. 187-190). The corresponding biblical episode is, of course, Saul's visit to the witch of Endor (I Samuel 28.3-25).

Saul seeks out the witch on the eve of his great battle against the Philistine army at Mt. Gilboa. In this battle Saul and three of his sons will be slain, and one consequence of these deaths will be the transference of the royal line from the House of Kish to the House of Jesse. David will be king. Henchard seeks out the weather prophet on the eve of his great commercial battle with Farfrae. He will stake his fortunes on Fall's predictions of a rainy harvest by purchasing grain early in the harvest season at a relatively high price. If the weather turns fair, prices will fall, he will be caught with the high-priced grain in his granaries and forced to sell at a tremendous loss on a low market. Fall's prediction does turn out to be wrong, and Henchard's business suffers a blow from which it never recovers. Subsequent to this fatal speculation, Henchard becomes bankrupt and Farfrae, who has speculated more wisely, succeeds him as the leading merchant of the town. To make the revolution in the fortunes of the two men complete and symmetrical, he also succeeds Henchard as mayor. When Farfrae buys up his former employer's corn stores and hay barns he orders the name of Henchard obliterated from the gateway and his own painted in, so that all may know that Henchard "ruled there no longer" (p. 223). A new commercial dynasty has been established.

Henchard, unlike Saul, does not die immediately after his visit to the seer, but his way is all downhill after he has acted on the basis of Fall's prediction of bad weather. Saul, unlike Henchard, does not receive bad advice, but the knowledge which he receives from Samuel's ghost—that he and his sons must die on the morrow, "because thou obeyedst not the voice of the Lord, nor executedst his fierce wrath upon Amalek" (I Samuel 28.18)—cannot help him to change fate.

Supporting the general resemblance between the episodes are a few more detailed parallels. Both Saul and Henchard arrive for their respective appointments by night, and both attempt to remain anonymous by muffling their faces. Henchard would be embarrassed to have it known that he believes in the superstition of weather prophecy. And in a sense Saul also is embarrassed, because as king he has been carrying on a campaign to rid his territories of wizards and witches. Fall knows Henchard at once and addresses him by name. To show off his prophetic powers he has even set a place at his dinner table for him, although Henchard had sent no advance warning that he was coming for a consultation. There is an uncanniness about this which is not matched by anything in the biblical episode. The witch penetrates Saul's disguise, but only after she has conjured up the ghost of Samuel. There is no immediate recognition.

Nevertheless, this incident of the pre-set dinner table in Hardy's novel does have a parallel in the full narrative of Saul's life, and our attention is directed specifically to this parallel by the sentence Hardy uses to express Henchard's surprise: "Henchard felt like Saul at his reception by Samuel" (p. 189). To make sense out of this we have to go back to a very early event in the life of Saul before he had become king. The prophet Samuel in his foreknowledge of events had gone to meet Saul at Ramah in the land of Zuph, where the young man had arrived while searching for his father's lost asses. Saul was amazed when the prophet, whom he had never seen before, escorted him into a banquet room where thirty persons were waiting and where a choice cut of meat had already been set aside for him: "And Samuel said, Behold that which is left! set it before thee and eat: for unto this time hath it been kept for thee since I said, I have invited the people. So Saul did eat with Samuel that day" (I Samuel 9.24).

Henchard refuses to eat with Fall for fear that "sitting down to hob-and-nob there would have seemed to mark him too implicitly as the weather-caster's apostle" (p. 190). Saul, likewise, refuses to eat but his servants prevail upon him to partake of a fatted calf and some unleavened bread which the woman prepares for him. In both stories the issue of breaking bread with the soothsayers adds a contrasting touch of homely realism to these encounters with the supernatural.

V

I believe that thus far I have demonstrated the existence of extensive parallels between Hardy's account of the Henchard-Farfrae rivalry and the biblical account of the Saul-David conflict. Whether these parallels result from the fully conscious intention of the artist, or whether we are dealing here with a degree of unconscious influence from the older narrative, are extremely difficult questions to answer. We do know that Hardy's mind was saturated in the imagery and episodes of the Bible and that he constantly employed a wide range of biblical allusions in his novels. Without going any farther than *The Mayor of Casterbridge* itself, it is a simple matter to collect references to characters, incidents and settings of several other books of the Old Testament. For example, Henchard freely compares himself to Cain and to Job; Farfrae in his commercial success is like Jacob in Padan-Aram; Elizabeth-Jane questions Lucetta about her love life in "Nathan tones"; the enterprise of cattle raising in Casterbridge is carried on with "Abrahamic success." These frequent allusions, by themselves, tend to bring the world of early nineteenth-century Wessex and the world of the early Hebrews into significant relation with one another. They prepare us for the more detailed correspondences we have been tracing.

In the midst of an inevitable uncertainty as to Hardy's intentions, there is one matter on which we can be certain; that is, that Hardy read his Bible not as fact and not as a foundation upon which to erect a system of religious belief or unbelief. Rather, he read the Bible narratives as fictional art, containing much to teach the modern novelist. On Friday, 17 April 1885, Hardy wrote in his diary that he had just completed the writing of *The Mayor of Casterbridge*. The entry immediately preceding is dated Easter Sunday of the same year and deals with "Evidences of art in Bible narratives":

They are written with a watchful attention (though disguised) as to their effect on their reader. Their so-called simplicity is, in fact, the simplicity of the highest cunning. And one is led to inquire, when even in these latter days artistic development and arrangement are the qualities least appreciated by readers, who was there likely to appreciate the art in these chronicles at that day?

Looking round on a well-selected shelf of fiction or history, how few stories of any length does one recognize as well told from beginning to end! The first half of this story, the last half of that, the middle of another. . . . The modern art of narration is yet in its infancy.

But in these Bible lives and adventures there is the spherical completeness of perfect art. And our first, and second, feeling that they must be true because they are so impressive, becomes, as a third feeling, modified to 'Are they so very true, after all?' Is not the fact of their being so convincing an argument, not for their actuality, but for the actuality of a consummate artist who was no more content with what Nature offered than Sophocles and Pheidias were content?[6]

What is the relevance for literary criticism in these parallels? No relevance whatsoever if one decides that I Samuel is merely the source for a set of characters and incidents in Hardy's *The Mayor of Casterbridge*. I would suggest, however, that we are dealing here with something more than a source. It seems to me that the Saul-David conflict represents a kind of framing action for the main dramatic situation of the novel, and that this frame, as soon as it is recognized, becomes a part of the novel's total organization or form. The form of Hardy's novel in this respect deserves comparison with that tour de force of framed narrative, James Joyce's *Ulysses*, although obvi-

[6]Florence Hardy, *The Early Life of Thomas Hardy, 1840-1891* (New York, 1928), pp. 222-223.

ously Joyce has exploited the parallels between Bloom's wanderings in early twentieth-century Dublin and Ulysses' adventures in the ancient world with a degree of system and of exhaustive detail that is quite unknown to Hardy's novel. We all accept the fact that an adequate response to *Ulysses* requires a reader constantly to make relations between the contemporary and the legendary levels of the action. I would suggest that *The Mayor of Casterbridge,* although a much less highly evolved example of the framed novel, requires a similar effort. In the end it is not simply that Henchard is like Saul, that his glooms and rages recall the glooms and rages of the Hebrew king, and that the pathos of his decline and death is reminiscent of the sad decline and death of the aging monarch. In another sense Henchard *is* Saul just as Farfrae is David, and the relationship of love and hate which exists between the older man and the younger is a permanently possible, endlessly recurrent relationship between successive generations. Through these identifications the unity of experience is stressed. We are back here to Miss Bodkin's archetype. In *The Mayor of Casterbridge* the evocation of the considerably more archaic version of essentially the same dramatic conflict fixes the significance of that conflict in unmistakable terms. It comes to be contemplated as a pattern or image of human action, of action which occurs in time but is not bound by the temporal limits of any historical epoch, since it may occur again and again. At the same time a situation which arises so naturally out of the local and narrowly restricted circumstances of a particular region has been universalized by its association with an ancient "Asiatic" prototype.

VI

If we turn our attention to the setting of the action in *The Mayor of Casterbridge* we may note a characteristic which suggests an analogy to the ancient-modern parallelism of person and incident in the dramatic situation. I am referring to the remarkable sense of continuity of the past with present times which is expressed through the archaeological features of the setting.

Roman soldiers lie buried in the fields and gardens of Casterbridge, and the city cemetery where Susan Henchard is interred has preserved its "continuity as a place of sepulture" since the days of Roman occupation: "Mrs. Henchard's dust mingled with the dust of women who lay ornamented with glass hair-pins and amber necklaces, and men who held in their mouths coins of Hadrian, Posthumus, and the Constantines" (p. 135). Although the townspeople "were quite unmoved by these hoary shapes" because "between them and the living there seemed to stretch a gulf too wide for even a spirit to pass" (p. 72), they avoided the great ruins of the Roman amphitheatre which stood near the town, "for some old people said that at certain moments in the summer time, in broad daylight, persons sitting with a book or dozing in the arena had, on lifting their eyes, beheld the slopes lined with a gazing legion of Hadrian's soldiery as if watching the gladiatorial combat; and had heard the roar of their excited voices; that the scene would remain but a moment, like a lightning flash, and then disappear" (p. 73). And there are monuments in the neighborhood of Casterbridge which date from before the period of Roman occupation, from a time perhaps as ancient as that recorded in I Samuel: "Two miles out, a quarter of a mile from the highway, was the prehistoric fort called Mai Dun, of huge dimensions and many ramparts, within or upon whose enclosures a human being, as seen from the road, was but an insignificant speck" (p. 313).

My point here is that the huge vistas of time opened up by these descriptions are quite in keeping with the discovery that the struggles of Henchard and Farfrae reflect the struggles of Saul and David. This distinctive feature of the setting works together with the framing narrative to supply a spacious context within which our response to the whole action may be ordered. And yet it would be a sentimental mistake to employ this larger context to obscure or scant the immediate, "contemporary" implications of that action.

Henchard, after all, is remarkable not because of the scope and intensity of his sufferings as King Saul, but because he suffers in his own person as hay trusser Henchard and as Mayor Henchard, the petty Wessex magistrate. The final comment we can reach here is not that Henchard is a king but rather that kings are men and that men are destined to suffer and decline in an orderly succession of generations.

VII The Biblical Layer in Franz Kafka's Short Story "A Country Doctor"

Hillel Barzel

Department of Comparative Literature, Bar Ilan University, Tel Aviv, Israel

I. Introduction

The Bible is frequently referred to specifically in Kafka's contemplative writings. His "Reflections on Sin, Suffering, Hope and the True Path" contain references to the Tower of Babel, the Garden of Eden, the Fall of Man, the Tree of Life, and the Tree of Knowledge. His other epigrammatic writings discuss themes drawn from the first chapters of Genesis, and Kafka speaks of Moses in the context of suspended animation. His diaries, too, contain references to the Bible: these include notably Kafka's famous dictum "Only the Old Testament sees."[1] His purely literary works, on the other hand, contain relatively few references to the Bible, and then only in limited contexts. In "The Bucket Rider" Kafka refers to the commandment "Thou shalt not kill." His use of biblical names appears deliberate. The hero of *The Trial* is called Joseph K., and the Land Surveyor in *The Castle* boasts the name of Joseph for a while. These are both heroes who, like Joseph in the Bible story, have accusations brought against them while personally quite unconscious of having transgressed. The emissary sent to assist the Land Surveyor is called Barnabas, like Paul's companion. One of the cities in *Amerika* is named Raamses, hinting unmistakably at that city's significance in the Old Testament (Exod. 1:11).

Several of Kafka's critics have raised the biblical layer to a position of dominant importance in their readings of his

---

[1] "Nur das Alte Testament sieht" *(Tagebücher,* entry for July 6, 1916). But the English translation prefers "Only the Old Testament knows" *(The Diaries of Franz Kafka, 1914–1923,* trans. Martin Greenberg and Hanna Arendt [New York: Schocken Books, 1965], p. 158).

works.[2] The enigmatic nature of Kafka's output has opened the door to a wide variety of allegorical interpretations which have attempted to read hidden biblical figures into all his protagonists. Many of these read the figure of Jesus into stories such as "A Hunger Artist" and "The Hunter Gracchus" (or into the scene of a mother holding her child in *The Castle*).

This discussion of the biblical layer in "A Country Doctor" does not intend to suggest some allegorical interpretation of the story, or to claim that while the author sketches the profile of any one figure in it he in fact has in mind some other. What is to be examined, in the hope of arriving at a new synthesis, is Kafka's working of elements drawn from the Bible into his molding of characters and plot. On the one hand it will be shown that his use of the Bible as source is by no means fortuitous or merely associative in origin, but highly intentional and intimately bound up with the story's particular and immediate meaning. By bringing out the biblical layer in other, even deeper, strata of the story, we may arrive at an understanding of "A Country Doctor's" overall essence which will help us interpret the story. It should, of course, be clear that the biblical layer is but one of a whole range of component elements.

II. Surrealistic elements

The basic materials out of which Kafka's stories are constructed are generally disguised. Thus the reader is unlikely, at first glance, to see any biblical elements in "A Country Doctor" at all. To single out these elements, it would be well to consider the story's surrealistic compo-

[2] Max Brod perceived a deep affinity between the basic questions raised in *The Trial* and Job's reflections on the ways of God as supreme judge of the universe and its creatures (*Über Franz Kafka* [Frankfurt-am-Main and Hamburg: Fischer, 1966], pp. 158-60). In his wake, Northrop Frye has called *all* Kafka's works commentaries on Job (*Anatomy of Criticism* [New York: Atheneum, 1967], p. 42). Brod saw in the affair of Amalia and Sortini in *The Castle* a somewhat removed version of the story of Abraham's sacrifice of Isaac.

nents; that is, those elements which deviate from linear narrative based on logical progression of circumstances and the depiction of recognizable realities. The country doctor's means of transportation—his gig and horses—are indeed strange and unreal. His previous steed is dead, and in its place a mysterious groom gives him a strange pair of horses. They are described in the story as unearthly, their provenance an unexpected source of aid: "'Yes,' I thought blasphemously, 'in cases like this the gods are helpful, send the missing horse, add to it a second because of the urgency; and to crown everything bestow even a groom'" (p. 151).[3] The horses loosen their reins, open the windows of the house, and look in on the patient, oblivious of the family's cries (*ibid.*). Their whinnying accompanies the doctor as he treats the patient, and he admits he has no control over the horses. Their whinnying together is ordained by heaven (p. 153). By being harnessed to the doctor's "earthly" vehicle, the unearthly horses transform it at the end of the story into the perpetually mobile carriage of the eternal wanderer.

No less strange is the method of treatment the doctor and his hosts adopt. Stripped of his clothes, the doctor is carried to the patient's bed: "They laid me down in it next to the wall, on the side of the wound" (p. 154). Included in the doctor's audience are a school choir that accompany his actions in song. Their ditty combines the motifs of threat and of deprecation of his person. At first they sing:

> Strip his clothes off, then he'll heal us,
> If he doesn't, kill him dead!
> Only a doctor, only a doctor. (*Ibid.*)

Later, as he leaves the village, this song resounds in his wake:

> O be joyful, all you patients,
> The doctor's laid in bed beside you! (P. 155)

[3] All quotations from "A Country Doctor" are from *Selected Short Stories of Franz Kafka*, trans. Willa and Edwin Muir (New York: Modern Library, 1952), pp. 148-56.

To the foregoing unreal components, which constitute a dreamlike sequence of events, the doctor's fur coat is to be added: "The gig swayed behind, my fur coat last of all in the snow" (*ibid.*). The old doctor is unable to pluck the saving fur coat off its hook, and in this lies his failure: "My fur coat is hanging from the back of the gig, but I cannot reach it, and none of my limber pack of patients lifts a finger" (p. 156).

III. Elijah and Elisha

It is not too difficult to see that the foundation of all these strange elements lies in the stories of Elijah and Elisha. Both prophets cure a sick boy by lying in bed with him: "And he said unto her, Give me thy son. And he took him out of her bosom, and carried him up into a loft, where he abode, and laid him upon his own bed. And he cried unto the Lord, and said . . . , O Lord my God, I pray thee, let this child's soul come into him again. And the Lord heard the voice of Elijah; and the soul of the child came into him again, and he revived" (I Kings 17:19-22). The version with Elisha reads similarly: "And when Elisha was come into the house, behold, the child was dead, and laid upon his bed. He went in therefore, and shut the door upon them twain, and prayed unto the Lord. And he went up, and lay upon the child, and put his mouth upon his mouth, and his eyes upon his eyes, and his hands upon his hands: and he stretched himself upon the child; and the flesh of the child waxed warm" (II Kings 4:32-34). In Kafka's story too, the boy is in genuine danger of death. Huge rose-red worms are already crawling over his wound. The worms are an obvious metaphor for death, a common symbol of which is worms taking possession of human flesh.

The significance of the horses and carriage is also readily understood from the stories of Elijah and Elisha. The last step on earth of the savior-prophet Elijah is marked by the appearance of fiery horses and a fiery chariot: "And it came to pass, as they still went on, and talked, that, behold, there appeared a chariot of fire, and horses of fire, and parted them both asunder; and Elijah went up by a whirlwind into heaven. And Elisha saw it, and he cried, My father, my father, the chariot of Israel, and the horsemen thereof" (II Kings 2:11-12). Elisha too is granted fiery horses and a fiery chariot: "And Elisha prayed, and said, Lord, I pray thee, open his eyes, that he may see. And the Lord opened the eyes of the young man; and he saw: and, behold, the mountain was full of horses and chariots of fire round about Elisha" (II Kings 6:17). Also among the special objects which mark the path of Elijah and his successor is a mantle. A powerful force is concealed within the mantle: its transfer from Elijah to the one who will continue on his path is also the signal for the bestowal of supernal powers from the former to the latter. With the aid of the mantle Elisha accomplishes deeds similar to those of Moses with his staff; for example, he crosses the Jordan on dry ground (II Kings 2:7-14). The boys' jeers at the bringer of deliverance also have their precedent in an episode in the story of Elisha: "And he went up from thence unto Beth-el: and as he was going up by the way, there came forth little children out of the city, and mocked him, and said unto him, Go up, thou bald head; go up, thou bald head" (II Kings 2:23).

IV. Antithetical affinities

Use of a biblical substratum in "A Country Doctor" is not, as it often is in other cases, designed merely to raise the hero of the tale to mythical or legendary dimensions. Kafka's intention is to contrive an antithetical tension between the all-powerful deliverer of old and the miserable country doctors whose capabilities are so limited. Elijah, especially in Jewish tradition, is the prophet of deliverance, the resolver of all problems in dispute, and herald of the Messiah. Elijah is the archetype of a savior who is close to man and his needs, and his presence in the popular imagination and in folklore is well-nigh uninterrupted. While the Messiah is a savior to be revealed only at the messianic age, Elijah, who is to accompany him when he comes, is already known. He is available to all who seek him and extends succor to all. The image of Elisha, even in the Bible, is that of an omnipotent healer. Elisha puts an end to the parched earth and useless water (II Kings 2: 19-22). He delivers Naaman, captain of the Syrian army, from his leprosy (II Kings 5:1-20). Ben-Hadad, the sick king of Syria, petitions Elisha for a cure (or perhaps merely for some fortune-telling): "Shall I recover of this disease?" (II Kings 8:8).

"I am no world reformer," declares the healer in our modern tale (p. 152). "World reformer" is, I suggest, a synonym for prophet. No powers are denied the biblical prophet in his capacity as bringer of deliverance. The source of aid is God himself. The fiery horses and fiery chariot are a conveyance transporting the prophet from this world of mortals to immortality. Through the omnipotence of the one who sends him, the prophet can revive the dead. He has means, such as the mantle, to work miracles. When children mock him the prophet curses them, and forty-two of them are torn apart by she-bears who come out of the woods. Kafka's protagonist is, on the face of it, above mortal man, close to the wellsprings of salvation. He too receives horses which transform his gig into an extraordinarily swift vehicle. He too has a mantle. He even uses the same method of treatment as the two prophets of old. But the similarity is false. The horses drive him to a feeling of impotence, at the end, to eternal wandering through the snowy wastes. The bringer of deliverance is not carried up to heaven by his horses and chariot, and his last cry is of having fallen victim to his professional duty: "Betrayed! Betrayed! A false alarm on the night bell once answered—it cannot be made good, not ever" (p. 156). Unlike Elisha, he is forced to put up with the children's jeers. He is, in fact, a victim of this "most unhappy of ages" (*ibid.*); he is not a formative force in it.

A yet sharper and more significant antithesis exists in the identity of the forces which come to the aid of the modern deliverer. We know whence the fiery horses of the Bible come; in Kafka's story the horses emerge from a pigsty, and the groom is a demonic figure. In accepting the horses from the pigsty, the doctor knows he has made a pact with Satan. Even in his treatment of his patient, he is not autonomous in his actions; these are, in fact, dictated by his sickroom audience. At a deeper level there emerges a philosophically significant contrast between the world of the Bible and that of the country doctor. The world of the Bible is anchored in absolute values. Both justice and salvation are by definition absolute. The prophets have no need to betray their values in order to fulfill their mission. Deliverance and the means used to achieve it are fully compatible with one another. This is not the case with the country doctor, however. Kafka's story throws the extending of medical aid to the sick boy into a conflict between means and ends. To save the boy, the doctor has to sacrifice Rose. The problem is also symbolically put in the play of metaphors. The servant-girl's name is Rose, which arouses associations with beautiful, sweet-smelling pink flowers. The sick boy's wound is described as a flower (p. 153). Pink appears in the description of the blossom-wound, and the color is worked into the description of the worms crawling about in the open wound. The doctor has had to sacrifice the one flower, Rose, the blossom of life, in his attempt to save the boy from the flower in his flesh, the blossom of death.

V. The nature of the wound

The very nature of the wound is to be understood in the context of the story's biblical substratum. It is probably a veiled reference to original sin, which is the impress of death that is stamped in man's flesh from the moment of his birth. Significantly, the wound is in the ribs: "This blossom in your side is destroying you" (p. 153). Adam's rib, in Genesis, is the origin of Eve, mother of all mankind. The rib is instrumental in revival and in birth. From it start the generations of man. This element, too, is antithetically used in Kafka's story: instead of the ribs being associated with life, we see a rib stamped with the impress of death. This, then, is the usage-spectrum of the biblical layer at both its ends. On the one hand we have Elijah, who was carried to heaven, who never felt the taste of death, and whose destiny differed from that of all other mortals. On the other hand is the boy with original sin festering in his side who cannot be delivered therefrom.

However, Kafka did not mean the antithesis between his story and the ancient substratum to be total. There is no polar opposition of prophet to Satan, of absurd death to eternity. True, the doctor is prodded into his mission by the demonic groom, but his purpose had been to bring deliverance. The horses may not have descended from heaven, but they do bring the doctor to his destination. The very symbol of death is described in terms of its antithesis, a flower. However, the doctor's conversation with the boy hints that even in the seal of death stamped in man's ribs there might be a degree of good. The sick boy says, "A fine wound is all I brought into the world; that was my sole endowment" (p. 155). Scripture looms large in the background to these words: on coming into this world, man is from the moment of his birth afflicted with sin; for this the penalty is death, and that is man's only true defense. Thus the doctor replies, "You have not a wide enough view. I have been in all the sickrooms, far and wide, and I tell you: your wound is not so bad. Done in a tight corner with two strokes of the axe. Many a one proffers his side and can hardly hear the axe in the forest, far less that it is coming nearer to him" *(ibid.)*.

The reply attaches overriding importance to hearing the axe. The impress of death that is stamped in man comes from God. Inasmuch as man understands this, he is acknowledging a dialogic relationship, admittedly on a tragic plane, that emerges between him and his creator. The doctor's answer is thus in the spirit of the reassuring ending of the contemplative lines of the book of Job: "I have heard of thee by the hearing of the ear: but now mine eye seeth thee" (42:5). The answer granted to Job does not dispel his doubts, but he may at least draw satisfaction from the dialogical relationship with God that he is thereby granted; God heard and answered him. The sick boy cannot be rid of his wound, even with the doctor's aid. But we learn from the doctor's words that the boy's wound is preferable to a wound made where the coming of the axe cannot be heard. The blow of the axe is the touch of God's hand upon man. This knowledge can render the injury, incurable as it is, more palatable. So even though the doctor has not succeeded in bringing deliverance from the illness, he has at least brought soothing tidings. Accepting the doctor's words of explanation, the boy lies still (p. 155).

Paradox, with all that it entails as regards the method of using the biblical source, is a technique which runs consistently through Kafka's works. He creates it, among other ways, by turning normal logic, or the order to which we are accustomed, on its head. "We are digging the Pit of Babel," says one of his aphorisms. This exemplifies a topsy-turvying attitude toward the ancient mold. And yet Kafka does not entirely depart from the pattern, for both in the original Tower of Babel story and in the aphorism the basic reference—to man's desire to achieve the unattainable—is maintained. So also in "A Country Doctor," as we have shown, the affinity to the ancient source is antithetical, while nevertheless fundamental patterns— here, the healer's duty to proffer aid even in such grave cases as are beyond deliverance by human hand—are maintained.

VI. The purpose behind use of the Bible

Kafka's extensive use of the biblical layer in constructing this story arises apparently from his wish to lend depth and variety to the unchanging thematic substructure in which all his works are grounded. The theme which pervades and embraces all of Kafka's novels and short stories is man's striving toward the unattainable, the absolute. Joseph K. strives for total acquittal; the Land Surveyor wants his authorization from the Castle; Karl Rossmann desires freedom and independence in his new life in America; Gregor Samsa wishes to shake off his insect nature. These protagonists are allowed to come just close enough to their purpose to gain the delusion that it is within their reach. They clutch at all sorts of intermediaries whom they imagine can bring them home to their long-sought goal. But this is by its very nature unattainable. Kafka's heroes are condemned to remain all their lives on the threshold, unable to cross it and attain their goal.

The village doctor is yet another hero who sets himself a lofty aim—to bring deliverance. The fulfillment of his mission is almost within his grasp. He comes very close to the patient, being laid by his very side. He even speaks the words of consolation he has prepared. But he is quite incapable of bringing relief to this patient, to any other patient, or even to himself: "Naked, exposed to the frost of this most unhappy of ages, with an earthly vehicle, unearthly horses, old man that I am, I wander astray" (p. 156).

Kafka's monothematic framework is by no means devoid of change. The goal changes, the characters differ, and the nature of the obstacles set in the path toward that goal, too, is varied from work to work. One of the techniques of gaining depth and variation is to construct the story over an ancient base, as in the case of "A Country Doctor." Underlying the story's foundations are the ideal savior and the condemned mortal of all times. Deliverance as presented in this story is clearly the counterpart of the absolute ends that figure in Kafka's other works. When Joseph K., hero of *The Trial*, meets the Law Court painter Titorelli, the latter says it is quite unimaginable for the Court to acquit anyone brought before it. He adds that complete acquittal is found only in legends. Transposing the language of the novel dealing with law courts and their ways, one could say that total acquittal is like reaching the boundless, the eternal. Guilt is finiteness, boundedness, and man's life in the shadow of death.

Among "legends" describing complete acquittal of mortal

men are those Bible stories in which the hero is seen to step out beyond mortal limitations into eternity. The only two Old Testament figures who are assumed directly into heaven and the divine presence are Enoch and Elijah. It is not surprising that the imagination of the writer, in whom the search for the absolute is the monothematic foundation of his entire output, should be caught by the figures of Enoch and Elijah. In juxtaposing the old doctor—image of the man who has never felt the taste of death—and the boy with an axe wound which symbolizes that which awaits man *qua* flesh and blood, Kafka has deepened the foundations of his permanent base and broadened its frontiers. Despite its setting within a recognizable period, the story rises to an "eternal present" outside of time. Like the doctor's ultimate endless wanderings, the entire story is raised beyond the wheels of time. It embraces two extratemporal images, the one referring to the road, barred till the end of days, by which man becomes like God, and the other to those immortal personages who have broken through that barrier which blocks off all ordinary mortals. The country doctor makes partial and limited use of the immortals' apparatus in his attempt to achieve the unattainable. Thus his fate is on the one hand identical with that of all Kafka's heroes; while on the other hand the figures of the doctor and the sick boy link up with ancient figures and consequently step out of all time and place.

VII. Metarealism

Overall consideration of "A Country Doctor" thus shows that what might be immediately perceived as surrealistic, i.e., what appears strange and unexplained, has, in fact, a carefully and intentionally directed meaning. The biblical substratum shows that in this story, at least, Kafka is raising basic universal problems concerning man as man. At the bottom of "A Country Doctor" lies no individual's psychological makeup, no private set of symbols, but a universal pattern. The story deals with Everyman, and its hidden structure is not psychological but metaphysical, if by the former word we mean the enactment of the peculiar destiny in the soul of one particular individual. Alongside the metaphysical aspect lent the story by the image of the prophets and of the Godhead striking with an axe lies the thread of real occurrences. The characters and plot are of earthly and local hue. The reader perceives not only the strange, which hints at abstract meaning in the story, but also the real. Thus the label "metarealistic" is eminently suited to define the essence of this genre of story.

The word "metarealism" is intended to point out the close links forged between the realistic and the metaphysical. The threads connecting "A Country Doctor" with its biblical source show that to refute the metaphysical in interpreting the doctor's journey is in effect to deny the foundations of the story. On the one hand, the effective camouflaging of base-materials shows that the writer is not concerned exclusively with the Bible, but also with the reality of human life in all ages. Thus the components of the story are not to be interpreted as one-way allegorical signs. Kafka talks of nonterrestrial and not superterrestrial horses. He has created a new genus of creatures with its own special peculiarities, and they are not merely unequivocal representatives of other creatures. The horses are neither those of the Bible nor the horses of a normal story. The symbols of "A Country Doctor" simultaneously embrace both concrete and abstract designates: they contain a synthesis drawn both from the realistic and concrete and from the biblical element, which here furthers the metaphysical bent of the text.

VIII. Additional elements

Obviously, beside the biblical stratum in "A Country Doctor" lie other strata which enrich the story. Links can be forged between this short story and the Hassidic-folkloristic tale. The founder of the Hassidic movement, the Baal Shem Tov, used to travel in his carriage on missions of urgent succor. Alexis, his famous charioteer, did not have to tell the horses where to go; they would make their way by themselves to the correct destination. The Hassidic tale is much preoccupied with problems of means and ends, and it also contains a recurring motif termed "delaying of mission." The setting out on perpetual wandering for a prolonged period of "exile" is another recurring motif in the world of Hassidism and its stories. Kafka was well acquainted with the world of Hassidic tales, and possibly his hero-figure is conceived as an archetype rolling into one the essentials of several bringers of deliverance drawn from the Bible as well as from other sources. Clearly, even if it is in this case only the Baal Shem Tov, he is presented via much the same technique as held good for Elijah and Elisha: by an antithesis which nevertheless retains within it a link of similarity between the old context and the new.

Autobiographical elements are also present. Kafka's uncle Siegfried Loewy was a country doctor and used to ride a horse. The figure of the doctor with his feeling of failure is linked with the typical Kafkan protagonist into whom much of the author's own life story has been woven. But of all these component elements, the Bible would appear to be preeminent. Through it the tale embraces the metaphysical perspective, which lends it depth and the timeless value of a myth.

IX. Conclusions

Many are the ways in which biblical motifs, characters, concepts, and other elements manifest themselves in literature. A work of literature's attitude to the Bible can be essentially imitative, in which case the writer sees himself as commentator on the Scriptures in poetry, drama, or narrative, and as broadener of their scope. This sort of attitude is manifest in the biblical works of Milton and Racine. The literary attitude can be expressive, and here the writer harnesses Holy Writ to contemporary aims arising from the specific needs of his work. In this case the basic biblical materials retain their identity but appear within totally new contexts. This is what Herman Melville does, for example, in *Moby-Dick*. There is also a third way, which might here be termed impressionistic, and which is characterized by extreme individualism. The basic elements lose their original identity, but can be seen to mold the manifest aspect of the work. That is Kafka's way. In every case it is Kafka who, in the last analysis, puts his own limits to his use of biblical materials and gives them whatever identity he chooses. In "A Country Doctor" the subordination of all component elements to the single theme and to the monolithic character of the author's viewpoint is very evident. Nevertheless, we see that beyond the limits of the world of literature, which is, as it were, constructed entirely out of the particular vision of the author, there lies a vision whose fount is in universal texts. Kafka's success in using this element from the common heritage determines in no small measure the success of the individualistically inspired story. We strongly sense the story's "intensity" and, even without grasping all its hidden wealth, perceive that it is constructed layer upon layer.

VIII The Theme of the Fall in Albert Camus' *The Fall**

William R. Mueller

Director of the Humanities Institute of Baltimore, Maryland, and Cambridge, England

> The two articles that follow should be read together as complementary statements on *The Fall*. Chapter VIII gives the theological background and discusses Camus' treatment of the Fall. Chapter IX discusses in detail the significance of the allusions to the Bible.
> —Ed.

There is an important distinction between the biblical doctrine of the fall and Jean-Baptiste Clamence's concept of his own fall. The innocence of Adam and Eve was a state of sinlessness; their fall was a disobedient succumbing to the sins of pride and idolatry. The innocence of Clamence was a state of unawareness of his sin; his fall from innocence was a gradual recognition of the fact that he had been a sinner without knowing it. Clamence's fall was more clearly a coming to a knowledge of good and evil than was Adam's, for Clamence had mistaken evil for good until he fell; his fall is actually a conviction of sin, an intellectual awareness of what really distinguishes the evil from the good. His fall frees him from self-righteousness, though not from unrighteousness.

Clamence's discovery was that his actions belied his motives, that the appearance of his outer self and the reality of his inner self bore no relationship. When he spoke of himself as "a double face, a charming Janus," he spoke with a penetrating accuracy. His discovery was the same as that of T. S. Eliot's Thomas Becket when he was confronted by the Fourth Tempter in *Murder in the Cathedral:* he was doing the right deed for the wrong reason. By delving into

*From "Theme of the Fall: Albert Camus' *The Fall*," chapter 2 of *The Prophetic Voice in Modern Fiction* by William R. Mueller. Copyright 1959. Association Press. Pp. 56-82 (74-82). Reprinted by permission.

his memory, Clamence realized that "modesty helped me to shine, humility to conquer, and virtue to oppress" (84),[1] that "the surface of all my virtues had a less imposing reverse side" (85). His every noble and helpful action before his fall had been motivated by his passion to feel above others, to take his stance on some summit, "well above the human ants" (24). His legal profession and success served perfectly to sustain his sense of freedom and superiority:

My profession satisfied most happily that vocation for summits. It cleansed me of all bitterness toward my neighbor, whom I always obligated without ever owing him anything. It set me above the judge whom I judged in turn, above the defendant whom I forced to gratitude. Just weigh this, *cher monsieur*, I lived with impunity. I was concerned in no judgment; I was not on the floor of the courtroom, but somewhere in the flies like those gods that are brought down by machinery from time to time to transfigure the action and give it its meaning. After all, living aloft is still the only way of being seen and hailed by the largest number. (25)

. . . Clamence is a perfect example of a person whose love of self is so complete that there is no room for other persons in his closed universe: "It is not true, after all, that I never loved. I conceived at least one great love in my life, of which I was always the object. . . . I looked merely for objects of pleasure and conquest" (58). "To be happy," he asserts, "it is essential not to be too concerned with others" (80). But the more he struggles for happiness and freedom, the more he becomes trapped in that hell of isolation and self-love. He lives in the most pretentious of all worlds, a world in which there exist only one person and many objects. The one person of Clamence's world is Clamence; all other human beings become for him objects to be used and manipulated for his own self-gratification. It is no wonder that he eschews friendships, for they are binding, calling for mutual obligations; it is little wonder either that he loves his acquaintances most upon their death, for death ends any possible claim which they may place upon him. His fall is the

1. Page numbers refer to the Justin O'Brien translation (Vintage Books; New York: Random House, 1956).

discovery that his world has always been one of "I-it" relationships.

In Christian thought a conviction of sin is an essential part of the process of redemption. By means of his vision of God through Christ the Christian becomes shockingly aware of that vast distinction between the Godhead and his own depraved and unhealthy state. His conviction is his knowledge that he has loved neither God nor neighbor, that he has, like Clamence, loved himself to the exclusion of all others. The vision is so stunning and gracious that it not only convicts him of sin but draws him toward itself, serving as a means to lead him from unrighteousness or self-righteousness to righteousness. The Christian is foreshadowed in the publican who knew of both his sin and his salvation: "God, be merciful to me a sinner!" (Luke 18:13).

Clamence is convicted of his sin but remains uncertain of the way to redemption; in fact, he is by no means certain that there is a way. He does have some impulse toward truth, toward showing himself as he really is, not simply to his cultured companion in Amsterdam, but to the fortunate beneficiaries of his selfishly motivated actions as well. He feels called upon to make known his duplicity: to jostle the blind, toward whom he really feels a degree of loathing, and to slap infants. Though he never went so far as this, he did ease his conscience by complaining to the proprietor of a sidewalk restaurant about a beggar who approached him while he was eating. And he did suggest in a lecture to a group of young lawyers that he was far more wicked than some murderer whom he might defend in court. But these overtures to truth were motivated not so much by an abstract love of truth as by a desire to escape the laughter and judgment of mankind. He sought to perfect his self-accusation not as a step toward Christian redemption, but as a means of maintaining his advantage over his fellow men:

You see, it is not enough to accuse yourself in order to clear yourself; otherwise, I'd be as innocent as a lamb. One must accuse oneself in a certain way, which it took me considerable time to perfect. I did not discover it until I fell into the most utterly forlorn state. Until then, the laughter continued to drift my way, without my random efforts succeeding in divesting it of its benevolent, almost tender quality that hurt me. (95-96)

Ironically, Clamence, seeking freedom, was instead making himself the perfect slave of mankind. Deaf to God's judgment, he lent his ear only to the judgment of men. Paul's question to the Galatians might very appropriately have been put to him: "Am I now seeking the favor of men, or of God? Or am I trying to please men?" (1:10). Paul's counsel to the Romans would also have a fine appropriateness: "Do not be conformed to this world but be transformed by the renewal of your mind, that you may prove what is the will of God, what is good and acceptable and perfect" (12:2).

Finally, does Clamence leave us with the belief that he is eternally damned to the concentric circles of hell so adequately suggested by the canal-imposed structure of Amsterdam? Is he to be forever enslaved in that last circle reserved for traitors to God? Is he to remain always touched by "the breath of stagnant waters, the smell of dead leaves soaking in the canal and the funereal scent rising from the barges loaded with flowers" (43)? Are we to accept his closing words that the chance for salvation is past?—"It's too late now. It will always be too late. Fortunately!" (147).

Possibly so, and yet one must ask several questions. How are we to account for the facts that the narrator has adopted the name of Jean-Baptiste or John the Baptist, that the waters near Amsterdam are referred to as an "immense holy-water font" (109), and that doves (traditional symbols of the Holy Spirit) are always hovering above the fog of the city? Has Camus placed Clamence in Amsterdam simply because it is a mecca for the kinds of persons who enable him successfully to ply his profession as judge-penitent, or because it suggests a wilderness awaiting a Messiah?

While traveling with his companion on the Zuider Zee,

Clamence recalls that day aboard the upper deck of an ocean liner when his sighting of a black speck on the ocean horrified him, reminding him of a body in the Seine some years before and the cry of a drowning woman. He realized that that cry, that conviction of his sin,

had never ceased, carried by the river to the waters of the Channel, to travel throughout the world, across the limitless expanse of the ocean, and that it had waited for me there [on the liner] until the day I had encountered it. I realized likewise that it would continue to await me on seas and rivers, everywhere, in short, where lies the bitter water of my baptism. Here, too, by the way, aren't we on the water? . . . We shall never get out of this immense holy-water font. (108-109)

Clamence, convinced of his sin and surrounded by baptismal water, is also aware of the doves flapping above Amsterdam and waiting to descend: "The doves wait up there all year round. They wheel above the earth, look down, and would like to come down. But there is nothing but the sea and the canals, roofs covered with shop signs, and never a head on which to light" (73). The prophet, the water, the doves are all present; only a Messiah is missing, the Christ at whose baptism the dove descended, alighting upon him. And what are we to make of Clamence's wandering and confused vision toward the end of his confession where the huge snowflakes approximate to him the descent of the doves, possibly the bearers of the good news, the messengers of salvation? Is Clamence to remain "a false prophet crying in the wilderness and refusing to come forth" (147), or is he to answer his call as John the Baptist, also a voice in the wilderness, but a voice whose conviction of sin leads him to cry, "'Repent, for the kingdom of heaven is at hand'" (Matthew 3:2)?

These are questions for us to ponder in this confession of a midtwentieth-century Mr. Anthropos to his cultured contemporaries, to you and to me; for the confessor is, as Camus suggests in his prefatory sentences from Lermontov, *"the aggregate of the vices of our whole generation in their fullest expression."* And the ear which attends

Clamence in the *Mexico City* bar and in the streets of Amsterdam and its environs is the ear of the educated, and presumably secular, man of our time, a time in which man exhibits only "two passions: ideas and fornication" (6), and in which he has no serious commitments, doing all things only "'in a way'" (8). The confession is made to one who, despite his familiarity with the subjunctive, his knowledge of the Bible and Dante and the Orient, nevertheless fails to understand the symbolic references to doves (73) and does not recognize van Eyck's painting of "The Just Judges" (128).

One's interpretation of the novel must rest ultimately on his judgment of its irony. Clamence, it would seem, is a supreme ironist who uses the images and symbols of the Christian faith finally to imply their meaninglessness to and emptiness for him and his generation. Clamence, it seems, sees or is aware of no hope. He feels that if faced again with a young woman's plunge from a bridge, he would repeat his cowardly withdrawal. But one can not with certainty equate the author's point of view with the narrator's, and in *The Fall* there may be irony within irony. Perhaps Camus is ironically implying that Clamence, not knowing himself as well as he thinks he does, has courageously made an agonizing descent into the lower depths and has been shattered to the point at which the Holy Spirit may claim his soul. In this matter each reader's own sensitivity must be his guide, for the artist is not called upon to furnish the kind of explicit resolution which may characterize theological exposition.

IX The Function of Christian Imagery in *The Fall**

Sandy Petrey

Department of French, State University of New York at Stony Brook

Before discussing in detail how Christian parallels affect the reader's reaction to Clamence, we should re-examine the manner in which Camus establishes what is by far the novel's most important Christian analogy, that between Clamence and John the Baptist. First, there is the name Camus' speaker gave himself, Jean-Baptiste Clamence. Jean-Baptiste needs no comment, and Clamence is, as many readers have noted, an echo of the Vulgate's epithet for John, *vox clamantis in deserto*. The figure of the Baptist permeates Clamence's self-conception. He chose to be known by his name, and his preoccupation with him, the "Elijah who was to return," is unmistakable when he describes his life and the death which would "consummate" his career.

In solitude and when fatigued, one is after all inclined to take oneself for a prophet. When all is said and done, that's really what I am, having taken refuge in a desert of stones, fogs, and stagnant waters, an empty prophet for shabby times, Elijah without a messiah, choked with fever and alcohol, my back up against this moldy door, my finger raised toward a threatening sky, showering imprecations on lawless men who cannot endure any judgment. (p. 117)[1]

I would be decapitated, for instance, and I'd have no more fear of death; I'd be saved. Above the gathered crowd, you would

---

*Adapted from "The Function of Christian Imagery in *La Chute*," *Texas Studies in Literature and Language*, 11 (1970): 1445-54 (1448-54). Copyright the University of Texas Press. Reprinted by permission.

[1] Translations of the author's nonbiblical quotations are taken from *The Fall*, translated by Justin O'Brien (Vintage Books; New York: Random House, 1956).

hold up my still warm head, so that they could recognize themselves in it and I could again dominate—an exemplar. All would be consummated; I should have brought to a close, unseen and unknown, my career as a false prophet crying in the wilderness and refusing to come forth. (pp. 146-47)

Phrases like "empty prophet," "false prophet," and "Elijah without a messiah" express the nature of Camus' prophet. Clamence offers only guilt, degradation, and despair, and the horror of his message is accentuated by the continuous comparison between his falseness and John's message of universal redemption and hope. "Elijah without a messiah" is an insulting absurdity, for without a messiah Elijah has no reason for being. Clamence adopts the posture and assumes the importance of a prophet, but Camus makes the reader aware of the emptiness of his pose by many varied references to what a prophet should be and has been. The plenitude of the Christian myth affords a mercilessly effective comparison to the void proclaimed by Clamence. As Camus said, prophets like Clamence "announce nothing at all," and the sham of such a man is underscored by setting him beside John the Baptist, the culmination of all the prophets who announced the salvation of mankind through the Incarnation and sacrifice of God himself.

The parallel between John and Jean thus gives the reader an ironic vision enabling him to assess the latter accurately; echoes of the dignity of a man with the most meaningful of purposes are woven into the presentation of a contemptible man whose only goals are self-serving. It should be emphasized that Camus accomplishes this fundamental task without strain, without interjecting his authorial voice into the narrative in any way. Clamence chose his own name, and it is his own mania which leads him to refer so directly to John in describing his career. His comparison of himself with the greatest of the prophets is completely consistent with his megalomania, and even expressions like "empty prophet" fit naturally into the speech of this memorable conversationalist who glorifies himself by describing his sins with a wink. Camus took what should be a novelistic obstacle—assigning the narrative entirely to the villain—and derived from it the advantage of being able to make the existence of a parallel between Clamence and John the Baptist so obvious that it cannot be missed.

This preliminary establishment of the parallel allows Camus to make the more subtle references to a prototype ordinarily found in modern fictional symbolism with greater assurance that they will serve their purpose. The following echoes of the Gospels' description of John are both subtle enough not to be oppressive and too striking to be mere coincidences in a novel where the analogy with John is unmistakable and where the reader is told at the very beginning, "If you are not familiar with the Scriptures, I admit that this won't help you" (p. 9).

Now John wore a garment of camel's hair, and a leather girdle around his waist. (Matt. 3:4)	The camel that provided the hair for my overcoat was probably mangy; yet my nails are manicured. (p. 9)
But when he saw many of the Pharisees and Sadducees coming for baptism, he said to them, "You brood of vipers! Who warned you to flee from the wrath to come?" (Matt. 3:7)	Do you have any possessions? Some? Good. Have you shared them with the poor? No. Then you are what I call a Sadducee. . . . Yes, I was rich. No, I shared nothing with the poor. What does that prove? That I, too, was a Sadducee. (pp. 9-10)
For he will be great before the Lord, and he shall drink no wine nor strong drink, and he will be filled with the Holy Spirit, even from his mother's womb. (Luke 1:15)	But after all, I presented a harsh exterior and yet could never resist the offer of a glass or of a woman. (pp. 85-86)
He who has the bride is the bridegroom; the friend of the bridegroom, who stands and	I had principles, to be sure, such as that the wife of a friend is sacred. But I simply ceased

hears him, rejoices greatly at the bridegroom's voice; therefore this joy of mine is now full. (John 3:29)

quite sincerely, a few days before, to feel any friendship for the husband. (pp. 58-59)

He who believes in the Son has eternal life. (John 3:36)

Because I longed for eternal life, I went to bed with harlots and drank for nights on end. (p. 102)

All these Biblical references contrast John's transcendent majesty and power with Clamence's cruel psychological games. The Baptist gives dignity to all he touches; Clamence attacks and vitiates all dignity. John's camel's-hair coat and diet of locusts symbolize his total commitment to a cause surpassing the things of men; Clamence's camel's-hair coat is a slight embarrassment compensated for by a manicure. John damned Sadducees with fire in his voice; Clamence welcomes them and slyly admits his membership in their sect. Mercenary sex replaces faith as the way to eternal life, and the husband's friend whose joy was perfect becomes, at the husband's voice, the husband's friend whose cuckolding technique is masterful.

Such echoes contrast John's integrity and commitment to Clamence's self-indulgence, but, more importantly, they condemn the artifice of Clamence's serpentine speech and epigrammatic wit by implicitly asking the reader to compare this reticulate style to the Gospels' noble simplicity. As Camus is careful to have Clamence say, in reference to his own speech, while introducing himself, "Style, like sheer silk, too often hides eczema" (p. 6). Appeals to our collective knowledge of the Bible's direct power help us see through to this disguised sore. Clamence's monologue has great intellectual appeal, and some stylistic standard, such as that furnished by the radiance of the Gospels, is necessary to prevent his charm and the memorable insights he undeniably expresses from hiding the egoistic cruelty of his words. Christian imagery furnishes a linguistic as well as moral standard by which to judge Clamence.

Analogies with other Christian figures help establish an

ironic counterpoint to Clamence. Camus' prophet is a burning bush, but he leads his people into rather than out of enslavement. He is Virgil guiding Dante, but both are condemned never to leave Limbo. He is Christ— "Fortunately, I arrived! I am the end and the beginning; I announce the law" (p. 118)—but, when he mocks the Savior whose way was prepared by the Baptist, he only emphasizes that he is the forerunner, not of God and redemption, but only of himself and the Fall. One of the Biblical texts he quotes is the first part of a verse whose unspoken conclusion is Christ's malediction of false prophets (p. 89, Luke 6:26). All Camus' Christian imagery cruelly betrays Clamence's poverty. There is a kind of contest between Clamence and the prophets to whom he refers, a contest as decisive as that between the 450 pagan priests and Elijah, another prominent symbolic character, one whom Christian tradition has constantly identified with the Baptist. In each case false prophets are mercilessly exposed. The reader sees that Clamence is on the side of Baal, and his vision of a fiery chariot descending for him, as it did for Elijah (p. 146), is ridiculous and pathetic.

Clamence thus becomes a negation of the Christian *figures* to whom Camus calls attention. Moreover, the meaning of a large number of Christian *symbols* is also negated in *The Fall*. In a kind of Black Mass, where traditional symbols are used to celebrate the opposite of the traditional God, *The Fall* reverses the significance of many Christian symbols to express the nature of the man it is describing. Water, that most important symbol of baptism and a rebirth into innocence, has a major role in the novel, but it has lost its purifying quality. Rain and fog add to Amsterdam's gloom, its canals are the concentric circles of Hell, and its misty sea despairs and disorients those who come to it. Water now resembles the water which cleanses only in its "color of a weak lye-solution" (p. 72). Religion, once "a huge laundering venture," is now transfer of filth: "soap has been lacking, our faces are dirty, and we wipe one another's noses" (p. 111). All water is contaminated by the

113

seminal baptismal experience occurring when the girl leapt (or might have leapt) into the Seine:[2] the "limitless expanse of the ocean" is an "immense holy-water fount" filled with "the bitter water of my baptism" (pp. 108-9), and the "holy-water fount" damns instead of blessing. Like his namesake, Clamence wants to "get everyone involved," but only "in order to have the right to sit calmly on the outside myself" (p. 137). Water initiates men into utter despair rather than into a new life. John proclaimed "the baptism of repentance for the remission of sins" (Mark 1:4 KJV), but for Clamence there is neither repentance nor remission of sins.

The metaphoric value of light, another important Christian symbol of redemption, is similarly reversed. Dawn is the time of the Fall rather than the image of hope: ". . . for the fall occurs at dawn" (p. 143). The gloom of Clamence's message is manifested in the darkness enveloping Amsterdam. Night, rain, fog, or snow holds back the light in each of the novel's six chapters. Clamence bears witness to crime which cannot be expiated, and his universe is lit only by gin. The contrast with true prophets can again be summarized by comparing Clamence's words with the Biblical description of John.

In him was life, and the life was the light of men. The light shines in the darkness, and the darkness has not overcome it. There was a man sent from God, whose name was John. He came for testimony, to bear witness to the light. (John 1:4-7)

Fortunately there is gin, the sole glimmer of light in the darkness. Do you feel the golden, copper-colored light it kindles in you? (p. 12)

Every man testifies to the crime of all others—that is my faith and my hope. (p. 110)

[2] The baptismal connotations attached to the girl's plunge into the river help explain Clamence's preoccupation with Christian symbols. He vicariously shared her immersion, as is indicated by his references to the cold and dark river water, and he emerges from his baptism with a new name, to lead a new life. His personal awareness of how deeply this spiritual rebirth affects him is evident in the hallucinations which make him see the girl whenever he looks at water and in his attempt to make his listeners aware of the immersion molding their lives.

The dove bearing the sign of God's love for man and announcing the Good News of Christ's mission when John was baptizing Him has become never-descending clouds moving only to help veil the light (p. 96) or snowflakes descending during Clamence's delirium to bring the self-deluding "good news" of his personal elevation (p. 145).

The specific symbolic references to the Christian tradition we have been examining lead to comparison of the general Christian message of redemption with Clamence's malice and cynicism. Continuous reminders of those who blessed men with the truth which would make them free mean that Clamence's charm is less likely to disguise the degeneracy of his denial of blessing and exaltation of slavery: "With me there is no giving of absolution or blessing. . . . You see in me, *très cher*, an enlightened advocate of slavery" (pp. 131-32).

Clamence perverts confession and penitence into an attempt to lessen the agony of his own guilt. He wants to "extend judgment to everybody in order to make it weigh less heavily on my own shoulders" (p. 137). The "judge-penitent" is a penitent because he finds this pose the most effective means of judging. His condemnation of mankind is cruel and petty, for it is intended only to alleviate his personal guilt and despair. Christian imagery, especially the parallel with John, is a powerful means of conveying the far-reaching significance of this cruelty. The two great events in the Christian view of world history are Adam's Fall and Christ's sacrifice. All men sinned in the Fall, all men are offered redemption by Christ. John the Baptist prepared the way for victory over the consequences of the Fall, but Clamence totally reverses the function of his namesake to proclaim a new Fall with no possibility of redemption. The name of his novel announced his mission as surely as John's movement in Elizabeth's womb during Mary's visit announced his. The three Christian virtues of faith, hope, and love are systematically denied. Clamence's "faith and hope" are, as we have seen, that "every man testifies to the crime of all the others" (p. 110) and his love is egoism: "I conceived at least one great love in my life, of which I was always the object" (p. 58).

The Christian message was eschatological: there was very little time left, the kingdom of God was at hand; in the Baptist's words "the axe is laid unto the root of the trees" (Matt. 3:10 KJV). But there was always enough time to repent and be saved, hope existed for all mankind. Clamence's message is that there is no time left, that there is absolutely nothing man can do to save his damned soul. The agonizingly bitter shout concluding his monologue—"It's too late now. It will always be too late. Fortunately!" (p. 147)—is more shocking because it is spoken by a character who has adopted the name and function of a man who offered the conquest of time and a new life in eternity.

Despite the immense number of Christian echoes in *The Fall* (there are many to which I have not referred), it is a serious mistake to assume that it contradicts all Camus' other writings and depicts Clamence's atheism as the cause of his emptiness. His sin is not to have rejected God, but to have attempted to replace Him with his own ego. Camus would agree with Clamence that "there is no lamb or innocence" (p. 130), but *The Fall* vehemently condemns the man who glories in the fact that van Eyck's "Honest Judges," who once adored the Lamb of God, now seem to be adoring the man himself. Christian forms are devoid of divine meaning. The purpose is to furnish a standard against which Clamence can be measured, a standard endowed with incalculable connotative power, even in an age which has lost its faith. As André Malraux said, "Of all the imprints that we bear, the Christian imprint, like a scar on our flesh, is the most deeply etched."[3] Rather than forging his own myth, Camus makes impressive use of a myth already permeating his readers' world. The force of the Christian frame of reference in *The Fall* depends not on faith, but on the common cultural heritage of Western man. It is employed not for specific religious purposes, not even

[3] *D'une jeunesse européene*, quoted in Henri Peyre, *Contemporary French Literature* (New York, 1964), p. 153.

for specific philosophical purposes, but for the absolutely basic technical purpose of directing the reader's reception of a novel. Camus reached back to the beginnings of Christianity to find a contrast to Clamence whose cosmic significance would communicate the debility of this "little prophet" and his "shabby times."

It is tempting to take the definition of Clamence's character derived by setting him beside his Biblical counterparts and compare his moralistic posture with that of Camus himself. But such a comparison would be contrary to the basic purpose of this essay, which is to evaluate the strictly novelistic value of one aspect of Camus' literary genius. There has been no attempt to discuss the place of *The Fall* in Camus' complete work, and for this reason the essay is perhaps as false to the overall spirit of the novel as discussions which neglect its literary qualities to examine its philosophical and biographical importance. The only justification for such distortion is that it is a reaction to criticism which furnishes lengthy analysis of the novels "without consulting the texts,"[4] as one recent work admits. Camus' philosophical significance is undeniable; he deserves the recognition he has been granted as a voice of his age, but the relevance of his writings to the real world should not obscure his skill in creating and defining an imaginary world. It was with the hope of leading to greater appreciation of one aspect of that skill that this essay was written.

[4] Pierre-Henri Simon, *Présence de Camus* (Paris, 1961), p. 172.

X The Humor of the Absurd: Mark Twain's Adamic Diaries*

Stanley Brodwin

*Department of English,
Hofstra University*

"Everything human is pathetic," wrote Mark Twain in *Following the Equator* (1897), adding that "The secret source of Humor itself is not joy but sorrow. There is no humor in heaven" (XX, 101).[1] A proper response to this statement may well be to attribute it to Twain's late, despairing mood and nothing more. And while such a response would be obvious and understandable, it would not embrace the profounder implications of the passage. We can penetrate to the heart of the passage's meaning, I believe, by seeing it as a crystallization or epitome of Twain's conviction that humor is, in its essence, implicit in the universal nature of things and in man's own response to the reality of his fallen condition. For Twain, humor ultimately derives from contradiction, absurdity and incongruity, the principle of irony triumphant; it functions as a theological sign of man's fall but at the same time enables him to deal with that pathetic state. The secret source is finally located in an existential awareness of a dread Divinity or Cosmos that renders man helpless before a determining and deterministic universe that somehow toys—as does a practical joker—with his innocence, compassion, curiosity and love, and turns them into forms of suffering or evil.

Mark Twain's pessimistic determinism, has, of course, been well examined in recent years, the criticism largely

*Reprinted from *Criticism*, 14, No. 1 (Winter, 1972): 49-64 by permission of the Wayne State University Press. Copyright 1972 by Wayne State University Press.

[1] *The Writings of Mark Twain*, ed. A. B. Paine, 37 vols. (New York, 1923). Unless otherwise specified, all further references are to this Stormfield edition.

dealing with his attack on the moral sense, the Bible, the idea of free-will and man's inability to reform morally. But Twain's perception of the nature and role of humor in relation to his theological determinism has not been fully delineated. Indeed, some of Twain's most profound and exciting insights about this relationship have been ignored. The dominant approaches to questions about the sources of Twain's humor and philosophy have been Freudian, or psychological in general, and historical. I propose to confront this problem in theological-literary terms. More specifically, I believe that an analysis of Twain's Diaries of Adam, Eve and Satan—theological folk stories, in effect—will reveal a variety of ideas illuminating one central concept: that humor is a theological element that binds God's creation to man's fall. Humor is both a cause and effect of the fall. The theological conceit becomes a theoretical basis on which Twain's own common genius can be explained. Through these Diaries, Twain makes a sustained effort to grasp the philosophical sources of his despair in its ironic relationship to his comic vision. The Diaries, in fact, circle the whole range of that comic vision. In "Extracts from Adam's Diary" (1893, 1897), and "Eve's Diary" (1905), we have the fall treated paradoxically in an Horatian, life-affirming way; while in "That Day in Eden" (1923), "Eve Speaks" (1923), and "Papers From the Adam Family," in *Letters from the Earth* (1962), we move toward the humor of the absurd, the practical joke, which finally breaks forth into bitter, Juvenalian satire. The total effect of this pattern is recognized by Twain's Satan, the detached observer in "That Day in Eden," who is made to reflect on the pathos of man's condition. What is finally encompassed by the diaries is the very relationship between man and God mediated through the nature of humor or the comic vision.

Clearly, Mark Twain's relationship to God—either the God of the Bible whom he hated, or the Deistic concept he professed to believe in—was to a large degree conveyed through his almost lifelong obsession with the Genesis story of the fall and its characters. Theologically considered,

Twain's relationship to the Bible as a whole was one of love and hate, rejection and attraction, the polar questions being the goodness or the evilness of Creation, and the conflicts between freedom and determinism, nature and conscience, man and God—questions which permeate a large body of his major work. And because Twain was a born questioner of the ways of God to man, the Genesis story provided him with a concrete-particular through which skepticism and belief could oscillate from comedy to pathos or tragedy. So, for example, comedy derives from skepticism in the anecdote Twain tells of the time when he was "only a Sunday school scholar":

I was greatly interested in the incident of Eve and the Serpent, and thought Eve's calmness perfectly noble. I asked Mr. Barclay [his school teacher] if he had ever heard of another woman who, being approached by a serpent, would not excuse herself and break for the nearest timber. (XXVI, 307)

. . . We may now turn to an examination of Mark Twain's cluster of Adamic fables. These works all employ many of the techniques and forms of the Southwestern American humor Twain knew and brought to perfection: exaggeration, linguistic distortion, slang, puns, and, above all, the tall-tale, the kind of story that makes fantasy real and the real fantastic. The mode is of course irony, either dramatic or verbal, which serves both as a technique and as a philosophic statement affirming that incongruity, disparity and uncertainty are the essential conditions of life.

In the Adamic fables, the irony is created by counterpointing myth and reality in a way which is comically absurd. Here, the mythic figures of Adam and Eve do not behave or speak as mythic figures, or figures in a fantasy, but rather as very "real" people who speak in a contemporary idiom although making naive assumptions about reality. Linguistic and intellectual anachronism is one of Mark Twain's devices for creating ironic humor in these fables. In "Adam's Diary," for example, Adam is constantly irritated by Eve's reckless naming of things:

Tuesday. Been examining the great waterfall. It is the finest thing on the estate, I think. The new creature calls it Niagara Falls—why, I am sure I do not know. Says it *looks* like Niagara Falls. That is not a reason, it is mere waywardness and imbecility. I get no chance to name anything myself. (XXIV, 342)

The device of Eve's intuitively correct naming of everything around her is continued throughout the diary. The anachronistic "Niagara Falls" brings the myth closer to home by heightening the disparity or gulf between myth and reality.

More pointed is the extension of this device to bear upon the fall. Eve has named the garden "Niagara Falls Park" and has already put up a sign "KEEP OFF THE GRASS." Adam ruefully comments that "My life is not as happy as it was" (XXIV, 343). In this instance, "reality" as known from contemporary experience ironically heightens the experience of the mythical fall: the knowledge of prohibition, as it were, makes the whole world kin.

Structurally, the incident anticipates what is the central event in the diary, the fall. The comic irony is maintained by showing how glad Adam is to have a snake who can talk to Eve, enabling him to "get a rest" (XXIV, 347). Then, Adam writes:

Friday.—She says the snake advises her to try the fruit of that tree, and says the result will be a great and fine and noble education. I told her there would be another result, too—it would introduce death into the world. That was a mistake—it had been better to keep the remark to myself; it only gave her an idea—she could . . . furnish fresh meat to the despondent lions and tigers. I advised her to keep away from the tree. She said she wouldn't. I foresee trouble. Will emigrate. (XXIV, 347)

Eve wishes to bring death into the world because she feels sorry for the carnivores who do not have anything to eat. The idea, potentially tragic, that the evil man creates is a result of the good he wishes to do, remains lightly humorous, however, because of the extreme naïveté of Eve. This naïveté is sufficiently exaggerated to make for the ironic contrast between her motives and their results. It was not pride that caused the fall, but the virtue of compassion for animals!

This is dramatized as Adam is shown riding through a plain filled with peaceful animals who suddenly begin eating each other: "I knew what it meant—Eve had eaten that fruit, and death was come into the world" (XXIV, 348). Eve comes in bringing the apples with her, dressed with boughs and leaves. Adam writes that he was "obliged to eat them, I was so hungry. It was against my principles, but I find that principles have no real force except when one is well fed . . ." (XXIV, 348). Adam and Eve are provided with motives opposite from the traditional ones of pride and disobedience.

But to further stress his differences from any traditional point of view, Mark Twain treats the personal consequences of the fall to Adam in a burlesque fashion, using an obvious comic device, the pun, which is itself a linguistic representation of the inversion of ideas:

Ten Days Later.—She accuses *me* of being the cause of our disaster! She says that . . . the Serpent assured her that the forbidden fruit was not apples, it was chestnuts. I said I was innocent, then, for I had not eaten any chestnuts. She said the Serpent informed her that "chestnut" was a figurative term meaning an aged and moldy joke. I turned pale at that, for I have made many jokes to pass the weary time, and some of them could have been of that sort. . . . She asked me if I had made one just at the time of the catastrophe. I was obliged to admit that I had. . . . I was thinking about the Falls, and I said to myself, "How wonderful it is to see that vast body of water tumble down there!" Then in an instant a bright thought flashed into my head, and I let it fly, saying, "It would be more wonderful to see it tumble *up* there!"—and I was about to kill myself with laughing at it when all nature broke loose in war and death and I had to flee for my life. "There," she said with triumph, "That is just it; the Serpent mentioned that very jest, and called it the First Chestnut, and said it was coeval with the creation." Alas, I am indeed to blame. (XXIV, 349)

It is at this point that the full import of Twain's theology of the comic can be grasped. Eve had caused the fall through compassion and now, in her attempt to blame Adam, we discover that humor, too, is guilty, although that humor was simply the result of Adam's curious, insightful mind, given to turning reality on its head. The joke may be as old as creation, "coeval" with it as the serpent says, but only when man makes the joke does war and death appear. Incongruity is at the heart of reality, existential, part of a cosmic joke that is not a very good one. Yet it is a latent joke in the nature of things until man apprehends the ludicrous. Man's comic sense is both a cause of suffering because it enables him to see into the absurdity of things, and it is also symptomatic of the fallen state of affairs in that the response to absurdity, even though war and death may follow, is very often the laugh of guilt. "I am indeed to blame," Adam admits. In this case, the tragic event of the fall is made to appear an object for laughter suggesting that in the end, the secret source of humor is sorrow.

Adam's last entry in his diary, however, marks a change in tone, concluding on a more personal note. Adam has learned to live with Eve and affirms that "It is better to live outside the Garden with her than inside it without her" (XXIV, 356). And "blessed be the chestnut that has brought us . . . together . . ." (XXIV, 356). Eve's compassion and Adam's humor, twin ideas that at best reflect man's celebratory, healing qualities, have caused the fall, caused the exile and at the same time created the means by which man is able to face that exile. What had begun as an irritating relationship between the couple, confused and filled with humorous difficulties, now affirms itself in the midst of its own joke and emerges strong and binding.

In "Eve's Diary" Twain uses different comic devices for his ideas and effects. Eve is presented as a tender, girlish creature who loves nature and Adam with the innocence of a child. In an interpolation in her diary, Adam describes her as "all interest, eagerness, vivacity, the world is to her a charm, a wonder, a mystery, a joy . . ." (XXIV, 372-73). Twain makes comic use of Eve's love of nature and her attempt to make order out of it:

There are too many stars in some places and not enough in others, but that can be remedied presently, no doubt. The moon got loose last night, and slid down and fell out of the scheme—a very great loss; it breaks my heart to think of it. (XXIV, 358)

Adam is concerned with other things, but Eve is filled with the wonder of Creation, which gives a kind of "realism," a touch of emotional authenticity, to the diary. Yet, characteristically, Mark Twain uses Eve's observations for more than primitive folk humor. Eve's analysis about the loss of the moon suggests another irony of human nature.

But of course there is no telling where it went to. And besides, whoever gets it will hide it; I know it because I would do it myself. I believe I can be honest in all other matters, but I already begin to realize that the core and center of my nature is love of the beautiful, . . . and that it would not be safe to trust me with a moon that belonged to another person and that person didn't know that I had it. I could give up a moon that I found in the daytime, because I should be afraid someone was looking; but if I found it in the dark, I am sure I should find some kind of excuse for not saying anything about it. For I do love moons, they are so pretty and romantic. (XXIV, 358-61)

This passage develops one of Twain's most trenchant ironies: our virtues make us sinners. For even though the diary purports to show man in a prelapsarian state, Mark Twain makes it abundantly clear that moral weaknesses, the inability to resist temptation, resides even in the most innocent breast. Only in this context he is able to feel a sympathetic humor towards human nature and its penchant for rationalization.

Man's tendency to self-delusion, his inability to distinguish between appearance and reality, and his essential egotism are most vividly portrayed, however, in the scene in which Eve sees herself in a pool of water (echoing Milton) and takes her reflection for a separate self. Although, in Adam's account, she jumps in to embrace herself, and almost drowns, for Eve, the image "comforts . . . with its sympathy" (XXIV, 367). Eve's narcissism, superficially seen as a fault in her character, is inverted to become a genuine source of comfort, a kind of "good" during that period in which she and Adam do not have a harmonious relationship. Eve tries to win over Adam, and it is part of the intertwined pathos and humor of the situation that she attempts this by getting him the forbidden apples:

I tried to get him some of these apples, but I cannot learn to throw straight. I failed, but I think the good intention pleased him. They are forbidden, and he says I shall come to harm; but so I come to harm pleasing him, why shall I care for that harm? (XXIV, 366)

It is now ironically love, not pride, that causes the fall in Mark Twain's comic view. Adam had confirmed that life is better out of the garden with Eve than in it without her. In her diary, Eve writes that "The Garden is lost, but I have found him, and am content. He loves me as well as he can. I love him with all the strength of my passionate nature . . ." (XXIV, 378). For Twain, these emotions transmute Eve into the Eternal Feminine, all love derived from her: "I am the First Wife; and in the last wife I shall be repeated" (XXIV, 381). Adam and Eve are archetypes from whose forms all humanity is taken.

The diary ends with Adam's famous line at Eve's grave, a line that Albert Bigelow Paine said is "the full tale of Mark Twain's love and sorrow, and is perhaps the most . . . beautiful line he ever wrote."[2]

ADAM: Wheresoever she was, *there* was Eden. (XXIV, 381)

Thus the diary ends on a plaintive, melancholy, but affirmative note. Together with its companion piece, it has again traced the fall with humorous depth, making love now to be part of that vision that emerges from a corruptible (and corrupting) world. We have seen that compassion and comically curious wit are other aspects of the vision which now completes itself with love. Yet the ultimate irony is that these values would find no place in the "real" world if they were not needed to cope with a Divine Nature which has no place for them; indeed, makes them the very causes

[2]*The Writings of Mark Twain*, 24, xii.

of the fall. The recognition of this fact is what makes human life pathetic, and makes man penetrate into his sorrow in order to transcend it, guilt-ridden and alienated though he may become from an empty Edenic state of being. Adam and Eve's very willingness—even compulsion to inquire, question and act on their insights—is the essence of their pathos and sorrow. Those inquiries and acts create humor for us, and by so doing, offer us a spiritual shield with which we can confront our predicament. Humor is at once the symptom and cure for the fall.

But this view of humanity was far from Twain's final statement. In "That Day in Eden" he confronted the theological issues of the fall in terms of his own fairly well-defined determinism. The tone now becomes melancholy, questioning, brooding. Gone is the domestic bickering, the amusing personal foibles, the comic experimentation with life that characterized "Adam's Diary" and "Eve's Diary." Seen from the point of view of a detached, patronizingly sympathetic Satan, Mark Twain achieves a certain artistic distance from these characters with whom he is so often passionately engaged. At the same time, this distance lends a more genuine "mythic" aspect to his treatment of the fall and prepares the way for the theological "joke" that is to take place.

The essential qualities of Twain's story are rendered in the opening paragraph:

Long ago I was in the bushes near the Tree of Knowledge when the Man and the Woman came there and had a conversation. I was present, now, when they came again after all these years. They were as before—mere boy and girl—trim, rounded, slender, flexible, snow images lightly flushed with the pink of the skies, innocently unconscious of their nakedness, lovely to look upon, beautiful beyond words. (XXIX, 339)

The tone is detached and suffused with a sense of the peaceful passing of time. Child-like innocence is aptly embodied in the metaphor of "snow images . . . flushed with the pink of skies," which at the same time establishes their relationship to a pure Nature. There is no sign of jealousy

or envy in Satan. He speaks as a grateful spectator looking
upon a work of art. He hears them, as always, puzzling over
the words "Good, Evil, Death" (XXIX, 339). This is the idea
upon which the story is structured, for it is their
puzzlement over these words that leads them to seek out
Satan, thus beginning the process of the fall. Satan, without
malice, tries to explain to them the meaning of "pain," but
they cannot comprehend it:

". . . Things which are outside of our orbit—our own particular
world—which by our constitution and equipment we are unable to
see, or feel, or otherwise experience—*cannot be made com-
prehensible to us in words.* There you have the whole thing in a
nutshell. It is a principle, it is axiomatic, it is a law. Now do you
understand?"
  The gentle creature looked dazed, and for all result she was
delivered of this vacant remark:
  "What is axiomatic?"
  She had missed the point. Necessarily she would. (XXIX, 341)

Satan continues his explanations and introduces the word
"death" to them, saying that it is a sleep:

  "Oh, I know what that is!"
  "But it is a sleep only in a way . . . . It is more than a sleep."
  "Sleep is pleasant, sleep is lovely!"
  "But death is a long sleep—very long."
  "Oh, all the lovelier! Therefore I think nothing could be better
than death." (XXIX, 341-42)

In this instance the irony is poignant, understated, and
foreshadows the fall itself. The simple, direct language
conveys Eve's naïveté well, introducing sympathetic humor
into the fable. The inevitable question of morals is,
however, finally introduced, the last of a progression of
terms that began with "pain." Satan asks if Eve would
drown her child on Adam's command, since "obedience to
constituted authority is moral law" (XXIX, 343). Eve
replied that she would if she wanted to. Satan then tries to
describe to her the innocence of her attitude:

It is a divine state, the loftiest and purest attainable in heaven and in earth. It is the angel gift. The angels are wholly . . . sinless, for they do not know right from wrong, and all the acts of such are blameless. No one can do wrong with knowing how to distinguish between right and wrong. (XXIX, 343)

The question of the moral sense is at last brought into the open and Satan is forced to define it as the "*creator* of wrong," since "wrong cannot exist until the Moral Sense brings it into being" (XXIX, 344). If the objection be raised at this point that the moral sense can also bring "right" into the world, Mark Twain has his answer that "right" exists already in the theory of the natural innocence of Adam and Eve. What Twain is trying to do in "That Day in Eden" is to define the moral sense not so much as a creator of evil, ontologically speaking, but of the capacity to know evil and feel guilt, thus dividing all human actions into "right" or "wrong." The moral sense makes an "amorality" into an "immorality." For example, Eve would drown her baby if she wanted to. But acquiring the moral sense would make her consciously guilty of such a desire or act. She would "know" good and evil.

"That Day in Eden," though it bears the bias against the moral sense that many of Mark Twain's other works do, is constructed to dramatize not only the difference between having and not having the moral sense, but also to establish the blamelessness of man. Eve is simply "wistful" (XXIX, 344) about having the moral sense and Adam is "indifferent" (XXIX, 345) to it. Satan's observations, suffused with Twain's own voice of ironic compassion, crystallize the point:

Poor ignorant things, the command of refrain had meant nothing to them, they were but children, and could not understand untried things and verbal abstractions which stood for matters outside their little world and . . . experience. (XXIX, 344-45)

Eve tastes the apple and all Satan can say is that "It was pitiful" (XXIX, 345). Pathos accompanies the creation of conscience, a pathos that was implicit in Satan's way of experiencing first their childishness and, finally, their loss of innocence. Satan and Adam watch Eve suddenly grow inexpressibly old. Indeed, the tone of sadness the story conveys is very much the product of this dramatic realization of the fast onrush of time and age. This sadness is exquisitely evoked by Twain's restrained style and his control over the responses of the characters: "All this the fair boy saw: then loyally and bravely he took the apple and tasted it, saying nothing" (XXIX, 346). Old age becomes a metaphor for their fall as they leave Eden together. In "Eve Speaks," Eve questions the justice of their expulsion:

We could not know it was wrong to disobey the command, for the words were strange to us and we did not understand them. We did not know right from wrong—how should we know? We could not, without the Moral Sense first—ah, that would have been fairer, that would have been kinder; then we should be to blame if we disobeyed. (XXIX, 347)

Painfully, she cries out: "They drove us out. Drove us out into this harsh wilderness" (XXIX, 348). Then they experience all the suffering of life, except for death. That experience comes when they discover their son, Abel, hurt and seemingly sleeping. Poignantly, Mark Twain shows them responding like ignorant children to some motiveless torture, or some vast practical and cruel joke. Eve brings the corpse of Abel food, and covers him with the down of birds in the hope of his awakening. She finally bemoans the discovery of the meaning of death. Satan comments:

Death has entered the world, the creatures are perishing; one of the Family is fallen; the product of the Moral Sense is complete. The Family think ill of death—they will change their minds. (XXIX, 350)

The consolation of death becomes Twain's version of the *felix culpa*. And yet a curious kind of sad humor suffuses the story. The reader, like Satan, is made to smile inwardly, a troubled and bemused smile that is witness to a scene of cosmic but logical absurdity. And, like Satan, we are prevented from empathizing in tragic terms because of the folk-mythic distance of the characters and situation. We see that the philosophic thrust of all Mark Twain's examinations of the fall is always to show the inability of innocence to cope with the moral demands of which it can have no true conception.

Finally, Twain shifted from theological exposition to social and political satire in the "Papers of the Adam Family" from *Letters from the Earth*. The significance of these papers lies in their strong postlapsarian emphasis, the life of man after the fall. The comic mode here breaks through to cold satire, the laugh of horror. It is in a "Passage From Eve's Autobiography . . . 920", that this emphasis begins. In this piece Eve is astonished that she should be the source of the most ". . . stupendous event which would happen in the Universe for a thousand years—the founding of the human race!" (*L. E.*, 89-90). All that saves man from overpopulation, however, is war: "War is a rude friend, but a kind one. It keeps us down to sixty billion and saves the hard-grubbing world alive. It is all the globe can support . . ." (*L. E.*, 92). War, the political extension of death, becomes a boon to mankind. The irony cuts into the purpose of life and makes that purpose death. Death becomes what man deserves, and is the final judgment of his worth. Twain's irony was never more bitter, or more artistically right, than in making Eve—The Mother of All Living—the fervent supporter of war and death.

The remaining papers extend the satire to baseball, the theatre, commercialism and patriotism, but do not reach the same pitch of satirical intensity, though Methuselah, writing in the year 747, makes this interesting observation:

This new actor, Luz, whose fame filleth the land of late, so wrought upon the multitude in the great part of Adam in the classic, venerable and noble play of the Driving Forth from Eden (there being nothing comparable to it written in these modern times), that they [the audience] wept aloud and many times rose up shouting. . . . (*L. E.*, 63)

Twain, too, was "wrought upon" by the tragedy of the fall but he was able to perceive its comic or absurd qualities as well. In "That Day in Eden" particularly, we have a tale that manifests the "logic of the absurd." For unlike his actor, Luz, Mark Twain does not over-emotionalize the fall; he simply presents it as a logical and inevitable process, given the nature of the characters, but also necessarily absurd. There is only an ignorant pair who do not know the meaning of words and concepts, and still are told— absurdly—that they must respond to and take responsibility for what they cannot know. Therefore, "That Day in Eden," "Eve Speaks," and much of the Adam papers in *Letters from the Earth* bear the stamp of a kind of cold grotesqueness, which is about as far as satire can go without becoming absurd in its effect on the reader. Yet there is still a strain of pathos carried over from the more ostensibly "comic" diaries, which serves to soften the coldly logical absurdity of the fall in "That Day in Eden." . . . In these diaries the fall derives from Adam and Eve's warm, loving, and witty qualities. There their hearts betray them. But in "That Day in Eden," and "Eve Speaks" they are betrayed by their intellectual failures and an absurd Deity. Only Satan is given a perspective on this. After the fall, when Adam and Eve recognize what has happened to them, their horror and despair are so great that death becomes genuine relief. Laughter still survives but it survives in a form of the triumphant relief Eve feels, for example when she learns that "sixteen hundred millions of people" have been killed in "nine months" (*L. E.*, 90). . . .

[Twain] saw yet another tragic dimension in the relationship between humor and a fallen world in *The Mysterious Stranger*. Humor, or its underlying concept, absurdity, may well be at the heart of the Cosmos, in the way God deals with man, Twain suggested in the diaries. But at least humor could also be a weapon against other, destructive manifestations of the fall. Yet what does man do with his laughter, be it satanic or benign? Satan's diatribe against man is withering:

For your race, in its poverty, has unquestionably one really effective weapon—laughter. Power, money, persuasion, supplication, persecution—these can lift a colossal humbug—push it a little—weaken it a little, century by century; but only laughter can blow it to rags and atoms at a blast. Against the assault of laughter nothing can stand. You are always fussing and fighting with your weapons. Do you ever use that one? No; you leave it lying rusting. As a race, do you ever use it at all? No; you lack the sense and the courage. (XXVII, 132)

God was responsible for man's moral sense, which makes innocence a dream and reality a nightmare of moral error. Yet it is man who rejects the grace and power of laughter and the comic sense. What we have seen in the diaries is Mark Twain's deepening theological insight into the nature of that laughter and comic sense, their uses and consequences, and how they are really inescapable—existential —despite man's failure to use them effectively. The statement referred to at the start of this essay, that "There is no humor in heaven," really means that there is no compassion in heaven. All that there is "in" heaven is the ontological ground of humor or the comic sense as it is revealed in logical absurdity and incongruity. Man may laugh affirmatively or despairingly at what is a kind of practical joke played on him by God or Providence, but he never doubts that the joke is intrinsically cruel. Even in a casually humorous way Twain could make this point. For he suggested that the hand of Providence was behind Noah's flood, explaining that it took place because "Somebody that liked dry weather wanted to take a walk."[3] And does not Herman Melville tread the same ground when Ishmael says that ". . . small difficulties and worryings, prospects of sudden disaster, peril of life and limb; all these, and death itself, seem . . . jolly punches in the side bestowed by the unseen and unaccountable old joker"? Indeed, Ishmael says there are times a man takes ". . . this whole universe for a vast practical joke, though the wit thereof he but dimly discerns, and more than suspects that the joke is at

[3] Quoted in Clara Clemens, *My Father, Mark Twain* (New York, 1931), p. 54.

nobody's expense but his own."[4] But, as we have seen, Twain's way of saying these things was to transmogrify the Adamic myth so that determinism and absurdity are shown to be two sides of the same coin. In one brief epigram from *Pudd'nhead Wilson* Twain captures this idea:

Adam was but human—this explains it all. He did not want the apple for the apple's sake, he wanted it only because it was forbidden. The mistake was in not forbidding the serpent; then he would have eaten the serpent. (XVI, 8)

The paradox is that we can only perceive this humor in sorrow.

In conclusion, Mark Twain's Adamic Diaries reveal his understanding that his profound comic sense had theological roots; that it was a manifestation of man's fallen state and a dread cure for it that few men knew how to use; and that his "kinship" with Adam gave him a universal relationship through which his deepest theological insights into the humor of the absurd could be illuminated.

[4] Melville, *Moby-Dick* (New York, 1948), p. 224. The chapter is fittingly called "The Hyena."

XI Biblical Interpretation in *Huckleberry Finn*, Chapter 14*

Stuart Lewis

Department of English,
University of Colorado

From *Huckleberry Finn*, chapter 14

"Well, but he [Solomon] *was* the wisest man, anyway; because the widow she told me so, her own self."

"I doan k'yer what de widder say, he *warn't* no wise man nuther. He had some er de dad-fetchedes' ways I ever see. Does you know 'bout dat chile dat he 'uz gwyne to chop in two?"

"Yes, the widow told me all about it."

"*Well*, den! Warn' dat de beatenes' notion in de worl'? You jes' take en look at it a minute. Dah's de stump, dah—dat's one er de women; heah's you—dat's de yuther one; I's Sollermun; en dish yer dollar bill's de chile. Bofe un you claims it. What does I do? Does I shin aroun' mongs' de neighbors en fine out which un you de bill *do* b'long to, en han' it over to de right one, all safe en soun', de way dat anybody dat had any gumption would? No; I take en whack de bill in *two*, en give half un it to you, en de yuther half to de yuther woman. Dat's de way Sollermun was gwyne to do wid de chile. Now I want to ast you: what's de use er dat half a bill?—can't buy noth'n wid it. En what use is a half a chile? I wouldn' give a dern for a million un um."

"But hang it, Jim, you've clean missed the point—blame it, you've missed it a thousand mile."

"Who? Me? Go 'long. Doan talk to *me* 'bout yo pints. I reck'n I knows sense when I sees it; en day ain' no sense in sich doin's as dat. De 'spute warn't 'bout a half a chile, de 'spute was 'bout a whole chile; en de man dat think he kin settle a 'spute 'bout a whole chile wid a half a chile doan' know enough to come in out'n de rain. Don' talk to me 'bout Sollermun, Huck, I knows him by de back."

"But I tell you you don't get the point."

"Blame de point! I reck'n I knows what I knows. En

* From *Explicator*, 30 (March, 1972): Item 61. Reprinted by permission.

mine you, de *real* pint is down furder—it's down deeper. It lays in de way Sollermun was raised. You take a man dat's got on'y one or two chillen; is dat man gwyne to be waseful o' chillen? No, he ain't; he can't 'ford it. *He* know how to value 'em. But you take a man dat's got 'bout five million chillen runnin' roun' de house, en it's diffunt. *He* as soon chop a chile in two as a cat. Dey's plenty mo'. A chile er two, mo' er less, warn't no consekens to Sollermun, dad fatch him!"

—Mark Twain

While Jim cites the famous incident of *I Kings*, III, 16-28, as an example of Solomon's lack of wisdom, Huck interprets the story in the traditional manner and believes that Jim has missed the point. In the past, Huck had shown a common-sense attitude toward the Bible, refusing to learn about Moses because he "don't take no stock in dead people" (Chapter I). Yet in this instance he argues for the usual meaning of the story and will not listen to a more down-to-earth interpretation.

As a boy, living in Missouri, Twain never really saw the harshest aspects of slavery, and the same is apparently true of Huck. Unlike Huck, Jim realizes the terror of one man's holding absolute power over another. The story of Solomon and the harlots affects him deeply because he has witnessed, or at least heard of, such atrocities as Solomon threatened actually being carried out on members of his own race. The threat which Huck cannot take seriously is very real to Jim because it relates to the immediate experience of the slaves. The test is too close for comfort.

Jim's speech shows his superior wisdom as well when he says that the point of the story "lays in de way Sollermun was raised." A major theme of Twain's writings was the effect that society had on a person's morals. Jim is speaking for Twain when he argues that Solomon's upbringing (and, by implication, that of the slave-owner) has made him insensitive to human suffering.

Jim's speech relates to another theme of the novel as well, the debased value of human life under slavery. Twain treats ironically the idea of putting monetary value on human life, as can be seen in Jim's comment at the end of Chapter VIII: "Yes, en I's rich now, come to look at it. I owns myself, en I's wuth eight hund'd dollars. I wisht I had de money, I wouldn' want no mo'." (See also the conclusion of *Pudd'nhead Wilson*.) In this context, Jim's use of a dollar bill in place of the baby in his reenactment of the story is significant, for it shows that to the slave-owner a slave's child is regarded as a commodity rather than as a human being. Finally Jim's question "what use is half a chile?" may be a comment on the fact that slavery robs a man of half his humanity.

Thus . . . Jim is the true teacher in this chapter. Though Huck does not learn anything immediately, this debate over Solomon's wisdom sets the stage for Huck's realization at the conclusion of the next chapter that Jim really is a man and prepares the reader for a whole new relationship between the two adventurers.

XII *Of Mice and Men:* John Steinbeck's Parable of the Curse of Cain*

William Goldhurst

Department of Humanities,
University of Florida

Of Mice and Men is a short novel in six scenes presented in description-dialogue-action form that approximates stage drama in its effect (about this fact there is no critical disagreement). The time scheme runs from Thursday evening through Sunday evening—exactly three days in sequence, a matter of some importance, as we shall see presently. The setting is the Salinas Valley in California, and most of the characters are unskilled migratory workers who drift about the villages and ranches of that area picking up odd jobs or doing short-term field work and then moving on to the next place of employment. Steinbeck focuses on two such laborers who dream of one day saving up enough money to buy a small farm of their own. One of these is George Milton, small of stature, clever, sensitive, and compassionate; the other is Lennie Small, who is oversized, mentally retarded, enormously strong, and prone to getting into serious trouble. Early in the story the prospect of their ever realizing their dream seems remote, but as the action develops (they meet a crippled bunk-house worker who wants to go in with them on the scheme, and who offers to chip in his life savings), the probability of fulfillment increases. If the three homeless migrants pool their salaries at the end of the current month, they can quit and move on to their farm, which as Steinbeck emphasizes repeatedly is a place of abundance and a refuge from the hardships of life.

Lennie manages to avoid disaster for exactly three days. He gets involved, innocently at first, with the flirtatious wife of Curley, the boss's violent son; and through a series

From "Of Mice and Men: John Steinbeck's Parable of the Curse of Cain," *Western American Literature*, 6 (1971): 123-35 (124-32, 134-35). Reprinted by permission.

of unfortunate circumstances, he becomes frightened and unintentionally kills the girl. Curley organizes a posse to apprehend Lennie—with the idea either of locking him up in an asylum or, more likely of killing him on the spot. George gets to Lennie first and out of sympathy for his companion shoots him in the head to spare him the pain of Curley's shotgun or the misery of incarceration.

The title of the story has a two-fold application and significance. First it refers to naturalistic details within the texture of the novella: Lennie likes to catch mice and stroke their fur with his fingers. This is a particularly important point for two reasons: it establishes Lennie's fatal weakness for stroking soft things and, since he invariably kills the mice he is petting, it foreshadows his deadly encounter with Curley's wife. Secondly, the title is of course a fragment from the poem by Robert Burns, which gives emphasis to the idea of the futility of human endeavor or the vanity of human wishes.

> The best laid schemes o' mice and men
> Gang aft a-gley
> An' leave us nought but grief an' pain
> For promised joy.

This notion is obviously of major importance in the novella, and it may be said to be Steinbeck's main theme on the surface level of action and development of character.

Other noteworthy characters and incidents in *Of Mice and Men* include Crooks, the Negro stable hand who lives in the harness room. Here on one occasion he briefly entertains Lennie and Candy, the bunk-house worker who wants to be a part of the dream-farm. Crooks tells them they will never attain it; he says he has known many workers who wanted land of their own, but he has never heard of anyone who has actually realized this ambition. Then there is Carlson, the blunt and unfeeling ranch hand who insists on shooting Candy's aged sheep dog, which having outlived its usefulness has become an annoyance to the men who occupy the bunk-house. This is a significant episode which anticipates George's mercy-killing of Lennie at the conclusion. ("I ought to of shot that dog myself," says Candy later. "I shouldn't ought to of let no stranger shoot my dog.") Steinbeck is also at some pains to establish an important aspect of the ranch-workers' existence: their off-hours recreation, which consists of gambling, drinking, and visiting the local brothel. Upon such indulgences, which they find impossible to resist, these men squander their wages and thereby remain perpetually penniless, tied to a monotonous pattern of work, transitory pleasure, homelessness, and dependence upon job-bosses for the basic needs of existence.

Of Mice and Men was published early in 1937, was a Book-of-the-Month Club selection and one of the year's top best sellers. In the closing months of 1937 Steinbeck adapted the novella for the Broadway stage, where it enjoyed immediate popular success, winning in addition the award of the Drama Critics' Circle. The Hollywood version, released in 1941, became one of the most widely discussed motion pictures of the decade. If my own high school experience was at all typical, spontaneous parodies of Lennie's speech and behavior were a common feature of adolescent get-togethers in the 1940's. But from that time to the present *Of Mice and Men* has been a favorite topic for serious discussion in college literature classes; and a sensitive television production in the late 1960's revealed new subtleties and power in the little tale which, critical controversy or no, has now assumed the status of an American classic.

Viewed in the light of its mythic and allegorical implications, *Of Mice and Men* is a story about the nature of man's fate in a fallen world, with particular emphasis upon the question: is man destined to live alone, a solitary wanderer on the face of the earth, or is it the fate of man to care for man, to go his way in companionship with another? This is the same theme that occurs in the Old Testament, as early as Chapter Four of Genesis, immediately following the Creation and Expulsion. In effect, the question Steinbeck poses is the same question Cain poses to the

Lord: "Am I my brother's keeper?" From its position in the Scriptural version of human history we may assume with the compilers of the early books of the Bible that it is the primary *question concerning man as he is*, after he has lost the innocence and non-being of Eden. It is the same question that Steinbeck chose as the theme of his later book *East of Eden* (1952), in which novel the Cain and Abel story is re-enacted in a contemporary setting and where, for emphasis, Steinbeck has his main characters read the Biblical story aloud and comment upon it, climaxing the discussion with the statement made by Lee: "I think this is the best-known story in the world because it is everybody's story. I think it is the symbol story of the human soul." *Of Mice and Men* is an early Steinbeck variation on this symbol story of the human soul. The implications of the Cain-and-Abel drama are everywhere apparent in the fable of George and Lennie and provide its mythic vehicle.

Contrary to Lee's confident assertion, however, most people know the Cain and Abel story only in general outline. The details of the drama need to be filled in, particularly for the purpose of seeing how they apply to Steinbeck's novella. Cain was a farmer, Adam and Eve's first-born son. His offerings of agricultural produce to the Lord failed to find favor, whereas the livestock offered by Cain's brother, Abel, was well received. Angry, jealous, and rejected, Cain killed Abel when they were working in the field, and when the Lord inquired of Cain, where is your brother, Cain replied: "I know not: Am I my brother's keeper?" For his crime of homicide the Lord banished Cain from His company and from the company of his parents and set upon him a particular curse, the essence of which was that Cain was to become homeless, a wanderer, and an agricultural worker who would never possess or enjoy the fruits of his labor. Cain was afraid that other men would hear of his crime and try to kill him, but the Lord marked him in a certain way so as to preserve him from the wrath of others. Thus Cain left home and went to the land of Nod, which the story tells us lies east of Eden.

The drama of Cain finds its most relevant application in *Of Mice and Men* in the relationship between Lennie and George, and in the other characters' reactions to their associations. In the first of his six scenes Steinbeck establishes the two ideas that will be developed throughout. The first of these is the affectionate symbiosis of the two protagonists, their brotherly mutual concern and faithful companionship. Steinbeck stresses the beauty, joy, security, and comfort these two derive from the relationship:

"If them other guys gets in jail they can rot for all anybody gives a damn. But not us."
Lennie broke in, "But not us! An' why? Because . . . because I got you to look after me and you got me to look after you, and that's why." He laughed delightedly.

The second idea, which is given equal emphasis, is the fact that this sort of camaraderie is rare, different, almost unique in the world George and Lennie inhabit; other men, in contrast to these two, are solitary souls without friends or companions. Says George in Scene One:

"Guys like us, that work on ranches, are the loneliest guys in the world. They got no family. They don't belong no place. They come to a ranch an' work up a stake and then they go into town and blow their stakes, and the first thing you know they're poundin' their tail on some other ranch."

The alternative to the George-Lennie companionship is Aloneness, made more dreadful by the addition of an economic futility that Steinbeck augments and reinforces in later sections. The migratory ranch worker, in other words, is the fulfillment of the Lord's curse on Cain: "When thou tillest the ground, it shall not henceforth yield unto thee her strength; a fugitive and vagabond shalt thou be in the earth." Steinbeck's treatment of the theme is entirely free from a sense of contrivance; all the details in *Of Mice and Men* seem natural in the context and organically related to the whole; but note that in addition to presenting Lennie and George as men who till the ground and derive no benefits from their labor, he also manages to have them "on the run" when they are introduced in the first scene—this no doubt to have his main characters correspond as closely as possible to the Biblical passage: "a fugitive and a vagabond shalt thou be. . . ."

To the calamity of homelessness and economic futility Steinbeck later adds the psychological soul-corruption that is the consequence of solitary existence. In Scene Three George tells Slim, the mule-driver on the ranch:

"I seen the guys that go around on the ranches alone. That ain't no good. They don't have no fun. After a long time they get mean."

"Yeah, they get mean," Slim agreed. "They get so they don't want to talk to nobody."

Again, in Scene Four, the Negro stable buck Crooks tells Lennie:

"A guy needs somebody—to be near him. . . . A guy goes nuts if he ain't got nobody. Don't make no difference who the guy is, long's he's with you. I tell ya, I tell ya a guy gets too lonely and he gets sick."

This is Steinbeck's portrait of Cain in the modern world, or Man Alone, whose fate is so severe that he may feel compelled to echo the words of Cain to the Lord: "My punishment is more than I can bear." In *Of Mice and Men* Steinbeck gives us the case history of two simple mortals who try to escape the homelessness, economic futility, and psychological soul-corruption which Scripture embodies in the curse of Cain.

If in Scene One Lennie and George affirm their fraternity openly and without embarrassment, in Scene Two George is more hesitant. "He's my . . . cousin," he tells the ranch boss. "I told his old lady I'd take care of him." This is no betrayal on George's part, but a cover-up required by the circumstances. For the boss is highly suspicious of the Lennie-George fellowship. "You takin' his pay away from him?" he asks George. "I never seen one guy take so much trouble for another guy." A short time later Curley also sounds the note of suspicion, extending it by a particularly nasty innuendo: when George says "We travel together," Curley replies, "Oh, so it's that way." Steinbeck is implying here the general response of most men towards seeing two individuals who buddy around together in a friendless world where isolation is the order of the day: there must be exploitation involved, either financial or sexual! At the same time Steinbeck is developing the allegorical level of his story by suggesting that the attitude of Cain ("I know not: Am I my brother's keeper?") has become universal. Even the sympathetic and understanding Slim expresses some wonder at the Lennie-George fraternity. "Ain't many guys travel around together," Slim says in Scene Two. "I don't know why. Maybe ever'body in the whole damned world is scared of each other." This too, as Steinbeck interprets the Biblical story, is a part of Cain's curse: distrust. Later on, in order to give the theme of Aloneness another dimension, Steinbeck stresses the solitude of Crooks and Curley's wife, both of whom express a craving for company and "someone to talk to."

Notwithstanding the fact that they are obviously swimming against the current, Lennie and George continue to reaffirm their solidarity all along, right up to and including the last moments of Lennie's life in Scene Six. Here a big rabbit, which Lennie in his disturbed state of mind has hallucinated, tells the half-wit fugitive that George is sick of him and is going to go away and leave him. "He won't," Lennie cries. "He won't do nothing like that. I know George. Me an' him travels together." Actually Steinbeck's novella advances and develops, ebbs and flows, around the basic image of the Lennie-George relationship. Almost all the characters react to it in one way or another as the successive scenes unfold. In Scenes One, Two, and Three, despite the discouraging opinions of outsiders, the companionship remains intact and unthreatened. Midway into Scene Three the partnership undergoes augmentation when Candy is admitted into the scheme to buy the little farm. Late in Scene Four Crooks offers himself as another candidate for the fellowship of soul-brothers and dreamers.

This is the high point of optimism as regards the main theme of the story; this is the moment when a possible reversal of the curse of Cain seems most likely, as Steinbeck suggests that the answer to the Lord's question might be: Yes, I am my brother's keeper. If we arrive at this point with any comprehension of the author's purposes, we find ourselves brought up short by the idea: what if this George-Lennie-Candy-Crooks fraternity were to become universal!

But later in the same scene, the entrance of Curley's wife signals the turning point as the prospects for the idea of brotherhood-as-a-reality begin to fade and darken. As throughout the story she represents a force that destroys men and at the same time invites men to destroy her, as she will finally in Scene Five offer herself as a temptation which Lennie cannot resist, so in Scene Four Curley's wife sows the seeds that eventually disrupt the fellowship. Entering into the discussion in Crooks' room in the stable, she insults Crooks, Candy, and Lennie, laughs at their dream farm, and threatens to invent the kind of accusation that will get Crooks lynched. Crooks, reminded of his position of impotence in a white man's society, immediately withdraws his offer to participate in the George-Lennie-Candy farming enterprise. But Crooks' withdrawal, while extremely effective as social criticism, is much more. It represents an answer to the question Steinbeck is considering all along: is man meant to make his way alone or accompanied? Obviously this is one occasion, among many others in the story, when Steinbeck suggests the answer. Crooks' hope for fraternal living is short-lived. At the conclusion of the scene he sinks back into his Aloneness.

From this point on, even though the dream of fellowship on the farm remains active, the real prospects for its fulfillment decline drastically. In Scene Five, after George and Candy discover the lifeless body of Curley's wife, they both face the realization that the little farm is now unattainable and the partnership dissolved. Actually the plan was doomed to failure from the beginning; for fraternal living cannot long survive in a world dominated by the Aloneness, homelessness, and economic futility which Steinbeck presents as the modern counterpart of Cain's curse. Immediately following his discovery of Curley's wife's body, George delivers a speech that dwells on the worst possible aftermath of Lennie's misdeed; and this is not the wrath of Curley or the immolation of Lennie or the loss of the farm, but the prospect of George's becoming a Man Alone, homeless, like all the others and a victim as well of economic futility:

> "I'll work my month an' I'll take my fifty bucks and I'll stay all night in some lousy cat house. Or I'll set in some poolroom til ever'body goes home. An' then I'll come back an' work another month an' I'll have fifty bucks more."

This speech represents the true climax of the novella, for it answers the question which is Steinbeck's main interest throughout. Now we know the outcome of the Lennie-George experiment in fellowship, as we know the Aloneness of man's essential nature. In subtle ways, of course, Steinbeck has been hinting at this conclusion all along, as for example in the seven references spaced throughout Scenes Two and Three to George's playing solitaire in the bunk-house. For that matter the answer is implied in the very first line of the story when the author establishes his setting "A few miles south of Soledad . . . ," Soledad being at one and the same time a town in Central California and the Spanish word for solitude or aloneness.

But there are still other suggested meanings inherent in the dream-farm and the failure of the dream. The plan is doomed not only because human fellowship cannot survive in the post-Cain world, but also because the image of the farm, as conceived by George and Lennie and Candy, is overly idealized, the probability being that life, even if they obtained the farm, would not consist of the comfort, plenty, and interpersonal harmony they envision. The fruits and vegetables in abundance, the livestock and domestic animals, and the community of people involved ("Ain't gonna be no more trouble. Nobody gonna hurt nobody nor steal from 'em")—these are impractical expectations. George and Lennie, who were to some extent inspired by questions growing out of the story of Cain in Chapter Four of Genesis, want to retreat to Chapter Two and live in Eden! Of all ambitions in a fallen world, this is possibly the most unattainable; for paradise is lost, as the name of Steinbeck's hero, George Milton, suggests. And though there will always be men like Candy, who represents sweet hope, the view of Crooks, who represents black despair, is probably a more accurate appraisal of the human condition: "Nobody never gets to heaven, and nobody gets no land. It's just in their head. They're all the time talkin' about it, but it's jus' in their head." Obviously in this context Crooks' comment about nobody ever getting land refers not to literal ownership, but to the dream of contentment entertained by the simple workmen who come and go on the ranch. . . .

At this point without, I hope, undue emphasis, we might attempt to answer some specific objections which have been raised by critics of *Of Mice and Men*. The faults most often cited are the pessimism of Steinbeck's conclusion, which seems to some readers excessive; and the author's attempt to impose a tragic tone upon a story which lacks characters of tragic stature. Both of these censures might be accepted as valid, or at least understood as reasonable, if we read the novella *on the surface level of action and character-development*. But a reading which takes into account the mythical-allegorical significance of these actions and characters not only nullifies the objections, but opens up new areas of awareness. For example, although Lennie and George are humble people, without the status of traditional tragic characters, their dream is very much like the dream of Plato for an ideal Republic. And their experiment in fellowship is not at all different from the experiment attempted by King Arthur. And at the same time it is reminiscent of at least one aspect of Christ's ministry.

These are remote parallels to *Of Mice and Men*, yet they are legitimate and lend some measure of substance, nobility, and human significance to Steinbeck's novella. Its pessimism is not superimposed upon a slight story, as charged, but has been there from the opening line, if we know how to read it. Furthermore, the pessimism is not inspired by commercialism or false theatrics, but by the Hebrew Testament. ("And Cain said unto the Lord, My punishment is greater than I can bear.")

But let us tie up our loose ends, not with reference to critics, but with a brief summary of our discoveries during this investigation. *Of Mice and Men* is a realistic story with life-like characters and a regional setting, presented in a style highly reminiscent of stage drama. Steinbeck's technique also includes verbal ambiguity in place names and character names, *double entendre* in certain key passages of dialogue, and a mythical-allegorical drift that invites the reader into areas of philosophical and theological inquiry. Sources for the novella are obviously Steinbeck's own experience as a laborer in California; but on the allegorical level, *Of Mice and Men* reflects the early chapters of the Book of Genesis and the questions that grow out of the incidents therein depicted. These consist primarily of the consideration of man as a creature alone or as a brother and companion to others. In addition Steinbeck's story suggests the futility of the all-too-human attempt to recapture Eden, as well as a symbolic schema which defines human psychology. Steinbeck also implies a critique of the Hebrew-Christian ethic, to the effect that the absolute suppression of the animal appetites misrepresents the reality of human experience.

Finally we should say that Steinbeck's emphasis, on both the allegorical and realistic levels, is on the nobility of his characters' attempt to live fraternally. Even though the experiment is doomed to failure, Steinbeck's characters, like the best men of every age, dedicate themselves to pursuing the elusive grail of fellowship.

XIII The Brand of Cain in "The Secret Sharer"*

Porter Williams, Jr.
*Department of English,
North Carolina State University*

In discussing the moral predicament of Leggatt, the murderer in Conrad's "The Secret Sharer," it at first seems unnecessary to emphasize the obvious appropriateness of passing allusions to the Biblical story of Cain. Thus early in the narrative, while describing his imprisonment aboard the *Sephora*, Leggatt remarks that the captain's wife would have gladly had him out of the ship and then adds that it was the "'Brand of Cain' business, don't you see. . . . I was ready enough to go off wandering on the face of the earth—and that was price enough to pay for an Abel of that sort."[1] The allusion reminds us of the "brand" presumably upon Cain's forehead, a mark traditionally recalled as a moral stigma, and of the murderer's punishment of becoming an outcast, "a fugitive and a vagabond" (Genesis iv. 11-16). But the passing allusion becomes more important in Part II of the story when Leggatt persuades his protector to maroon him. Here Leggatt explains that he is not afraid of what a judge and jury can do to him, but he does not see himself returning as a prisoner to protest how his crime was almost forced upon him as he struggled desperately to save the *Sephora* in the face of a terrific storm and the angry attack of a half-crazed seaman: "What can they know whether I am guilty or not—or of *what* I am guilty, either? That's my affair. What does the Bible say? 'Driven off the face of the earth.' Very well. I am off the face of the earth now. As I came at night so I shall go" (pp. 131-132). The Biblical account of Cain's punishment be-

*From *Modern Fiction Studies*, 10 (Spring, 1964): 27-30. *Modern Fiction Studies*, © 1964, by Purdue Research Foundation, West Lafayette, Indiana. Reprinted by permission.

[1] Joseph Conrad, "The Secret Sharer," in *'Twixt Land and Sea* (New York, 1924), p. 107. Further references to this edition are cited in the text.

comes for Leggatt something of a legal precedent. He will accept the punishment decreed by Scripture but nothing more, for he can hardly expect in a court the kind of understanding he has received from the captain who has sheltered him. In short, the Cain story seems to be entering into the life of Conrad's tale as a precise symbol of Leggatt's predicament. For a man like Leggatt, being driven off the face of the earth was "price enough" to pay for his crime, and we know how painful this punishment was when we are informed how desperately Leggatt needed "to be seen, to talk with somebody" (p. 111) before going on. Above all, he needed to explain, to find someone who could understand. As Leggatt implies in a remark to the captain, he can face his punishment only "as long as I know that you under-stand" (p. 132). Certainly the Genesis story should be recalled here also with Cain's blunt complaint to the Lord, "My punishment is greater than I can bear. . . . I shall be a fugitive and a vagabond in the earth; and it shall come to pass, that every one that findeth me shall slay me" (Genesis iv. 13-14). Furthermore, Cain also received understanding and protection when the Lord pronounced sevenfold vengeance upon "whosoever slayeth Cain" and "set a mark upon Cain, lest any finding him should kill him" (Genesis iv. 15). Too often it is forgotten that the traditional brand upon Cain's forehead was really a mark of God's compassion and not a stigma, except in the sense that a crime had made such a protective mark necessary. Both murderers, Cain and Leggatt, have asked for protection and received it.

That Conrad was obviously aware of the protective aspect of Cain's "brand" is revealed at the close of the narrative when Leggatt finally leaves behind his protector and strikes out on his own. Once he has left the shelter provided aboard the ship, he appears in the mind of the captain as one "to be hidden for ever from all friendly faces, to be a fugitive and a vagabond on the earth, with no brand of the curse on his sane forehead to stay a slaying hand . . . too proud to explain" (p. 142). Leggatt, after all, is not a creature of the Old Testament world and receives no divine dispensation to protect him from enemies, though interestingly enough Conrad's language suggests through its ambiguous phraseology that although there is no mark "to stay a slaying hand," there is also "no brand of the curse" to make his shame permanent. Taken realistically, we need hardly wonder why no mark has appeared on the forehead of our British seaman, either as heavenly protection or as a stigma, though we might well ask whether Conrad wishes to imply something more than the obvious in reminding us again of the details of the Cain story. There is almost the suggestion that Leggatt, even while swimming away to take his punishment, has been relieved of at least part of his guilt. The last sentence of the story repeats this ambiguous note by recording how the captain gazes at the white hat which marks the spot where his second self has entered the water "to take his punishment: a free man, a proud swimmer striking out for a new destiny" (p. 143). To say the least, Leggatt's "punishment" carries with it a surprisingly hopeful blessing that dispels the gloom of the previous passage which had described the wanderer as "hidden for ever from all friendly faces." Albert Guerard writes that "Leggatt is perhaps a free man in several senses, but not least in the sense that he has escaped the narrator's symbolizing projection. He has indeed become 'mere flesh,' is no longer a 'double.' And the hat floating on the black water now defines a necessary separateness." [2] But in a less abstract sense, we should also consider what Leggatt has done to deserve this "new destiny" which seems to have placed him nearer the moral level of the captain, who has more clearly won the right to feel a "perfect communion" with his first command (p. 143).

Here the captain's white hat, already burdened with symbols, suggests the moral significance of the close of the story. It enters the plot a few pages from the close when the captain sees Leggatt for the last time and rams the hat upon Leggatt's head in a sudden gesture of compassion: "I saw myself wandering barefooted, bareheaded, the sun beating

[2] *Conrad the Novelist* (Cambridge, Mass., 1958), p. 25.

on my dark poll" (p. 138). And shortly afterwards when the hat saves the ship, it is the captain himself who points the moral by reminding us that the hat had been an expression of "pity for his mere flesh" (p. 142). It was this very pity for Leggatt that had first endangered the ship but had then finally saved it from destruction. But Leggatt too has known his moments of compassion for his protector, if not in his very insistence upon removing his embarrassing and dangerous presence, at least in his sincere warning to the captain to "be careful" (p. 135), for Leggatt understood well the dangers of bringing a ship about close under the rocks of Koh-ring. Beyond this, in a very real sense Leggatt has saved the captain by leaving behind the floppy hat which the captain assumes "must have fallen off his head . . . and he didn't bother" (p. 142). Regardless of intention, Leggatt has given up an object that "had been meant to save his homeless head from the dangers of the sun," and the captain has received what he needed most, "the saving mark for my eyes" (p. 142). To identify this "saving mark," a protective hat, with the saving "mark" set upon Cain may appear to be gratuitous symbol hunting, yet it is the very next sentence that describes the suddenly bareheaded fugitive as now having "no brand of the curse on his sane forehead to stay a slaying hand." As the captain repeats it, the hat "meant to save his homeless head" was now "saving the ship, by serving me for a mark to help out the ignorance of my strangeness" (p. 142). Surely Conrad has returned to the details of the Cain story at the close of his narrative to emphasize the supreme importance of the white hat as a symbol of compassion and protection and to identify it briefly with the mark intended to save Cain.

A final point, a mere conjecture, remains. Can we not assume that Conrad wishes us to guess why his fugitive, after losing the protective hat as if he were losing the very "brand of the curse," is now rightfully free, proud, and deserving of a new destiny? As we already know how Leggatt had warned the captain of the dangers of Koh-ring, it is worth considering that at the moment of his departure

151

Leggatt obviously knew that the ship was near disaster and therefore quite intentionally left the hat upon the water to serve the helpless captain as a mark. The hat appeared upon the black water before the captain saw the "flash" of Leggatt pass under it, allowing for the possibility that Leggatt had consciously thrown the hat before he left. The captain assumes that Leggatt "didn't bother" to retrieve it when he slid quietly into the water, although we are told that it was "within a yard of the ship's side" (p. 142). If this "neglect" had been purposeful, Leggatt would indeed have earned some right to become a "free man" and a "proud swimmer." He had saved his second ship by releasing the captain from further trying obligations of protection and by leaving behind the symbol of that protection at the very moment it was so desperately needed to save the ship. In giving up the hat meant to "save his homeless head," this new Cain sacrifices a kind of "saving mark" on his forehead in order to protect another from the perils of "ignorance" and "strangeness." Just as the original Cain set out to take his punishment and meet a new destiny with the confidence that something had been done for him to make that punishment endurable, so our new Cain sets out in the same way but with the additional confidence that he had himself done something for his own redemption. The heavier burden of compassion accepted by the two sharers has of course been borne by the captain, but it is tempting to think that Conrad's outcast has become for a moment his brother's keeper. Whether the dropping of the hat was merely one of those accidents "which counts for so much in the book of success" (p. 123) or a final gesture of gratitude on Leggatt's part, the happy outcome would have been the same for the generous captain. The idea that it might have been a sacrificial return of a gift that was redeeming Leggatt was a secret neither Conrad nor the proud swimmer wished to share. All we know is that the lost hat is a symbol of compassion and a "saving mark" and that both sharers have somehow been saved by it before striking out proudly for new destinies which both seem to have deserved. For as long as the abandoned hat remains of use, it is still true that it is "as if the ship had two captains to plan her course for her" (p. 134). Even if Leggatt does not know of his part in "navigating" the ship, his freedom and pride, so carefully emphasized in the closing words of the story, would stand as surprisingly bountiful rewards.

XIV The Rending of the Veil in W. E. B. DuBois's *The Souls of Black Folk**

Jerold J. Savory

Department of English, Benedict College (Columbia, South Carolina)

The book discussed here contains both fiction and expository essays. It contains many allusions to the Bible, but the allusion to the veil is the one that occurs most frequently.—Ed.

W. E. B. Du Bois's *The Souls of Black Folk* begins and ends with the symbol of the "Veil," Du Bois's apt metaphor for "the color line" of racial oppression and injustice which, in 1903, he prophetically announced to be "the problem of the twentieth century." "I who speak here," he says in "The Forethought" to his collection of poetic essays, "am bone of the bone and flesh of the flesh of them that live within the Veil" (p. xxviii).[1] At the conclusion of fourteen chapters of stirring commentary on the strivings and gifts of Black Americans, he adds his word of hope that "if somewhere in this whirl and chaos of things there dwells Eternal Good, pitiful yet masterful, then anon in His good time America shall rend the Veil and the prisoned shall go free" (p. 216).

The Veil motif recurs throughout the essays, expressing aspects of the problems contributing to the color line barrier separating Blacks from Whites. At times it is the Veil of ignorance which education must lift from the faces of the sons of slavery. This, of course, reminds one of the famed Tuskegee statue of Booker T. Washington lifting the veil from the face of a kneeling slave and of the Washington–Du Bois controversy over the kind of educa-

*From *CLA Journal*, XV (March, 1972): 334-37. Reprinted by permission of The College Language Association.

[1] The page references for *The Souls of Black Folk* are to the Washington Square paperback edition with an introduction by Truman Nelson (New York: Washington Square Press, 1970). Du Bois first published his book in 1903.

tion that would most effectively and lastingly remove the blinding curtain. At other times the Veil symbolizes the blindness of Whites who from fear, foolishness, and blatant racism, refuse to step beyond it to see the powerful potentials and the sorrowful spectacle of their oppressed brothers on the other side. In yet another sense, Du Bois seems to use the Veil as a symbol of a moral and spiritual paralysis which evil fate has inflicted upon American Blacks *and* Whites, an illness curable only by some kind of divine intervention (pp. 174, 216).

Keeping in mind that Du Bois's uses of the symbol and particularly his conviction that the rending of the Veil must begin "at the top" through the enlightened efforts of the "Talented Tenth" (p. 86) of liberally educated Blacks qualified to assume positions of educational, economical, and political leadership, let us turn for a moment to another and more ancient reference to the Veil, an image that Du Bois may have had in mind when he wrote *The Souls of Black Folk*. The reference is in the Bible, the contents of which Du Bois knew well and to which he alludes throughout his writings.

Apart from Old Testament Temple regulations and, later, St. Paul's recommendation that veils are properly modest worship apparel for women (I Corinthians 11:4-16), the most frequent Biblical use of the term is in reference to the Temple in which a large curtain (sometimes a double curtain) was hung to separate the "holy of holies" from the public (Exodus 26:31-37). Only the high priest had authority to enter the place of sacred power "within the veil" to commune with God on behalf of the people. By the time of the ministry of Jesus, the masses were increasingly oppressed by corrupt leadership of men "at the top," the men in positions of power against whom Jesus railed his most vehement rebukes and upon whom he declared that God's judgment would rest most heavily. Thus, the writers of the Gospels say that when Jesus had died on the cross, "the veil of the temple was rent in twain from the top to the bottom" (Matthew 27:51, and parallel passages in Mark and Luke).

155

This suggests, first, that Jesus's sacrifice gave all the people access to God's power and, secondly, that divine judgment had come upon corrupt leaders who had been false to the covenant through a misuse of their power. When the veil is torn, it is from "top to bottom," beginning with the attack upon the priests and governmental officials who had misused the veil to elicit fearful obedience from the common folk. It is further significant that the early church seized the symbol of the torn veil to demonstrate a belief that Christ's sacrifice had shattered all false barriers between the bond and the free and had given all men equal status with a freedom in "bondage" only to the God who had torn down the Veil through the death of His Son.

Although Du Bois does not specifically point out that he has this dramatic Biblical story in mind, his use of the Veil symbol as a metaphor for his philosophy of education and civil rights receives an added depth of meaning when seen against this background of Biblical theology. Both Du Bois and Booker Washington knew the ominous presence of the shadow of the Veil of racism. They differed primarily over how it might be removed. At the risk of over-simplifying the positions of either man, we might say that Washington advocated lifting the Veil from the bottom[2] by giving young Blacks the kind of technical training that would enable them to earn some of the White man's wealth, while Du Bois advocated rending the Veil from the top by giving Black students the kind of education that would equip them to fight for positions of decision-making power along with the Whites. Only if Blacks could break through the top of the Veil where they could influence the political, economic, and educational policies that affect the lives and shape the destinies of *all* Americans, only then, declared Du Bois, would America begin to move "toward a larger, juster, and

[2] Booker T. Washington, *Up From Slavery*, in *Three Negro Classics*, Avon Discus Edition (New York: Avon Books, 1969), p. 147. *Three Negro Classics* also contains Du Bois's *The Souls of Black Folk* and James Weldon Johnson's *The Autobiography of An Ex-Colored Man. Up From Slavery* was first published in 1901 and contains Washington's "Atlanta Exposition Address," delivered in 1895.

fuller future" (p. 87) in which its citizens, regardless of race, would have the *freedom to decide* whether they would cultivate the soil or cultivate their minds.

However disillusioned Du Bois may have become in his later years when he chose to end his days in Africa, he is clear in *The Souls of Black Folk* about how his vision of social change must be realized, if it is ever to come about in America. It is not enough for those who live "in the shadow of the Veil" to dream of a life "*above* the Veil." At one point, Du Bois, the cultured scholar, tells of how the enlightenment of great literature and philosophy has permitted him to move across the color line to "sit with Shakespeare," to "move arm in arm with Balzac and Dumas," and to "summon Aristotle and Aurelius." "So, wed with Truth," he says, "I dwell above the Veil" (pp. 88-89). Again, Du Bois, the grieving father of a dead first-born baby cradled briefly under the awful shadow of the Veil, hopes that "above the Veil," the innocent may sleep in the bosom of a Love and Wisdom that transcends the wretched of the earth (pp. 169-75).

But Du Bois's hope does not rest in dreams of a life *above* the Veil, whether through an aesthetic retreat into a world of books or through the weary longing for becoming free at last in death. Rather, his hope is for the *rending* of the Veil in this life by which the song, sweat, and spirit of Black folk may pass through the whirl and chaos of the color line to liberate America's imprisoned native sons and daughters, thus to liberate America.

XV Hemingway's Ancient Mariner*

*Department of English,
Princeton University*

At first sight of the second shark, Santiago utters the single word *Ay*. "There is no translation for this word," writes Hemingway, "and perhaps it is just a noise such as a man might make, involuntarily, feeling the nail go through his hands and into the wood." For some hours now, of course, Santiago's hands have shown the fisherman's equivalent of the stigmata of a saint. Both have been cut in the "working part," which is the palm, by the unpredictable lurchings of his quarry. The right hand is cut first, at a time when the old man's attention is momentarily diverted by the warbler's visit. Another of the marlin's sudden accelerations awakens him from the only sleep he permits himself. The line is burning out through his already wounded right hand. When he brings up his left for use as a brake, it takes all the strain and cuts deep.

The old man's involuntary epithet, and Hemingway's explanation of it, is fully in line with what has gone before. Throughout the ordeal, Santiago has been as conscious of his hands as any crucified man might be. He speaks to them as to fellow-sufferers, wills them to do the work they must do, and makes due allowances for them as if they were, what he once calls them, "my brothers." He also carefully distinguishes between them in a manner which should not be lost on any student of paintings of the Crucifixion. The right hand is the good one, dextrous and trustworthy. The left hand, the hand sinister, has "always been a traitor."

Our Lord might well have entertained a similar reflection

---

*Selections from Chapter XII, "The Ancient Mariner," in Carlos Baker, *Hemingway: The Writer as Artist*, published by Princeton University Press, 4th rev. edn. (copyright © 1972 by Carlos Baker), pp. 313, 314, 319 and 320. Reprinted by permission of Princeton University Press.

about the man who was crucified on his own left. The allusions to Santiago's hands are so carefully stylized that such a statement becomes possible. On the naturalistic plane, of course, the meaning of the distinction between the two hands is apparent to all normally right-handed persons; the left is never as good as the right. But on the plane of what we have called *Dichtung,* and in the light of the tradition of Christian art as it pertains to the Crucifixion, it is clear that a moral judgment is to be inferred. Of the two who were crucified with Jesus Christ, the one on the left failed Him, insulting and upbraiding him. But the man crucified on Jesus' right hand rebuked his companion, and put his fortunes into the hands of the Savior. In paintings of the Crucifixion, as Hemingway is well aware, the distinction between the two malefactors is always carefully maintained. It even carries over into pictures of the Last Judgment, where those who are to be saved are ranged on the right hand of the Savior, while the damned stand dejectedly on the left. . . .

. . . It is clear that Hemingway has artfully enhanced the native power of his tragic parable by enlisting the further power of Christian symbolism. Standing solus on the rocky shore in the darkness before the dawn of the fourth day, Santiago shows the wounded hands. Dried blood is on his face as from a crown of thorns. He has known the ugly coppery taste in his mouth as from a sponge filled with vinegar. And in the agony of his fatigue he is very much alone. "There was no one to help him so he pulled the boat up as far as he could. Then he stepped out and made her fast to a rock. He unstepped the mast and furled the sail and tied it. Then he shouldered the mast and started to climb."

Once he paused to look back at the remains of his fish. At the top of the hill "he fell and lay for some time with the mast across his shoulder. He tried to get up. But it was too difficult and he sat there with the mast on his shoulder and looked at the road. A cat passed on the far side going about its business and the old man watched it. Then he just watched the road." The loneliness of the ascent of any

Calvary is brilliantly emphasized by the presence of the cat. The Old Masters, as Auden wrote long ago, were never wrong about suffering. "How well they understood its human position; how it takes place while someone else is eating or opening a window or just walking dully along . . . They never forgot that even the dreadful martyrdom must run its course anyhow in some corner, some untidy spot where the dogs go on with their doggy life"—and where the innocence of ignorance never so much as bats an eye. The cat on the far side of the road from Santiago is also proceeding about its private business. It could not help the old man even if it would. Santiago knows and accepts this as he has accepted the rest. There is nothing else to be done—except to reach home, which he manages at last to do, though he has to sit down five times to rest between the hilltop and the door of his shack.

On the newspapers that cover the springs of the bed, and below the colored chromos of the Sacred Heart of Jesus and the Virgin of Cobre, the old man now falls heavily asleep. He sleeps face down with his arms out straight and his body straight up and down: cruciform, as if to sum up by that symbolic position, naturally assumed, all the suffering through which he has passed. *In hoc signo vinces.* Santiago has made it to his house. When Manolo looks in next morning, he is still asleep. There is a short conversation as he drinks the coffee the boy brings, and they lay plans for the future even as they allude laconically to the immediate past. "How much did you suffer?" Manolo asks. "Plenty," the old man answers. Outside, a three-day blow has begun. Inside the shack, the book concludes, the old man falls again into the deep sleep of renewal, of diurnal resurrection. "He was still sleeping on his face and the boy was sitting by him watching him. The old man was dreaming about the lions." In my end is my beginning.

XVI The Ironic Christ Figure in *Slaughterhouse-Five*

Dolores K. Gros Louis

Honors Division, Indiana University

"Why are English teachers always asking us to look for the Christ figures in fiction?" is a question I've received from students more than once. The query frequently implies that teachers are reading between the lines, projecting meanings that are not in the fiction at all. The answer, usually supported if not offered by other students (the perceptive ones!), is that teachers ask students to look for the Christ figure because it is there and it is important to the author's meaning. Why is it there? First, the redeemer theme and the death-and-resurrection theme are archetypal, appearing around the world in various forms. Second, in Western culture the story of Jesus is "still the greatest story ever told, or at least, the most familiar one."[1] If the story of Jesus is still the greatest or the most familiar story, then writers may draw on it freely with the assumption that most of their readers will recognize the major parallels to the gospel story.

Novelists use the gospel story in many ways and for many different purposes. Some use it to structure their work of fiction. Some use it as an aid in characterization, either to elevate a protagonist or to deflate him by his contrast to Jesus. Others adapt the story to show how Jesus himself might exist and act in a particular modern situation. Some writers use only casual allusions and metaphors to broaden the meaning of certain incidents and events. Some create a Christ figure, either ironic or serious, to convey a contemporary religious, political, or social theme. Still others use the Christ story as a rhetorical device for indirect authorial comment.

In *Slaughterhouse-Five*, Kurt Vonnegut is using the

[1] Theodore Ziolkowski, *Fictional Transfigurations of Jesus* (Princeton: Princeton University Press, 1972), p. 232.

Christ story in the last two ways. Through Billy Pilgrim's similarities to Jesus, Vonnegut creates a Christ figure who is a resurrected survivor with a philosophical message for the world. Vonnegut's own, contrasting message is conveyed indirectly, through his deflation of Billy Pilgrim as an ineffectual and immoral messiah. Vonnegut's implied moral is the antithesis of the gospel preached by his ironic Christ figure.

In his excellent study *Fictional Transfigurations of Jesus*, Theodore Ziolkowski describes fictional transfigurations as adaptations with essentially formal parallels, not ideological ones. In a fictional transfiguration, a modern Christ figure's qualities and actions are described in terms paralleling those of Jesus as he is portrayed in the Gospels; but the *meaning* of the Christ figure may have little or nothing to do with Christianity. Ziolkowski's five categories of fictional transfiguration are Christian socialist, psychiatric, mythic, Marxist, and Fifth Gospels. He doesn't discuss *Slaughterhouse-Five;* but it clearly belongs in the category of Fifth Gospels, which Ziolkowski defines as ironic adaptations by writers who are detached and neutral toward the New Testament, who view the story of Jesus primarily as a myth and feel free to adapt it in any way they wish.

Slaughterhouse-Five is a complex novel. A *Christian Science Monitor* reviewer states "To quote that rarity, a truthful book jacket blurb, Mr. Vonnegut's book is 'a miracle of compression.' One could write a Talmudic commentary on every other paragraph."[2] In this compressed, complex novel, the Christ motif is not immediately apparent to a casual reader, nor even to some serious readers. My commentary concentrates on the descriptions, situations, and actions of Billy Pilgrim which parallel those of Jesus in the Gospels. When seen all at once—"many marvelous moments seen all at one time"—these parallels form a pattern which is, clearly, consciously intended by Vonnegut. I have not rearranged these parallels to follow

[2]John Reed, "Billy Pilgrim's Progress: A Fable About Sanity," *Christian Science Monitor*, April 17, 1969, p. 15.

the gospel story chronologically, because Vonnegut, as is well known, has not used the story of Jesus to order his time scheme. Thinking about this, one realizes a major ironic contrast between Billy Pilgrim and Jesus: when Billy Pilgrim lives again after having been shot, there is no change in his life nor in anyone else's; through time-travel, he simply repeats again and again various moments of his life.

There are, however, many similarities between Billy and Jesus. The epigraph, a quatrain from the carol "Away in the Manger," hints that in some way "the little Lord Jesus" is related to the meaning of the novel. Early in the novel, in two oblique references to the carol, "Billy Pilgrim would find himself weeping. . . . It was an extremely quiet thing Billy did, and not very moist." "But sleep would not come. Tears came instead. They seeped." [3] The emphasis upon the moderateness of Billy's crying suggests that it is motivated by a profound and sincere grief. As Vonnegut quoted Shakespeare in his 1970 Bennington College address, "To weep is to make less the depth of grief." Much later in the novel, after stating again that Billy "would weep quietly and privately sometimes, but never make loud *boohooing* noises," Vonnegut repeats the epigraph and explicates it explicitly:

Which is why the epigraph of this book is the quatrain from the famous Christmas carol. Billy cried very little, though he often saw things worth crying about, and in *that* respect, at least, he resembled the Christ of the carol. (P. 197)

This authorial comment—"in *that* respect, at least, he resembled the Christ of the carol"—indicates that Vonnegut is certainly conscious of other possible resemblances between Billy and Jesus. We may note that here, as throughout the novel, it is only Vonnegut who is aware that

---

[3] Kurt Vonnegut, Jr., *Slaughterhouse-Five* (New York: Dell Publishing Co., 1971), pp. 61 and 62. Subsequent quotations, cited parenthetically in the text, are to this edition. The novel was first published in 1969 by Delacorte Press.

Billy Pilgrim is a Christ figure. Billy himself is never conscious of any similarity between himself and Jesus.

A second major resemblance is Billy's compassionate desire to comfort people, "Billy's belief that he was going to comfort so many people with the truth about time" (p. 28). The solace he offers is in his extraterrestrial message, the essence of which is the negligibility of death—or, in Christian terms, the eternity of life. "Isn't that comforting?" he asks the fatherless boy after informing him "that his father was very much alive still in moments the boy would see again and again" (p. 135). The first part of Billy's Tralfamadorian message has to do with the true nature of time; that is, the fourth-dimension, omniscient, Godlike view of time: "All moments, past, present, and future, always have existed, always will exist. . . . How permanent all the moments are" (p. 27). The second part of the message follows from that: if all the moments always were, always are, and ever will be, then "we will all live forever, no matter how dead we may sometimes seem to be" (p. 211; see also pp. 26-27).

After learning this comforting truth on Tralfamadore, Billy develops a somewhat messianic sense of having a special mission to the poor souls on Earth:

. . . he was devoting himself to a calling much higher than mere business.

He was doing nothing less now, he thought, than prescribing corrective lenses for Earthling souls. So many of those souls were lost and wretched, Billy believed, because they could not see as well as his little green friends on Tralfamadore. (P. 29)

"He was going to tell the world about the lessons of Tralfamadore" (p. 199) on the New York City radio talk show, in his letters to the Illium newspaper, and later, in public lectures.

At the beginning of his teaching, Billy encounters the same reaction as Jesus did early in his ministry: "When his family heard it, they went out to seize him, for people were saying, 'He is beside himself'" (Mark 3:21). Billy's family, especially his daughter Barbara, and other people in Illium think "that Billy [is] evidently going crazy" (p. 135) when he teaches the lessons of Tralfamadore. On several occasions Barbara attempts to take charge of him (pp. 25-26, 29-30, 135). After the publication of his first letter in the Illium *News Leader*,

She said he was making a laughing stock of himself and everybody associated with him.

"Father, Father, Father—" said Barbara, "what are we going to *do* with you? Are you going to force us to put you where your mother is?" . . . .

"It's all just crazy. None of it's true!" (P. 29)

Billy, like Jesus, persists nevertheless, with serenity and confidence. He maintains his sense of mission, his compassion for people, and his belief in his otherworldly message about the eternal nature of time and the insignificance of death. And like Jesus, Billy will eventually gain a large following. At the time of his death, which he has foreseen happening on February 13, 1976, "Billy is speaking before a capacity audience in a baseball park. . . . There are police around him as he leaves the stage. They are there to protect him from the crush of popularity" (p. 142).

Billy's foreseeing his own death is one example of his belief that whatever happens to him had to be so; that since all time is all time, all the moments in his life have already been structured. This reminds us that Jesus frequently does certain things "so that the prophecies might be fulfilled," though Jesus, of course, freely chooses to fulfill the prophecies. Billy's foreknowledge of his own death is mentioned several times in the novel:

He has seen his birth and death many times. . . . (P. 23),

His attention began to swing grandly through the full arc of his life, passing into death, which was violet light. (P. 43).

Billy Pilgrim says now that this really *is* the way he is going to die, too. (P. 141).

Billy predicts his own death within an hour. (P. 142).

165

The conscious modern difference is that, instead of telling his disciples, Billy describes his death to a tape recorder:

As a time-traveler, he has seen his own death many times, has described it to a tape recorder. . . . I, *Billy Pilgrim*, the tape begins, *will die, have died, and always will die on February thirteenth, 1976*. (P. 141).

The description of Billy's death includes several gospel parallels. When the crowd protests his announcement of his imminent death, "Billy Pilgrim rebukes them. 'If you protest, if you think that death is a terrible thing, then you have not understood a word I've said'" (p. 142). Not only the verb "rebukes" but also the rebuking statement recall Jesus' words: "Do you not yet perceive or understand? Are your hearts hardened? Having eyes do you not see, and having ears do you not hear? And do you not remember? . . . Do you not yet understand?" (Mark 8:17-18, 21). Then there are the offers to help save his life—"The police offer to stay with him. They are floridly willing to stand in a circle around him all night, with their zap guns drawn" (p. 142)—offers which Billy rejects. "'No, no,' says Billy serenely. 'It is time for you to go home to your wives and children, and it is time for me to be dead for a little while—and then live again.' . . . So Billy experiences death for a while" (pp. 142-43). This passage echoes John 16:16-19, "A little while, and you will see me no more; again a little while, and you will see me. . . . A little while, and you will not see me, and again a little while, and you will see me."

Some thirty years before his death, Billy is compared several times to Jesus on the cross. First is the near-identification of Billy (a non-Catholic) with the "ghastly crucifix" which he had contemplated twice daily as a child:

Billy, after all, had contemplated torture and hideous wounds at the beginning and the end of nearly every day of his childhood. Billy had an extremely gruesome crucifix hanging on the wall of his little bedroom in Illium. A military surgeon would have admired the clinical fidelity of the artist's rendition of all Christ's wounds—the spear wound, the thorn wounds, the holes that were made by the iron spikes. Billy's Christ died horribly. He was pitiful. (P. 38)

Just four pages later, "He was pitiful" is Roland Weary's evaluation of Billy as a footsoldier. As a war prisoner on a crowded boxcar, Billy is repeatedly described in terms of the crucifixion:

Billy stood by one of these [ventilators], and, as the crowd pressed against him, he climbed part way up a diagonal corner brace to make more room. (P. 67)

And Billy let himself down oh so gradually now, hanging onto the diagonal cross-brace in the corner in order to make himself seem nearly weightless to those he was joining on the floor. He knew it was important that he make himself nearly ghostlike when lying down. He had forgotten why, but a reminder soon came. . . . So Billy stood up again, clung to the cross-brace. (P. 78)

Billy Pilgrim was lying at an angle on the corner-brace, self-crucified, holding himself there with a blue and ivory claw hooked over the sill of the ventilator. (P. 80)

Besides reinforcing the Christ parallel fairly early in the novel, these apparently conscious references to the crucifixion suggest that being a war prisoner is a crucifying experience.

After he is shot in 1976 and "experiences death for a while," Billy experiences a Tralfamadorian resurrection as "he swings back into life again" (p. 143). The first place he returns to is the stage setting of the prisoners' production of *Cinderella,* a story which is an analogue of the theme of rebirth. Vonnegut himself suggests a particular analogy when he describes *Cinderella* as the gospel story is usually described—"the most popular story ever told" (p. 96). In Cinderella's silver boots, Vonnegut tells us, "Billy Pilgrim was Cinderella, and Cinderella was Billy Pilgrim" (p. 145). Cinderella is reborn in her transformation from an abused, humble servant into a princess; Billy is reborn when he swings back into life again, to relive the moment when he discovered that Cinderella's boots "fit perfectly"; and man's servant, Jesus, arises from death to eternal life.

Later in the novel (though much earlier in his life), Billy experiences a miraculous survival which is almost a resurrection: after the firebombing of Dresden, he emerges from "an echoing meat locker which was hollowed in living rock under the slaughterhouse" (p. 165). Jesus rose, we recall, from a tomb "hewn in the rock" (Matt. 27:60). After climbing the staircase out of the tomblike meat locker, Billy Pilgrim sees a new kind of world he never could have imagined. Dresden after the firebombing is an apocalyptic scene of total destruction; everything organic has been killed, including 135,000 human beings. Under the city, Billy Pilgrim was very close to death; when he emerges, he sees nothing but death. Yet he goes on living.

The psychohistorian Robert J. Lifton calls *Slaughter-house-Five* "Vonnegut's great survivor novel."[4] In his book *Death in Life*, Lifton defines the survivor in terms of rebirth applicable to Billy Pilgrim: "We may define the survivor as one who has come into contact with death in some bodily or psychic fashion and has himself remained alive."[5] In his later essay "Survivor as Creator," Lifton describes the survivor as "dying and 'being reborn,'" as "rejoining the living" after his "death immersion" (p. 40). In Lifton's terms, then, we may view Billy's survival of the Dresden firebombing as a psychic resurrection.

In addition to the major parallels between Billy and Jesus, further occasional biblical allusions reinforce the identification. First, before his capture by the Germans, Billy is "a dazed wanderer" in the wilderness "without food or maps" (p. 32). Second, in the German boxcar moving slowly toward the war prison, Billy is scorned and reviled by his fellow prisoners (pp. 78-79) just as Jesus is "mocked," "derided," and "reviled" by soldiers, passersby, chief priests, scribes, and even by the two robbers who were crucified with him (Mark 15:17-32). Billy is falsely accused,

---

[4] Robert J. Lifton, "Survivor as Creator," *American Poetry Review*, January/February, 1973, p. 41.

[5] Robert J. Lifton, *Death in Life: Survivors of Hiroshima* (New York: Random House, 1967), p. 479.

as Jesus is, and is made a scapegoat by Roland Weary; in 1976, he will be unjustly killed by Paul Lazzaro's hired murderer.

Fourth, as Billy leads the parade of prisoners to the Dresden-bound train, he had some resemblance to Jesus: "He had silver boots now, and a muff, and a piece of azure curtain which he wore like a toga. Billy still had a beard" (p. 147). His arrival in Dresden is an ironic parallel to the triumphal entry into Jerusalem:

> And then they saw bearded Billy Pilgrim in his blue toga and silver shoes, with his hands in a muff. . . . Billy Pilgrim was the star. He led the parade. Thousands of people were on the sidewalks, going home from work. (Pp. 149-50)

Then, after the destruction of Dresden, Billy and one hundred other prisoners of war "came at nightfall to an inn" where they are allowed to sleep in the stable, to bed down in the straw (pp. 180-81). Finally, if Jesus is the new Adam, the New Testament Son of God who will atone for Adam's fall, Billy Pilgrim is the old Adam before his fall. Immediately after he sees Adam and Eve in the highly polished boots of a German corporal, he looks up into the face of "a blond angel . . . as beautiful as Eve" (p. 53)—a juxtaposition suggesting that Billy is Adam. More important, Billy resembles Adam in the zoo on Tralfamadore where he lives naked and innocently ("guilt-free") with his mate in the Tralfamadorian ideal of human paradise.

With these minor allusions and the major parallels to the gospel story, Vonnegut endows his time-traveling optometrist with many similarities to Jesus. In descriptions, he compares Billy to the infant Jesus, to Jesus in his triumphal entry into Jerusalem, and to the mocked and crucified Christ. Even more parallels exist in Billy's actions: he wanders in the wilderness, he acts out of a sense of mission to the world, he preaches a message about eternal life, he is thought by many people to be out of his mind, he preaches to crowds, he foresees his own death, he is mocked and scorned, he is falsely accused and unjustly killed, and he

169

returns to life after death. This extensive pattern of parallels makes Billy Pilgrim a modern Christ figure.

The elaborate and conscious identification is undercut, however, by the important ways in which Billy Pilgrim differs from Jesus. By important differences I don't mean omitted gospel details such as the Last Supper but, rather, morally significant contrasts. First, Billy's death is not a sacrifice. Second, his death has no redemptive value for other people. And third, unless we believe the Tralfamadorian values taught by Billy, his teaching is unlike Jesus' in that it doesn't change our lives or suggest new values worth living by. Vonnegut clearly rejects—and wants us to reject—the Tralfamadorian view of time and its implications for human life.

Why, then, does Vonnegut make Billy Pilgrim a Christ figure of this sort? Isn't Billy Pilgrim a Vonnegut hero? What is the point of a savior who saves no one?

There are several answers to these questions. Since he is so ineffectual, Billy Pilgrim is an ironic Christ figure, that is, one resembling Jesus in many ways but ultimately lacking the all-important redemptive, sacrificial death. This irony is appropriate in a novel, and in a world, where there is such irony as Edgar Derby's being executed for stealing a teapot while no one is punished for the destruction of Dresden.

Then, too, an ironic Christ figure fits in with Vonnegut's pessimistic and satiric view of humanity in today's world. A poor imitation of Jesus may be all we can expect in a society which covers up and then justifies the needless firebombing of Dresden. Maybe an ironic Christ figure is appropriate in a society whose values are reflected in the American dream that is Billy's miserable life in Illium.

At the same time, Vonnegut's use of the gospel story, his allusions ranging from the first Christmas Eve to the resurrection, suggest a nostalgia, a kind of yearning that the Christ story might be true. This yearning is part of Vonnegut's search for meaning in an absurd world (he alludes to the Creator, Jesus, or God in his other novels).

His use of the gospel story is nearly blasphemous; yet the fact that he does use it, doesn't ignore it, suggests that it has some appeal for him. As one critic has stated, "The question [of God] haunts Vonnegut at every turn."[6]

The most important reason for Billy's being an ineffectual, ironic Christ figure, however, is that this allows Vonnegut indirectly to counter Billy's Tralfamadorian message with his own very different, very worldly message. Vonnegut is qualified to oppose Billy's teachings because, as he tells us several times, his experiences in the prison camp and in Dresden were the same as Billy's. Vonnegut is very conscious of this; Billy is a semi-autobiographical character, at least in the war parts of *Slaughterhouse-Five*. There are many similarities between Vonnegut and his protagonist: both were born in 1922; both have the same souvenir of war (a Luftwaffe ceremonial saber [pp. 6 and 195]); both are interested in science fiction as a help in "trying to re-invent themselves and their universe" (p. 101); both have messages to help mankind. Most important, both rise from near-death "in an echoing meat locker which was hollowed in living rock" and cannot understand why they were among the 105 survivors of the massacre of 135,000 people. Vonnegut comes close to identifying himself with Billy when he intrudes into the narrative four times to say, "I was there." Yet, though he was there, and though he had many of the same war experiences as Billy, Vonnegut's ultimate reaction to those experiences differs greatly from Billy's ultimate reaction.

Vonnegut's survival of the Dresden raid, like Billy's, ironically occurred in a slaughterhouse. It is well known from his other writing and from interviews that, to Vonnegut, his survival of Dresden was more than an irony—it seemed like a miracle. The sight of Dresden was an unforgettable nightmare. The absurd massacre, the total destruction of everything living, was an experience it took

[6] Ernest W. Ranly, "What Are People For?" *Commonweal*, May 7, 1971, p. 209.

him twenty-three years to write about. He did, of course, allude to it in other novels, most specifically in his preface to *Mother Night;* and fires and firemen appear often in his fiction. He had seen an apocalyptic vision of the end of the world ("Dresden was like the moon now, nothing but minerals" [p. 178]), and he had "survived to tell the tale"—not to escape to a science fiction paradise. In an interview in 1966, Vonnegut talked about Dresden and the writing of *Slaughterhouse-Five:*

> Yes, I'm working on it now. It's what I've been working on for a long time, and it's extremely hard to think about. You know, you have these enormous concentration camps full of corpses, and then you have a city full of corpses, and, you know, is the city full of corpses right or wrong? . . . Well, I think the only thing I have been able to think of doing as a result of seeing the destruction of that city there and knowing at the same time about the great crimes of Germany, is to become the impossible thing, which is a pacifist, and I figure I'm under an obligation, having seen all this, you know, that that's the only possible conclusion I can come to, is that we must not fight under any conditions.[7]

This statement of pacifism, "that we must not fight under any conditions," combined with his compulsion to *look back* at Dresden and other appalling massacres in history, marks the most important distinction between Kurt Vonnegut and Billy Pilgrim. In 1967, Vonnegut goes *back* to Dresden (p. 1), while in the same year Billy goes *away*, to Tralfamadore (p. 25). True, this first time Billy goes as a captive, but he is nevertheless an enthusiastic learner of the Tralfamadorian views; in 1968 he writes to the newspaper, "They had many wonderful things to teach Earthlings, especially about time" (p. 26).

Through his Tralfamadorian lessons, Billy Pilgrim learns a resigned tolerance of war ("So—I suppose that the idea of preventing war on Earth is stupid, too" [p. 117]) and an acceptance of whatever will be, will be (and always was, and always will be). Vonnegut, most obviously in his

[7] Robert Scholes, "A Talk with Kurt Vonnegut, Jr.," *The Vonnegut Statement,* ed. Jerome Klinkowitz and John Somer (New York: Delacorte Press, 1973), pp. 117-18.

autobiographical first chapter but also throughout the novel, challenges Billy's postwar philosophy of serene acceptance. Billy's office sign and Montana Wildhack's locket say, "God grant me the serenity to accept the things I cannot change. . . ." According to Billy's view of time, he can change *nothing;* but Vonnegut, on the other hand, is only ironic when he says, "So it goes."

The Tralfamadorian lesson taught by Billy is "All moments, past, present, and future, always have existed, always will exist" (p. 27). Therefore, "we will all live forever, no matter how dead we may sometimes appear to be" (p. 211). Therefore, also, there is nothing we can do to prevent war, nothing we can do to prevent the end of the world ("A Tralfamadorian test pilot presses a starter button, and the whole Universe disappears. . . . He has *always* pressed it, and he always *will*" [p. 117]). So the thing to do as we visit various moments during eternity is to select the happy moments, the pretty moments. The Tralfamadorian guide tells Billy, "On other days we have wars as horrible as any you've ever seen or read about. There isn't anything we can do about them, so we simply don't look at them. We ignore them. We spend eternity looking at pleasant moments . . . " (p. 117). This is the gospel from outer space, the view of history that leads Billy Pilgrim to say about the destruction of Dresden, "It was all right. *Everything* is all right . . ." (p. 198).

This complacent gospel, preached by the ironic Christ figure, is rejected by Vonnegut himself. The author's extensive research on Dresden, and his writing of this novel with its overt pacifism, show that for him everything is *not* all right. Unlike the Tralfamadorians, Vonnegut the narrator looks back at many *horrible* moments: the destruction of Sodom and Gomorrah, the drowning or enslavement of the thousands of children in the Children's Crusade, the 1760 devastation of Dresden by the Prussians, the extermination of millions of Jews by the Nazis, the firebombing of Dresden, the atomic bombing of Hiroshima, the bombing of North Vietnam, the napalm burning of the

Vietnamese, the assassination of Robert Kennedy, the assassination of Martin Luther King, the daily body count from Vietnam.

Like Billy Pilgrim, Kurt Vonnegut also has a message for the world. If we are to avoid another Dresden, if we are to break out of the Tralfamadorian inevitability of war and the end of the world, "we must not fight under any conditions." "I have told my sons," he writes,

that they are not under any circumstances to take part in massacres, and that the news of massacres of enemies is not to fill them with satisfaction or glee.

I have also told them not to work for companies which make massacre machinery, and to express contempt for people who think we need machinery like that. (P. 19)

Comparing himself to Lot's wife, Vonnegut says it is human to look back on a massacre; he implies that it is *inhuman* to forget or ignore it. Looking back in *Slaughterhouse-Five*, he reminds us that war is awful, that it is absurd, that it creates many grotesque ironies.

Slaughterhouse-Five is not a Christian book, but it is a compassionate and moral one in its concern for man and his fate. Through an ironic Christ figure, Vonnegut presents and rejects an extraterrestrial gospel which leads away from moral responsibility, away from guilt, away from active protest against war. As reborn survivor, Billy preaches a view of life which negates guilt, negates responsibility, negates active concern for the past or for the future. *"Everything* is all right." As reborn survivor, Vonnegut transcends Billy's Tralfamadorian vision of life. He transcends it by offering us his own earthly vision, a vision which has nothing to do with science fiction. Although he is skeptical about the success of his message, Vonnegut teaches the "impossible" pacifism to which he converted after his experience of Dresden: Do not kill. Do not burn. Do not fight in war. Do not condone war. Everything is *not* all right.

Although Billy Pilgrim ends up as a resurrected time-traveler whose gospel helps no one, there *is* a positive aspect to some of his other similarities to Jesus. Billy's genuine suffering, and his deeply sincere desire to help humanity, suggest that there may be something of Jesus even in a nobody. In *these* respects, at least, Billy seriously resembles the Christ of the Gospels. This identification extends the significance of Billy's role in the novel. He is, however, also a pilgrim traveling away from the city of destruction. The inverted parallels to Jesus, such as the negative quality of Billy's message and the inefficacy of his death, add an ironic dimension of meaning to his role. As an ironic Christ figure whose gospel is both untrue and ultimately immoral, Billy Pilgrim is opposed by the moral, real narrator, who travels *back* to the city of destruction and arrives at an active pacifism.

To understand Billy's ambivalent role as a modern version of Jesus, we and our students must be familiar with the gospel story. Knowledge of that story is necessary for the aesthetic pleasure of recognizing the biblical allusions in *Slaughterhouse-Five* and for the intellectual pleasure of recognizing both the serious and the ironic parallels between Billy Pilgrim and Jesus. Most important, however, we and our students need the gospel background in order to recognize Billy's *failure* as a *savior,* to recognize the immorality and the ineffectiveness of his serene vision of time and death. If we perceive Billy as a Christ figure, then we will perceive the important ways in which he is *unlike* Jesus: his death redeems no one; and his particular vision of eternal life leads to a passive acceptance of war, which if not unchristian is certainly immoral, inhuman, and uncompassionate. Only unfeeling and unthoughtful readers could find anything of positive value in the guilt-free, passive Tralfamadorian gospel. Vonnegut's pacifism and active moral concern are much closer to the teachings of Jesus as recorded in the Gospels.

XVII Christ Figures in Modern Literature: An Annotated Bibliography

Dolores K. Gros Louis

Bowman, Frank P. "On the Definition of Jesus in Modern Fiction," *Anales Galdosianos*, 2 (1967), 53-66. Discussing the Jesus story as a myth used in fiction, Bowman analyzes the influence of its two peculiar attributes—historicity and alleged total validity—not shared by other Western myths. Describes and evaluates seven categories of narrative imitations of Christ, exemplified by British, American, Spanish, and French novels, 1780–1940. Concludes that, in a majority of these works, Jesus and Jesus figures "reflect the social and political preoccupations of the society in which the fiction is written, and the study of Jesus in literature must be a study in the sociology of literature concerned with politics as well as theology and esthetics."

Brumm, Ursula. "The Figure of Christ in American Literature," *Partisan Review*, 24 (1957), 403-13. Suggests that the Christ figure is part of the American literary tradition. Surveys the changing role of Jesus in the American cultural tradition, up through the humanization of Jesus. Sees Jesus as "an emblem for the man who suffers in spite, or perhaps because, of his innocence"; the Jesus analogy may also add to the hero's downfall a "victorious transcendence of fate," claimed to be a mark of tragedy. Discusses the figure of Jesus in works of "tragic quality" by Melville, Hemingway, Wolfe, Faulkner, West, and Ellison.

Detweiler, Robert. "Christ and the Christ Figure in American Fiction," *The Christian Scholar*, 47 (1964), 111-24. Argues against criticism which assumes that the fictional Christ figure should be the same as the historical, biblical, doctrinal Jesus; says that the Christ figure, as a literary creation, must be evaluated according to literary criteria. In presenting a Christ figure, the novelist is free from theological interpretations of Jesus and therefore creates a character "with the traits of Christ [especially a redemptive role] but in the image of man." Then, the Christ figure *may* point to a reality beyond itself, may suggest the question of faith, may lead the reader "to rethink existence in terms of God." Includes brief comments on a dozen American novels.

Dillistone, F. W. *The Novelist and the Passion Story* (New York: Sheed & Ward, 1960). Divides novels about Jesus and Jesus figures into two categories—historical novels, and novels set in the author's contemporary culture; finds in the latter category both greater literary value and greater religious value. Views the retelling of the Passion story as "the supreme need of our time." Using the thematic criterion of "the power of redemptive suffering," Dillistone selects four novels which have "a central character who is ready to accept suffering and even death in the service of a transcendent value, a worthy end." Devotes a chapter each to Mauriac's *The Lamb*, Melville's *Billy Budd*, Kazantzakis' *The Greek Passion*, and Faulkner's *A Fable*. No bibliography; no index.

Moseley, Edwin M. *Pseudonyms of Christ in the Modern Novel: Motifs and Methods* (Pittsburgh: University of Pittsburgh Press, 1962). Individual chapters on fourteen great novels, ranging from Turgenev's *Fathers and Sons* to Hemingway's *The Old Man and the Sea*, whose protagonists have Christlike qualities and experiences (some more, some less). Implied definition of the Christ archetype is too broad—"learning through suffering"—and thus allows inclusion of some heroes whose lives and deaths, while perhaps tragic, are not analogous to Jesus' life and death. Bibliographical index.

Schatt, Stanley. "The Whale and the Cross: Vonnegut's Jonah and Christ Figures," *Southwest Review*, 56 (Winter

1971), 29-42. Perceives four Vonnegut protagonists who assume the role of a Jonah figure when urged to do so by a Messiah figure. Says Vonnegut is aware that "at the heart of the Jonah story is a struggle between the benevolent forces of human and divine love and mercy and those malevolent forces of human selfishness and hardheartedness." His Jonah figures are "perplexed by the difficulty of loving mankind once they discover humankind's weaknesses"; his Messiah figures are usually poor imitations of Jesus. The Jonah and Messiah figures are: Dr. Paul Proteus and Finnerty in *Player Piano;* Malachi Constant and Rumfoord in *The Sirens of Titan;* John, Bokonon (false Messiah), and Dr. Felix Hoenikker (ironic Jesus figure) in *Cat's Cradle;* Eliot Rosewater and Kilgore Trout in *God Bless You, Mr. Rosewater.*

Ziolkowski, Theodore. *Fictional Transfigurations of Jesus* (Princeton: Princeton University Press, 1972). Distinguishes the fictional transfiguration from four other types of literary treatments of Jesus: fictional biography, *Jesus redivivus, imitatio Christi,* pseudonym of Christ. Fifty of these other literary treatments are listed in the bibliography. Analyzes twenty fictional transfigurations (American, British, European, and Greek) from 1872 to 1966. Argues convincingly that none of these novels can be properly understood without consideration of the shaping force of the fictional transfiguration's conventions and formal limitations. Indexed.

XVIII Brief Comments on Other Works of Fiction with Biblical Allusions
Roland Bartel

A. "Flowering Judas," Katherine Anne Porter

The Judas tree, according to one tradition, is the tree on which Judas Iscariot hanged himself after he betrayed Christ. Miss Porter alludes to this tradition and to several scenes in the New Testament as she exposes the various forms of betrayal in the lives of the characters in her story.

According to Matthew 26, Mark 14, Luke 22, and John 13, Jesus interrupted the observance of the Last Supper with his disciples by announcing that one of them would betray him. Mark and Luke provide the information that the Last Supper took place in an upper room, and John adds the fact that the meal was followed by the washing of feet. John also tells us that one of the disciples was leaning on the breast of Jesus when the betrayal was announced. Matthew, Mark, and Luke agree that Jesus asked the disciples to accept the bread and wine as his body and his blood. Matthew and Mark state that at the conclusion of the meal the group sang a hymn and departed for the Mount of Olives.

Miss Porter refers to all these facts in her story, but she does not give us a reenactment of the Last Supper. Her allusions serve rather to remind us from time to time that the actions of the characters constitute serious betrayals of various kinds. Although these allusions are basic to the structure of the story, they are not so prominent as to divert our attention from the story to the Bible. They are brief enough and infrequent enough to keep the Bible in the background, but it is a background that provides important information and impressions at crucial moments. An example of this practice can be seen in the occasional allusions to Jesus in the description of Braggioni, the flabby leader of the revolution. At the beginning of his career Braggioni seems to have impressed his followers with some Christlike attributes, but he has degenerated to the point where he has become the antithesis of Jesus. The allusions to Jesus, instead of building Braggioni into a Christ figure, emphasize the extent of his depravity and the seriousness of his betrayal.

The story opens with Braggioni sitting in an "upper room" in Laura's house during a political revolution in Mexico in the 1920s. He is still recognized as the leader of the revolution: his followers "are closer to him than his own brothers, without them he can do nothing"—an echo of the words of Jesus "I can of mine own self do nothing" (John 5:30) and "without me ye can do nothing" (John 15:5), and possibly of a passage from the Old Testament, "there is a friend that sticketh closer than a brother" (Prov. 18:24). The allusion also suggests that his activities as the leader of the revolution should be compared with the high ethical standard proclaimed in Mark 3:35, "Whosoever shall do the will of God, the same is my brother." His skin has been punctured during his revolutionary work, a possible allusion to the stigmata of Jesus. He sings discordantly about his exploits and of his desires, an apparent travesty of the hymn sung at the Last Supper. When he leaves the upper room he does not go to a Mount of Olives but to his own house where his wife washes his feet and leans her head on his arms as John leaned his head on the breast of Jesus. These allusions imply that Braggioni may at one time have had a Christlike incentive to help others, but he has long since betrayed his trust and his potential and become the very opposite of Jesus. He is using his power for sensual gratification, as indicated by his concern with food, sex, and perfume, and for financial gain. He has become "a professional lover of humanity" for selfish reasons. *"He will never die for it.* He will live to see himself kicked out from his feeding trough by other world-saviors." He has degenerated beyond the point where he might be considered a flawed Christ figure; he must, instead, be looked upon as a perverted Christ, a person whose betrayals have destroyed his humanity.

It is in the character of Laura, however, that the theme of betrayal is worked out to the fullest extent. Like Braggioni, she has joined the revolution but lost her idealism. Everything said about her points to the consequences of her betrayals of herself and others. Unlike Braggioni, she has not become selfish and gluttonous; she has, instead, lost her will and has become incapable of involving herself in anything constructive.

In the opening scene Laura is reluctant to enter her own house because she does not have the courage to ask the disagreeable Braggioni to leave—a striking example of her inability to act. She conceals her femininity and rejects those who admire her beauty and seek her attention. Her impotence as a lover is symbolized in the scene where she cleans Braggioni's ammunition and admits that she cannot combine romantic love with revolutionary activity. Her impotence in the revolution is dramatized when she plays one agitator off against another and leaves the people wondering why she came to Mexico. When she knocks on doors, she does not enjoy the rewards promised to the faithful: "knock, and it shall be opened unto you" (Matt. 7:7), and "Behold, I stand at the door, and knock: if any man hear my voice, and open the door, I will come in to him, and will sup with him, and he with me" (Rev. 3:20). Instead, she sees only strangers when she knocks on doors, like the unworthy who knock on the door too late and are told by the master of the house, "I know you not whence ye are; depart from me, all ye workers of iniquity" (Luke 13:27). Her life has become an everlasting "nay"; she considers the possibility that time may stand still and leave her permanently at rest. She relies on the word "no" as her substitute for the Lord's Prayer, for she believes that the magic of that word will not "suffer her to be led into evil." She remembers some philosophical axioms from her childhood, but they enslave rather than guide her. She knows that life will not permit her to remain on dead center indefinitely, so she stoically awaits an unknown disaster. When it comes, her betrayals culminate in a scene that once again draws heavily on the descriptions of the Last Supper in the New Testament.

Laura has poisoned her own life to such an extent that one of her efforts to help others ends in disaster. She takes food and money and secret messages to the imprisoned revolutionists, and those who are bored and confused she provides with narcotics. Eugenio, one of the distressed prisoners, kills himself with an overdose of her tablets; the would-be angel of mercy has become an angel of death. With Braggioni's help she tries to absolve herself from responsibility for Eugenio's death, but to no avail. The tolling of the midnight bell distracts her mind, and in the hallucination that follows Eugenio drags her to the land of death. Three times she searches for security by asking for Eugenio's hand, but the hand turns out to be fleshless. Instead of offering her security, Eugenio compels her to take part in a travesty of the communion sacrament. He holds the flowers of the Judas tree to her lips and orders her to eat them as his body and his blood. When she refuses with a loud "no," she awakens and is afraid to sleep again. The guilt of her many betrayals has destroyed her effectiveness as a human being.

The betrayal theme is developed also in the lives of the minor characters. Lupe tells Laura how she can get rid of her unwelcome serenading lover, but he betrays her when he doesn't tell her that if she follows his instructions she will actually encourage her lover to come back. Laura denies the love of the young captain when she frightens away his horse. She denies her schoolchildren when she cannot respond to their admiring comments. Her denials of herself and others have paralyzed her will. Her withdrawal from life and Braggioni's perversion of his ideals have similar effects: they have both lost their humanity because they have permitted the symbolic values of the Judas tree to flower in their lives.

B. "Judas," Frank O'Connor

If one fails to recognize the biblical allusions in Frank O'Connor's story "Judas," one misses a good bit of the humor. Jerry Moynihan, the narrator and central character, is going through the turmoil of falling in love and rethinking his relationship with his widowed mother. He reveals his confusion through some hilarious exaggerations conjured up by his hyperactive imagination. The ultimate exaggeration is the one implied in the title—O'Connor's hint to the reader that Jerry sees himself as a potential Judas when he agonizes about transferring his loyalty from his mother to his girl friend.

When the immature Jerry finally stumbles into the presence of Kitty Doherty, his girl friend, he receives some quick lessons in realism and independence. He is shocked to learn that she is a normal human being and not the angel of his dreams; she talks casually about her earlier flirtations, and she berates her suspicious and solicitous mother. This behavior apparently emboldens Jerry to reject his own mother and accept Kitty's love. However, when he returns home late at night, the striking of the clock reminds him that he had reneged on his promise to his mother that he would never stay out late—a parallel to Peter's despair when the crowing of the cock reminds him that he has broken his promise that he would never deny Jesus (Matt. 26:69-72; Mark 14:66-72; Luke 22:56-62). But Jerry remains true to Kitty and separates himself from his solicitous mother; he rejects her offer of a cup of tea; he lies about his reason for being late, and, for the first time in his life, he feels like a stranger in her presence. His new loyalty, however, does not last through the night. Whenever he tries to imagine Kitty's face during his sleepless hours, his mother's face crowds it out. He lies awake until the cocks crow, a second allusion to Peter's denial of Jesus. He apologizes to his mother and cries "like a kid" (Peter "went out and wept bitterly"). His mother hugs him and rocks him, and, in the culminating irony of the story, calls him her "little man."

How does O'Connor avoid offending when he alludes to Judas' betrayal and Peter's denial of Jesus to enhance the humor in his story? He does it through restraint and subtlety. The allusions are brief and unobtrusive. They do not detract from the central character, because they are consistent with his other exaggerations. They also remind us that the humor comes not only from the first person narrator in the foreground but also from the voice of the author who provided the title and created the character of Jerry.

The title should also be considered in relation to the mother. Is she not betraying her son by denying him his independence and his needs as he enters manhood? The final regressive scene may be read as a triple betrayal. Jerry betrays the maturation he has experienced the preceding night, and he betrays his declaration of love for Kitty; his mother betrays her responsibility to her growing son. Fortunately, the tone of this scene is consistent with that of the rest of the story and these betrayals do not lack a touch of humor.

C. "Judas," John Brunner[1]

In John Brunner's science fiction narrative "Judas," twelve brilliant cyberneticists (parallel to the twelve apostles) have invented a super-robot. While they were creating their "mechanical analogue of a human being," one of them aspired to create human intelligence and imagined that he was God. His megalomania was transferred from his mind to that of the robot, and the robot promptly usurped the role of God and Christ. The guilty cyberneticist repented and spent twenty years designing and building a miniature weapon with which to destroy the false God. When his weapon is finished he hides it in his pocket and attends a worship service in a sanctuary of polished steel and plastic where he hears a choral rendition of "The Word

[1] Brunner's story can be found in Harlan Ellison (ed.), *Dangerous Visions* (Garden City, N.Y.: Doubleday & Co., 1967), pp. 451-60.

Made Steel." After the congregation disperses, he elbows his way into the throne room and confronts the deified robot. With his secret weapon he drills a hole in the side of the robot and cripples it. Those who come to investigate observe that it is Friday and that the damage can be repaired in three days. When they ask the attendant the name of the person who caused the damage, they are told that his name must be Iscariot.

The Judas theme should be applied to the story in at least two places. The twelve cyberneticists who created the mechanical God betrayed society as well as their own humanity when they dedicated their talents to the mechanization of man's spiritual life. The second application is entirely ironic: the cyberneticist who repents and tries to restore some humanity to life is called a Judas by his associates.

The consequences of overweening ambition in this story might be compared with the building of the Tower of Babel (Gen. 11), the story of Icarus in Greek mythology, and the stories of overweening ambition in Aesop's fables.

D. *A Separate Peace*, John Knowles

John Knowles' novel *A Separate Peace* contains only two allusions to the Bible, but they occur at a crucial moment in the story and help us understand its theme and its characters. Gene and Phineas, the two central characters, are fighting boredom at Devon prep school during World War II. Phineas takes the lead in improvising pastimes and bending the rules, and Gene is a willing follower, though he soon begins to resent the successful leadership and disruptive activities of his friend. Gene's envy is subconscious at first; but as the story unfolds, he becomes aware of his inner emotions and sees himself and his friends in a new light.

Significantly, the references to the Bible occur in the part of the story dealing with the idyllic summer session of 1942, prior to Phineas' disastrous fall from the tree. During the first part of the summer session Phineas has involved Gene in a series of impromptu diversions—inventing blitzball; breaking the school swimming record; jumping from the tree a year ahead of schedule; forming the Super Suicide Society of the Summer Session; and finally, as a climax to these activities, taking an illegal bicycle trip to the ocean and spending the night on the beach. Before they fall asleep, Gene is strangely confused when Phineas calls him his best pal. Gene tries to return the compliment but can't: "Perhaps I was stopped by a level of feeling, deeper than thought, which contains the truth" (last sentence of chapter 3). At this time his dark feelings are still at the subconscious level; for when he awakens the next morning and sees the sun gradually illuminating the beach, he observes that his surroundings have become totally white and stainless, "as pure as the shores of Eden." When he looks at Phineas, still asleep on a nearby sand dune, he is reminded of Lazarus "brought back to life by the touch of God" (second paragraph of chapter 4). Phineas is also impressed with the beauty of the beach and the restful sleep; in answer to Gene's question he says that his last bad night's sleep occurred when he broke his ankle in football, a foreshadowing of the catastrophe about to follow.

When the two friends return to their dormitory that night and are studying for an examination, Gene suddenly discovers what he believes to be Phineas' motivation for interfering with his studies so frequently. Phineas must be jealous of a potential rival who may reach the level of excellence in his classes that he has reached in athletics! Gene says that this realization "broke as clearly and bleakly as dawn at the beach." The innocent relationship between these two residents of Eden is spoiled, and later that summer (still in chapter 4) Gene bounces Phineas from the tree and cripples him.

The central theme of this story, the fall from innocence, is part of a literary archetype that goes back to Genesis 2 and 3. The description of the original fall and Knowles' modern variation of it can be compared in various ways. Is the tree that so drastically changes the lives of Gene and Phineas comparable to the tree of the knowledge of good and evil in the Garden of Eden? Are the events in the Garden of Eden before and after the fall similar to some of the contrasts in the novel, such as Gene's understanding of himself at the beginning and the end of the story, and the sheltered life at Devon giving way to the reality of World War II?

The reference to Lazarus raised from the dead suggests, among other things, the mystery often associated with Phineas. Gene is puzzled by the near-hypnotic power Phineas has over him and understandably links him with the supernatural when the sunrise reminds him of Eden. It is also possible to interpret the end of the story as a return from the dead. After Phineas dies, the meaning of life becomes very real to Gene, and Gene himself returns from the dead through the discoveries he makes about himself and others. The possibility that the broken body and death of Phineas are a Christlike sacrifice for Gene is considered by Milton Foster in *The English Record*, 1958, pp. 34-40.

E. *The Pearl*, John Steinbeck

In Matthew 13:45-46 we learn of a merchant who finds a pearl of great price, the kingdom of heaven, and sells everything else to obtain it. In Steinbeck's novel Kino also finds a pearl of great price, called the pearl of the world. He sees it as a way of obtaining a material kingdom of heaven: respectability through a marriage ceremony and new clothes; improved earning power and self-protection through the purchase of a harpoon and a rifle; and, most important of all, an education for Coyotito that will protect them from further exploitation by the members of the predatory upper classes. As it turns out, Kino's pearl of great price brings him nothing resembling a kingdom of heaven, but a crushing defeat. Like the merchant in the parable, Kino sacrifices lesser things to obtain the new life that he envisions with the finding of the pearl. He endures the disruption of his domestic and social life; he refuses to yield when his boat and his grass hut are destroyed; and he defiantly starts walking, with his wife and infant son, to the big city where he hopes to get fair value for his pearl. But this journey does not fit the usual pattern of a journey in literature; there is no spiritual rebirth, no self-discovery, no Pilgrim's Progress. Instead, the journey brings to a shattering climax the frustrations that began with the finding of the pearl. Before he started on his journey, he killed an assailant in self-defense and lost his house, his boat, and his old way of life. During the journey he kills the three trackers, but in the scuffle his own son is slain. The pearl that was to open a new life for Coyotito is now without value, and Kino gives up the struggle and returns to his native town.

The conclusion is tragically ironic. Kino has not been able to get full value for the pearl; so instead of surrendering it to the greedy oppressors of his people, he throws it back into the sea, realizing that the pearl that gave him a momentary vision of a better life has actually uprooted him from his old way of life and totally destroyed him together with his vision. To the merchant in Matthew 13 the pearl of great price is the realization of the kingdom of heaven; to Kino the pearl of great price is the very opposite: he risks everything to improve his lot but loses everything when he clashes with his oppressors.

F. "By the Waters of Babylon," Stephen Vincent Benet

When an author uses a biblical phrase in the title of a story, he must satisfy the curiosity of his readers about the reason for his choice. In Katherine Anne Porter's "Flowering Judas" and Frank O'Connor's "Judas" it becomes obvious that the biblical allusions in the titles help us understand the central characters in the stories. The biblical allusion in the title of Benet's story serves a different purpose.

The title of Benet's story is a popular phrase in literature, and whenever it is used one assumes that it refers to Psalm 137. Byron, for example, versified parts of the psalm in two of his poems, "By the Rivers of Babylon" and "By the Waters of Babylon." Swinburne drew heavily on it in his poem "Super Flumina Babylonis," in which he expressed his feelings about the condition of Italy in the nineteenth century. A contemporary Italian poet and Nobel prize winner, Salvatore Quasimodo, incorporates several lines of the psalm into his poem describing the suffering of the Italians under Nazi occupation. Perhaps the best-known recent allusion to the psalm is T. S. Eliot's "By the waters of Leman I sat down and wept" in his poem *The Waste Land*.

The first three lines of Psalm 137 are probably the most poignant expression in literature of the despondency experienced by those who have been isolated from their homeland and all the values associated with it. The citizens of Judah were taken to Babylon as captives; and Jerusalem, the political and spiritual center of their lives, was destroyed. The psalmist expresses the despair of these exiles whose loyalty to Jerusalem (Zion) and all it stands for keeps them from adjusting to their new environment:

> By the rivers of Babylon,
> there we sat down, yea, we wept,
> when we remembered Zion.

In a sense the psalm is a requiem for a nation that has been liquidated.

Benet's allusion to Psalm 137 in the title creates an apprehensive mood that characterizes the entire story. The allusions to the Bible within the story contribute to this mood. The main character and narrator, a survivor of a nuclear war, says three times, "How shall I tell what I saw," a possible echo of "How shall we sing the Lord's song in a strange land?" (Ps. 137:4), and near the end of the story he says, "It was darkness over the broken city and I wept," a possible echo of "there we sat down, yea, we wept" (Ps. 137:1). When he says, "If I went to the Place of the Gods, I would surely die," he is echoing God's warning to Adam about the tree of the knowledge of good and evil, "for in the day that thou eatest thereof thou shalt surely die" (Gen. 2:17). The biblical allusions within the story have the same effect as the allusion in the title: they cast a pall over the story as a whole and help the reader experience the destruction of American civilization much more deeply. The psalm that expresses the longing of the citizens of Judah for the way of life from which they have been forcibly removed is indeed an appropriate background for Benet's story.

G. "Exodus," James Baldwin[2]

The two parts of James Baldwin's story "Exodus" show how the meaning of the title is worked out in the lives of two people. In the first part Florence recalls the stories about slavery told by her mother, Rachel, who had been a slave until the age of thirty-five when the end of the Civil War provided her with the occasion for an exodus into freedom. In the second part Florence arranges for her own exodus when she decides to leave her dying mother and her dissolute brother, to fend for herself in New York.

When Rachel and her fellow slaves were longing for freedom before the Civil War, they were sure that their plight and their dreams were similar to those of the Hebrew children who were led from bondage in Egypt to freedom in the Promised Land. The slaves identified their experiences with the biblical exodus in several ways: they believed that their suffering was like that of the Hebrew children, they believed that their cruel masters were like the hard-hearted pharaohs, and they were confident that the promises of deliverance given to the Hebrews were applicable to them also. Other parts of the Bible bolstered their confidence as well. They believed that their white masters had built their happiness on a weak foundation, an allusion to the house

---

[2] Published in *The American Mercury* in 1952 and then made a part of "Florence's Prayer" in Part II of *Go Tell It on the Mountain.*

built on sand (Matt. 7:24-27). They believed that their masters were walking on the edge of a precipice and would soon fall over the edge to their death as did the swine of the Gadarenes when they were possessed by the devils cast out from a mad man (Luke 8:33). When some liberated slaves were said to have killed the children of their masters, the information was passed along among the slaves in biblical language, "they dashed their children to death against the stones," an echo of the call for vengeance on the part of the Israelites in captivity in Babylon, "Happy shall he be, that taketh and dasheth thy little ones against the stones" (Ps. 137:9).

Rachel uses her knowledge of the Bible to strengthen her conviction that God will in the fullness of time bring freedom to the slaves. Her speech is filled with echoes of biblical words and phrases—the trumpet of the last judgment, the day of his wrath, children of her old age, prayers of the faithful, wait but a little season, the word going forth from the mouth of God, deliverance, salvation, whirlwind, and others—all of which help to convey the depth of her feeling; but it is the assurance with which she identifies her people with the slaves of Egypt that establishes her absolute confidence in her eventual exodus into freedom.

As Florence recalls all these stories about slavery and emancipation that she learned from her mother, she becomes more and more convinced that she, too, is in need of emancipation, not from white masters but from her mother and brother. Even though it was the immoral advances of her white employer that precipitated her decision to leave, it was her own family she wanted to leave because she "would not let herself be strangled by the hands of the dead." She abruptly informs her dying mother that she is leaving and ignores her mother's fears that Florence may be headed for eternal punishment in the burning lake (Rev. 20:15, 21:8). The fact that Florence hesitates only a moment indicates how important the need for freedom has become in her own life.

The title of the story applies to the events in the lives of two generations: the exodus of Rachel from her white oppressors, narrated with many allusions to the Bible, and the exodus of Florence from her mother Rachel and her brother Gabriel.

Part Two:
The Bible in Poetry

Introduction

The material in this section has been arranged to illustrate three approaches to the vast amount of poetry that has been influenced by the Bible. We begin with the poets who have used the Bible frequently, we then discuss the Negro spirituals that have used the Bible in a special way, and we conclude with poems on two biblical passages that have appealed to several poets. Authors, special poetic categories, and biblical passages—each approach has certain advantages, but all three approaches can be combined or even supplemented with others, such as historical periods or national literatures.

Studying an author's poems as a group may reveal distinctive patterns and themes in that author's use of the Bible which, if recognized, may help our understanding of both the poems and the Bible. Our knowledge of other things the poet has written may also shed some light on his biblical poems. The poems of the first six authors—Owen, Cullen, Housman, Bontemps, Eliot, and Shapiro—are discussed in some detail; the poems of the last five— Longfellow, Lindsay, Masters, Muir, and Lawrence— receive only brief comments in the headnotes.

Advanced students may wish to study authors not included here. Those who like the challenge of the poems by Shapiro, Muir, and Eliot should have no difficulty with the biblical allusions in the poems of such authors as Emily Dickinson, E. A. Robinson, Robert Browning, Alfred, Lord Tennyson, Thomas Hardy, John Milton, Christina Rossetti, Edith Sitwell, Wallace Stevens, and Robert Lowell.

Studying the Negro spirituals separately has obvious advantages because of the unique ways in which they use the Bible. Those wishing to make a unit on the Bible in the works of black writers should add to their study of the spirituals the material on Cullen, Bontemps, Baldwin, and Du Bois, and Ford's comment on Connelly in this book as well as some of the poems of James Weldon Johnson, Owen Dodson, Sterling Brown, Melvin B. Tolson, and Joseph S. Cotter. Those wishing to study the influence of the Bible on other categories of poetry might concentrate on biblical allusions in narrative poetry, lyrical poetry, protest poetry, war poetry, nature poetry, medieval ballads, etc. Another possible category might be the many translations and paraphrases of the Psalms that were published in England during the sixteenth, seventeenth, and eighteenth centuries.

Bringing together various poems on the same biblical passage permits the reader to compare the way in which several poets have responded to the same part of the Bible and to consider such questions as the following: What is the special attraction that a given passage has had for the poets? What is the source of the inspiration? Is the passage so terse that its very brevity has stimulated the imagination of the poets and prompted them to expand it? Are the poets impressed with the language of the passage as well as the substance? What kinds of details are added by each poet? Is it possible to generalize about the kinds of details poets tend to add to the passages that inspire their poems? How diverse are the poets' responses? How much freedom does each poet take with the biblical material he is using? Does the passage serve as the substance for the body of the poem, or is it the stimulus for a poem that deals with other matters? How interesting are the poets' additions?

We have illustrated this approach to biblical poetry with only two biblical passages, but the same approach could be used with just about every part of the Bible. In fact, one could organize quite a comprehensive study of the Bible and of poetry by assembling a large number of poems with biblical allusions and arranging them according to the appropriate biblical passages. The many anthologies of religious poetry found in most libraries usually identify biblical topics in either the table of contents or the index. Of special value is the topical section (Part III) of *Granger's Index to Poetry*, a standard library reference work. One anthology that is particularly helpful for poems dealing with the Old Testament is George Alexander Kohut's *A Hebrew Anthology*, published by S. Bacharach in Cincinnati in 1913.

No matter which approach seems most appropriate for a given time and place, the reader should have in mind certain questions when he encounters biblical allusions in a poem.

1. What is the function of the allusion?

2. How important is the allusion to the understanding of the poem? Would anything be lost if the allusion were not recognized and understood?

3. Is the allusion used in a straightforward manner, or is it used ironically, humorously, angrily, or in some other way? Is the spirit of the allusion in the poem the same as in the biblical context?

4. Has the allusion been integrated successfully with the tone and the method of the poem, or is it so prominent or so obscure that it is distracting?

5. Does the allusion affect only its immediate context or is it central to the entire poem?

Roland Bartel

I Teaching Wilfred Owen's War Poems and the Bible*

Roland Bartel

> Of the many English poets who fought in France in World War I, Wilfred Owen (1893–1918) is the best-known and probably the most original. He and Siegfried Sassoon shocked their readers by including in their poems the ugly details of trench warfare that they observed firsthand in France. Owen was killed in action on November 4, 1918, one week before the Armistice.—Ed.

Wilfred Owen is represented in most high school textbooks by "Dulce et Decorum Est," a realistic anti-war poem of World War I. I suggest that this poem is only one of a half dozen or more war poems by Owen that could be taught successfully in high school. Assuming that we would not want to teach all thirty-two of Owen's war poems, I suggest that we teach those poems containing allusions to the Bible and thereby accomplish several things at once: introduce our students to a recent poet whose reputation is steadily rising, illustrate the complexity and effectiveness of successful allusions, familiarize students with important episodes in the Bible, and provide students with a nucleus of war poems that can serve as a frame of reference for much of the war poetry written today.

Owen's most extensive use of the Bible occurs in his short poem "The Parable of the Old Man and the Young," an adaptation of Abraham's sacrifice of Isaac as told in Genesis 22. In the original story Abraham is portrayed as a devout patriarch who obeys without hesitation God's terrifying command that he slay his only son; he is rewarded for his obedience by being released from the command just in time

*From *English Journal*, 61 (January, 1972): 36-42. Copyright © 1972 by the National Council of Teachers of English. Reprinted by permission of the publisher.

to save his son. In Owen's poem he is portrayed as a war lord whose pride causes him to slay his son and half the youth of Europe as well.

Owen's choice of Abraham to represent the older generation of war makers seems rather puzzling, especially if we consider the context of the original story. In Genesis the story stands as the culminating episode of Abraham's long life of devout obedience to God. Before the story opens Abraham has obeyed without question or protest God's command to leave his homeland for an unknown country, he has sacrificed personal gain on several occasions to live in peace with his neighbors, he has twice rescued Lot from adversity, he has interceded for the inhabitants of Sodom, and he has received with humility the many promises of God that he would, though old and childless, become the founder of a great nation. His name has become synonymous with humility, peacefulness, obedience, and divine favor—all of which are confirmed in this final crisis of his life.

Such a humble and peace-loving man is a good choice for the role of a proud war lord in a parable whose basic technique is shock. Owen's parable, like many other parables, withholds its meaning until the very end. Owen keeps the reader off guard by following the account in Genesis closely in the first thirteen lines of his poem, then changing the original story abruptly to create the shock. He converts the ram caught in the thicket to the Ram of Pride and makes Abraham into a war lord whose refusal to slay his pride causes him to slay his son, "And half the seed of Europe one by one." This surprise ending reminds the reader of the conclusion of other great parables, such as Nathan's reproach to David—"Thou art the man" (II Samuel 12:7) and Jesus' admonition to the clever lawyer— "Go, and do thou likewise" (Luke 10:37). In each instance the surprise ending drives home the moral of the parable.

However, to be successful, a surprise ending requires more than a reversal of the reader's expectations. While he leads the reader along to expect one thing, the writer must subtly introduce details pointing in another direction so that when the ending is revealed the reader's shock is reinforced by a recognition of consistency within the poem. This delicate balance between plausibility and incredibility is maintained superbly by Owen as we shall see if we examine the source and then study his adaptation.

Abraham Tempted To Sacrifice His Son Isaac

And it came to pass after these things, that God did tempt Abraham, and said unto him, "Abraham."

And he said, "Behold, here I am."

And he said, "Take now thy son, thine only son Isaac, whom thou lovest, and get thee into the land of Moriah; and offer him there for a burnt offering upon one of the mountains which I will tell thee of."

And Abraham rose up early in the morning, and saddled his ass, and took two of his young men with him, and Isaac his son, and clave the wood for the burnt offering, and rose up, and went unto the place of which God had told him. Then on the third day Abraham lifted up his eyes, and saw the place afar off. And Abraham said unto his young men, "Abide ye here with the ass; and I and the lad will go yonder and worship, and come again to you."

And Abraham took the wood of the burnt offering, and laid it upon Isaac his son; and he took the fire in his hand, and a knife; and they went both of them together. And Isaac spake unto Abraham his father, and said, "My father."

And he said, "Here am I my son."

And he said, "Behold the fire and the wood: but where is the lamb for a burnt offering?"

And Abraham said, "My son, God will provide himself a lamb for a burnt offering." So they went both of them together.

And they came to the place which God had told him of; and Abraham built an altar there, and laid the wood in order, and bound Isaac his son, and laid him on the altar upon the wood. And Abraham stretched forth his hand, and took the knife to slay his son. And the angel of the Lord called unto him out of heaven and said, "Abraham, Abraham."

And he said, "Here am I."

And he said, "Lay not thine hand upon the lad, neither do thou any thing unto him: for now I know that thou fearest God, seeing thou hast not withheld thy son, thine only son, from me."

And Abraham lifted up his eyes, and looked, and behold behind him a ram caught in a thicket by his horns; and Abraham went and took the ram, and offered him up for a burnt offering in the stead of his son.

The Sacrifice of Isaac is a masterpiece of compact narration, certainly one of the finest stories in the Bible. Abraham receives the command to sacrifice his son, and he obeys promptly, a fact dramatized by the simple phrase "and rose up early in the morning." His unquestioning faith is suggested by the absence of any reference to inner conflict. The story concentrates on outward preparations: saddling the ass and proceeding with the two young men, his son Isaac, the wood, the fire, and the knife. The omission of details of time and place and condition of the journey focuses the reader's attention exclusively on the approaching sacrifice—we are simply told that "on the third day" Abraham recognized the appointed spot. The focus narrows still further when he asks the servants to remain behind while he and Isaac complete the journey. He divides the load with Isaac, giving him the wood and keeping the fire and the knife in his own hands. When Isaac asks about the lamb for the offering, Abraham's answer, "God will provide," reveals his complete trust and his ability to allay Isaac's fears. When they reach the top of the mountain the details of the altar and the movements of Abraham— binding Isaac and reaching for the knife—are depicted with frightening clarity. When the angel intervenes, Abraham again demonstrates his faith. Without being told to do so, he sacrifices a ram whose appearance he apparently considered providential.

In a story as compact as this one (four hundred words), the few repetitions that do occur take on special significance. "Take now thy son, thine only son Isaac, whom thou lovest" (v. 2) and "Thy son, thine only son" (v. 12) emphasize Abraham's love for his son and thus magnify the horribleness of the temptation. It is well to remember in this connection that Abraham does not know that the command is given to tempt him. The reader is given that information but Abraham proceeds on the assumption that the sacrifice will be consummated. The other repetition— "They went both of them together" (vv. 6 and 8) also serves to emphasize Abraham's attachment to his son.

Such, then, is the story that climaxes and confirms Abraham's long record of obedience to divine law, a story sharply etched on the reader's mind because it is told with such economy and precision.

In converting the story into sixteen lines of anti-war poetry, Owen reduced the story to a third of its length and added a few significant details. His deletions and additions reveal a great deal about the formation of a successful poem.

The Parable of the Old Man and the Young[1]

So Abram rose, and clave the wood, and went,
And took the fire with him, and a knife.
And as they sojourned both of them together,
Isaac the first-born spake and said, My Father,
Behold the preparations, fire and iron,
But where the lamb for this burnt-offering?
Then Abram bound the youth with belts and straps,
And builded parapets and trenches there,
And stretched forth the knife to slay his son.
When lo! an angel called him out of heaven,
Saying, Lay not thy hand upon the lad,
Neither do anything to him. Behold,
A ram, caught in a thicket by its horns;
Offer the Ram of Pride instead of him.
But the old man would not so, but slew his son,—
And half the seed of Europe, one by one.

Understandably Owen changed those details that might remind the reader of Abraham's saintly qualities. He makes no reference to the fact that Abraham acts in obedience to God's commands. He quotes Isaac's question about the lamb almost verbatim, but he omits Abraham's reply, "My son, God will provide himself a lamb for the burnt offering." Instead of answering his son's question Abraham responds by binding him with belts and straps. The next major change concerns an addition rather than omission. In

[1] Poems quoted in article are from Wilfred Owen, *Collected Poems.* Copyright Chatto & Windus, Ltd., 1946, © 1963. Reprinted by permission of New Directions Publishing Corporation.

Genesis the angel that told Abraham to spare his son said nothing about the ram, but in the poem the angel commands Abraham to slay the Ram of Pride. Abraham disobeys and precipitates a world war.

Of major importance is another change introduced by Owen. He changes Abraham's name back to Abram, suggesting a person less wise and less experienced than the devout man of Genesis 22. Abram's name had been changed to Abraham in Genesis 17 to commemorate his faithfulness and the renewal of God's promises of a son, a great progeny, and great prosperity. Using the earlier name, though an anachronism, strips Abraham of some of the superhuman qualities he had acquired at the end of his life and makes him more suitable for the role of war maker in the parable.

Owen's minor changes also contribute to the success of the poem. *Iron* (l. 5), *belts and straps* (l. 7), and *parapets and trenches* (l. 8) are words not found in Genesis but are needed to prepare for the conclusion. Beginning the poem with *So* may be a faint echo of God's command in Genesis, but its effect may well be to arouse curiosity about the journey. Adding the words *sojourn* and *first-born* does not contribute to changes in connotation, but it does help to condense longer passages in the original.

Does the omission of the reminders of Abraham's good qualities reduce the shock and weaken the parable? Not necessarily. Owen could assume that his readers would respond in a traditional manner to a retelling of the familiar story whose central character had become legendary for obedience to God. To make the conclusion plausible enough to produce shock rather than rejection, Owen altered just enough of the details to give the poem a consistent tone.

The tempo of the poem should also be considered. Not only has the story been reduced to a third of its length; the story is retold so rapidly that Abram's actions seem abrupt and cruel, devoid of the spiritual significance they have in Genesis. This pacing becomes all the more effective in view of the fact that many of the cadences of the original story are preserved in the poem. The tempo suggesting the new parable and the cadences suggesting the original story thus prepare for and reinforce the final juxtaposition: a Biblical saint serving as a modern war lord.

Another of Owen's poems that relies heavily on the Bible for its full meaning is "Greater Love." The title is taken from Jesus' discourse with his disciples at the last supper when he said, "Greater love hath no man than this, that he lay down his life for his friends" (John 15:13).

Greater Love

Red lips are not so red
  As the stained stones kissed by the
    English dead.
Kindness of wooed and wooer
Seems shame to their love pure.
O Love, your eyes lost lure
  When I behold eyes blinded in my
    stead!

Your slender attitude
  Trembles not exquisite like limbs
    knife-skewed,
Rolling and rolling there
Where God seems not to care;
Till the fierce love they bear
  Cramps them in death's extreme
    decrepitude.

Your voice sings not so soft,—
  Though even as wind murmuring
    through raftered loft,—
Your dear voice is not dear,
Gentle, and evening clear,
As theirs whom none now hear,
  Now earth has stopped their piteous
    mouths that coughed.

Heart, you were never hot,
  Nor large, nor full like hearts made
    great with shot;
And though your hand be pale,
Paler are all which trail
Your cross through flame and hail:
  Weep, you may weep, for you may
    touch them not.

The soldiers, according to Owen, are making a mockery of civilian concepts of love and beauty and sacrifice. Soldiers whose "eyes are blinded in my stead," whose love forces them into "death's extreme decrepitude," whose coughing ceases only when their mouths are stopped with earth, whose hearts are large and full because they are "made great with shot"—they are the ones who demonstrate Jesus' greater love and reenact his sacrifice even while they are being forced to violate his command against murder.

The comparison of the soldiers with Jesus in the title and in the heart of the poem becomes a complete identification in the last line where the soldiers carry the cross "through flame and hail," and the young girl, who has served as a foil for the soldiers throughout the poem, is told that she cannot approximate their supreme sacrifice: "Weep, you may weep, for you may touch them not." In Luke 23:28, Jesus tells the women who are following him to the crucifixion, "Daughters of Jerusalem, weep not for me, but weep for yourselves, and for your children." In both instances the sacrifice is of such a nature that weeping is futile, even irreverent.

With some hesitation I now recommend that other Biblical echoes be explored. I hesitate because finding allusions and parallels can easily get out of hand and impoverish rather than enhance the study of literature. As a general guide, I suggest that we rule out discussions of allusions and parallels that do not clearly illuminate the poem. If we proceed cautiously we can on occasion deepen the student's experience with a poem by bringing in parallels and analogues that may or may not be a direct allusion. The question is not, Can I prove that the author consciously referred to this passage, but rather, Will I add anything to the students' enjoyment and understanding of the poem if I present other passages of literature brought to my mind by something in the poem—a scene, a theme, a mood, a phrase with unusual word order, the rhythm or cadence of a group of words, perhaps even a single word.

The depth of Owen's veneration for his fallen comrades

(and, conversely, his outrage over the war) comes through with greater force if we consider the implications of the word *touch* in the last line. Now that the sacrifice of the soldiers has been equated with that of Christ, it is relevant to recall the significance of the word *touch* in the Gospels. We are told that many wanted to touch Jesus to be freed from the plague, that others wanted to touch him "for there went virtue out of him, and healed them all," that he was asked to heal a blind man by touching him, that many were healed by touching the hem of his garment. Owen is saying, by implication, that civilians might well experience some cleansing themselves if they could touch the true nature of the soldiers' sacrifice, but he asserts that they cannot hope to understand or share what the soldiers have been through.

Reviewing the prohibitions against touching can also enhance the last line. After the resurrection Jesus told Mary Magdalene, "Touch me not, for I am not yet ascended to my Father." In I Chronicles 16:22 David praises God that heathen were not permitted to touch the Lord's anointed and in Numbers 4:15 the sons of Kohath are forbidden to touch any holy thing in the tabernacle. Because of the rich connotations acquired by the word *touch*, Owen's prohibition against touching the bodies of the soldiers thus serves to sanctify the soldiers and criticize those to whom the words are addressed.

If the class is receptive and the time is available, the matter of allusions and parallels could be carried still further. The impact of the eighth line, "Where God seems not to care," can be strengthened by placing it alongside other expressions of loneliness, despair, abandonment by God: Coleridge's Ancient Mariner describing his isolation at sea with "So lone it was that God himself/Scarce seemed there to be"; the exiled Jews weeping by the rivers of Babylon because they cannot sing "the Lord's song in a strange land" (Psalm 137:4); the many cries of despair in the other Psalms when the speaker feels that he has been abandoned by God.

A consensus seems to be developing that "Greater Love" is one of Owen's very best poems. I say this to indicate that many things besides Biblical allusions should be taught in this poem, such as the counterpointing of sexual love and sacrificial love and the dramatic progression from comparison to identification, from a caustic tone to an elegiac tone.

The theme of "Greater Love" reappears in "At a Calvary near the Ancre," where the soldiers are again depicted as possessing the greater love because they "lay down their life; they do not hate." According to the poem, Jesus has been deserted by civilian Christians who prosecute the war, but he has found his true disciples among the soldiers.

Advanced students will find many rewards in studying "Strange Meeting," one of Owen's more difficult poems. It demonstrates the successful use of half-rhymes. It illustrates Owen's skill in merging external and inner dialog. It raises many ethical questions involving both individual soldiers and the larger community. To get the full impact of the poem, teachers will again need to bring in the Bible. When the "enemy" in the poem completes his recital of his attempts to help mankind, he says that he would have been willing to make any sacrifice for others except by means of war.

I would have poured my spirit without stint
But not through wounds; not on the cess of war.
Foreheads of men have bled where no wounds were. (lines 37-40).

The reference to the agony of Christ on the Mount of Olives prior to the betrayal—"and his sweat was as it were great drops of blood" (Luke 22:44)—once again links the sacrifice of the soldiers with that of Christ. The allusion suggests that when the speaker in the poem failed to convince mankind to get rid of war, his disappointment was comparable to that of Christ when he was betrayed by his disciples at the conclusion of his ministry.

The phrase "poured my spirit" also has Biblical overtones. It is used several times to express great travail and devotion. Citing a few examples should add significance to the speaker's assertion that he was willing to do anything for humanity. Hannah desired a son so fervently that in her prayers she "poured out her spirit before the Lord" (I Samuel 1:15). To emphasize the extent of his suffering, Job says "and now my soul is poured out upon me" (Job 30:16). In the famous passage on the suffering servant, the prophet says that after enduring many hardships the servant will be rewarded "because he hath poured out his soul to death" (Isaiah 53:12). These passages illustrate once more that poets and others skilled in the use of language can multiply the effectiveness of a passage by using language that has acquired appropriate connotations in earlier literature.

One of the central problems in the poem is the enemy, the person who speaks all but the first part of the poem. On the literal level he is an enemy soldier, but on the symbolic level he is a part of Owen himself—his alter ego, his conscience, his idealistic self. As we have seen, the enemy has many Christ-like qualities—in the sacrifices he wants to make for others, in his commitment to non-violence, in the reference to foreheads bleeding without wounds. So far so good—the teaching of the poem is improved by citing these parallels. But to go on to say that the enemy is Christ himself, as one critic has done, confuses the reading of the poem. I consider it an example of pushing Biblical allusions to the point where they hinder rather than help the teaching of the poem.

For the sake of completeness I will mention briefly Owen's other uses of the Bible. "Sonnet: on Seeing a Piece of our Artillery Brought into Action" begins with the words "Be slowly lifted up, thou long black arm," a parody of the words of Jesus to Nicodemus: "And as Moses lifted up the serpent in the wilderness, even so must the Son of man be lifted up: that whosoever believeth in him should not perish, but have eternal life" (John 3:14-15) and of Jesus' words to his disciples: "And I, if I be lifted up from the earth, will draw all men unto me" (John 12:32). The parody succeeds because it serves Owen's purpose of showing how armaments have become the false gods of the war makers.

Armaments have a fatal attraction for man; he sees in them his way to salvation. The hubris in such thinking is suggested in the allusion to the Tower of Babel in the second line: "Great gun towering towards Heaven."

"Insensibility" begins with "Happy are the men who yet before they are killed/Can let their veins run cold," an echo of "Blessed is the man that walketh not in the counsel of the ungodly" (Psalm 1:1) and probably of "happy is the man whom God correcteth" (Job 5:17). The juxtapositioning of solemn Biblical admonitions with situations of war again helps Owen express his outrage over the effects of war on the human spirit.

In summary we can say that Owen uses the Bible to exalt the suffering of the soldiers, sometimes to the level of the passion of Christ, but he also uses the Bible satirically to shock his readers into seeing the hypocrisy of their endorsement of war. We can also say that when an understanding of Biblical allusions and parallels illuminates a work of literature, extended digressions in pursuit of their meaning and function are justified in the cause of improving the teaching of literature. Finally, if the poems mentioned above arouse any interest in Owen at all, they might well be supplemented with poems by Owen that do not allude to the Bible. I would recommend especially "The Send-Off," "Arms and the Boy," "Insensibility," "S.I.W.," "Mental Cases," "Fertility," "Disabled," "The Next War," "Miners," "Inspection," and "Spring Offensive"—all of which are found in *The Collected Poems of Wilfred Owen*, a New Directions Paperbook.

II Countee Cullen (1903–1946)*

Countee Cullen was a prominent figure in the group of black writers of the 1920s often referred to as the Harlem Renaissance, a group that included Claude McKay, Jean Toomer, Wallace Thurman, Langston Hughes, W. E. B. Du Bois, Arna Bontemps, James Weldon Johnson, and possibly other writers who did not publish their works till later, such as Sterling Brown and Melvin B. Tolson. When he was eleven years old, Cullen was adopted by the pastor of the Salem Methodist Episcopal Church in Harlem, Frederick Ashbury Cullen. He traveled to Europe and Palestine with his father and spent two years in France on Guggenheim Fellowships. His marriage in 1928 to Yolande Du Bois, daughter of W. E. B. Du Bois, ended in a divorce in 1929.

Cullen's seven volumes of poetry reflect all the major experiences of his life—his classical education, his travels abroad, his exhilaration and disappointment in love, his agony over the suffering of the members of his race, his concern about the opportunities for black writers, and particularly his upbringing in a parsonage, which probably accounts for the large amount of biblical material in his poetry.

Simon the Cyrenian Speaks

He never spoke a word to me,
  And yet He called my name;
He never gave a sign to me,
  And yet I knew and came.

*Commentary by Roland Bartel.

At first I said, "I will not bear
   His cross upon my back;
He only seeks to place it there
   Because my skin is black."

But He was dying for a dream,
   And He was very meek,
And in His eyes there shone a gleam
   Men journey far to seek.

It was Himself my pity bought;
   I did for Christ alone
What all of Rome could not have wrought
   With bruise of lash or stone.

This poem is based on a single verse in each of the Synoptic Gospels (Matt. 27:32; Mark 15:21; Luke 23:26) which states simply that the crowd that drove Jesus to the scene of the crucifixion met Simon, a Cyrenian, and compelled him to carry the cross. The Bible does not identify Simon's race; Cullen follows the assumption of many commentators that Simon was black since Cyrene was a town in northern Africa. Cullen describes Simon as being transformed by the mystical power of Jesus' vision. At first he resents having to carry the cross, but then his pity for the meek man dying for his dream causes him to accept Jesus voluntarily, a decision that could never have been forced on him by all the power of Rome.

This poem is written in ballad stanzas—quatrains with alternating tetrameter and trimeter lines (4-3-4-3)—which on first reading may seem inappropriate for the subject. One feature of the ballad stanza, however, should not be overlooked. Some scholars have observed that there is a quality of inevitableness in the ballad measure, that in poems like "The Rime of the Ancient Mariner" and "Sir Patrick Spence" the pronounced meter provides an irresistible forward movement to the story. Is this element present in the poem, and if so, is it appropriate? See the comments on the next poem for some additional suggestions.

Colors

(Black)

1

The play is done, the crowds depart; and see
That twisted tortured thing hung from a tree,
Swart victim of a newer Calvary.

2

Yea, he who helped Christ up Golgotha's track,
That Simon who did *not* deny, was black.

These lines are taken from a series of epigrams with the general title "Colors" and with subtitles "Red," "Black," and "The Unknown Color." The first epigram reprinted above refers to a lynching as a reenactment of the crucifixion of Jesus. The second praises the black Simon the Cyrenian (see comments on previous poem) for carrying the cross of Jesus in contrast to the white Simon who denied him. The angry tone of the first epigram is supported by the sarcastic reference to a lynching as a play, and the accusatory tone of the second is enhanced by the brevity of the statement.

Cullen's two poems on Simon the Cyrenian should be compared with the four additional poems on the same subject (below, pp. 284-86), and with six poems on Peter's denial of Jesus (below, pp. 286-93).

A Thorn Forever in the Breast

A hungry cancer will not let him rest
Whose heart is loyal to the least of dreams;
There is a thorn forever in his breast
Who cannot take his world for what it seems;
Aloof and lonely must he ever walk,
Plying a strange and unaccustomed tongue,
An alien to the daily round of talk,
Mute when the sordid songs of earth are sung.

This is the certain end his dream achieves:
He sweats his blood and prayers while others sleep,
And shoulders his own coffin up a steep
Immortal mountain, there to meet his doom
Between two wretched dying men, of whom
One doubts, and one for pity's sake believes.

This sonnet should be compared with "Simon the Cyrenian Speaks" because both poems describe the suffering of a man of vision. Although the sestet refers to Gethsemane and Golgotha, the poem is not limited to Jesus. It portrays the isolation and doom experienced by an idealist who is driven to try to realize his dream of a better world. The restlessness of the dreamer is portrayed in a series of powerful images arranged in order of dramatic climax: it is a cancer, it is a thorn in his breast, it causes him to pray and sweat blood while others sleep (Gethsemane), and it forces him to carry his coffin up a steep mountain to meet his doom between two dying men (Golgotha). This portrait of an idealist driven to his death by his dreams seems almost too prophetic in the light of the murder of the famous black leader with a dream, Martin Luther King.

Yet Do I Marvel

I doubt not God is good, well-meaning, kind,
And did He stoop to quibble could tell why
The little buried mole continues blind,
Why flesh that mirrors Him must some day die,
Make plain the reason tortured Tantalus
Is baited by the fickle fruit, declare
If merely brute caprice dooms Sisyphus
To struggle up a never-ending stair.
Inscrutable His Ways are, and immune
To catechism by a mind too strewn
With petty cares to slightly understand
What awful brain compels His awful hand.
Yet do I marvel at this curious thing:
To make a poet black, and bid him sing!

This poem is a sarcastic sonnet, something a bit unusual in literature. It derives much of its strength from this unusual feature, especially since the first twelve lines pretend to accept on faith those aspects of creation that are hardest to explain: physical defects, death, and unproductive labor. "Inscrutable His ways are" (line 9) echoes the faith proclaimed in Romans 11:33, "O the depth of the riches both of the wisdom and knowledge of God! how unsearchable are his judgments, and his ways past finding out!" It also echoes the acceptance of God's power and wisdom in Job 9 and 42. This buildup of the traditional Judeo-Christian attitude toward God's omniscience, omnipotence, and omni-benevolence through twelve lines makes the reversal in the couplet all the more effective, especially since the couplet avoids stridency and continues the tone of restraint and apparent respect of the preceding lines. The deceptive verbal irony of the first twelve lines prepares for the striking situational irony of the couplet.

The final couplet should be compared with Psalm 137: how can anyone be expected to sing when he is in captivity, physical or psychological? This poem asks the question raised in Blake's "Tyger" (line 12 alludes to Blake's poem)—did the same Creator create both good and evil? It also asks the question underlying Milton's *Paradise Lost* and much of Fitzgerald's *Rubáiyát of Omar Khayyám*—can the ways of God be justified to man?

Black Magdalens

These have no Christ to spit and stoop
    To write upon the sand,
Inviting him that has not sinned
    To raise the first rude hand.

And if he came they could not buy
    Rich ointment for his feet,
The body's sale scarce yields enough
    To let the body eat.

The chaste clean ladies pass them by
    And draw their skirts aside,
But Magdalens have a ready laugh;
    They wrap their wounds in pride.

They fare full ill since Christ forsook
    The cross to mount a throne,
And Virtue still is stooping down
    To cast the first hard stone.

This poem combines several biblical allusions to deplore the wretched condition of black prostitutes. The first line refers to Jesus' healing of the blind and the deaf and the dumb with spit (John 9:1-6; Mark 7:31-35, 8:23-24). Lines 2–4 refer to Jesus' remonstrance to those who were critical of the woman taken in adultery (John 8:3-11). The second stanza refers to Jesus' defense of the fallen woman who washed his feet with her tears, dried them with her hair, and treated them with ointment (Luke 7:37-50). This woman is not named, but she is frequently identified with the Mary Magdalene of Luke 8:2 who had seven devils cast out of her. The third stanza alludes briefly to the priest and Levite who passed by on the other side rather than help the victim of a holdup. The black Magdalens, not having a good Samaritan to bind their wounds, wrap their wounds in pride (cf. Luke 10:30-37). The last line takes us back to the first stanza and Jesus' challenge to the accusers of the woman taken in adultery, except that now we have a significant reversal, and Virtue (capitalized) casts the first stone.

Cullen draws on all these vivid demonstrations of sympathy in the New Testament to show how much is being denied to the black Magdalens. Society has become hypocritical, has moved Jesus from the cross to the throne, and has caused Virtue to stoop down, not as Jesus did to defend someone in need, but to cast the first stone in a self-righteous manner.

For Daughters of Magdalen

> Ours is the ancient story:
> Delicate flowers of sin,
> Lilies, arrayed in glory,
> That would not toil or spin.

In this quatrain the fallen women speak for themselves and distort with great effect one of the most beautiful passages in the Bible in order to describe their dilemma. Jesus observed that the lilies of the field achieve their beauty without toiling or spinning, and urged his followers to demonstrate a comparable faith in the providence of God: "Consider the lilies of the field, how they grow; they toil not, neither do they spin: And yet I say unto you, That even

Solomon in all his glory was not arrayed like one of these"
(Matt. 6:28-29). The fallen women have refrained from
toiling and spinning—literally, not metaphorically as in the
Bible; as a result they have not lost their anxiety, as
promised by Jesus, but have instead become "delicate
flowers of sin."

Some readers may prefer a less serious interpretation of
the poem. The text and the allusion permit the poem to be
read in a variety of tones.

Comments on Other Poems by Cullen*

a. "The Litany of Dark People" *(Copper Sun)*

In "The Litany of Dark People" Cullen has reconciled the
conflict that appears in many of his other poems, the
difficulty of expecting black people to accept the white
man's Christianity. He asserts that the healing power of the
hem of Jesus' garment (line 6, cf. Matt. 9:20, 14:36) can help
the black people endure their suffering, provided they
approach it in the manner of Jesus. If they learn to merge
love and suffering, Bethlehem and Calvary, they will
develop a Christian spirit that will enable them to be
merciful to their persecutors on the judgment day.

Line 17 probably refers to Matthew 25:31-46 where Jesus
teaches that at the time of the last judgment the righteous
will be separated from the unrighteous on the basis of
whether they helped those in need. Cullen implies that if
the blacks are thrust into the role of a judge "when heaven's
constellations burst" they should display the spirit of Jesus
toward their adversaries, or "withholders."

Incidentally, the hem of Jesus' garment appears as a
metaphor in three other poems by Cullen. In "Little Sonnet
to Little Friends" the hem is a metaphor for the healing
influence he seeks in his lover, apparently deceased. In
"After a Visit" it expresses the attraction that poetry has

*The title of the Cullen book in which each poem appears is given in
parentheses.

for the Irish poets he met during a visit in Padraic Colum's rooms. He was inspired by the total commitment of the Irish poets to their poetry: they could not believe "That Poetry could pass and they not grasp her hem,/Not cry on her for healing. . . ." In "The Black Christ" the hem of beauty was the attraction that brought a black man and a white woman together and caused the lynching that is dramatized in that poem. Another poet who frequently used the same metaphor is John Greenleaf Whittier (see his poems "The Healer," "The Chapel Hermits," "Our Master," "The Human Sacrifice," "A Spiritual Manifestation," "A Legacy," and "At Washington").

b. "Never the Final Stone" *(The Black Christ)*

Poets have frequently observed that perfection is monotonous, that imperfection adds interest and variety to life. In "Never the Final Stone" Cullen looks upon imperfection and incompleteness in a slightly different way; it is an inducement to man to improve himself. He changes the story of the Tower of Babel in Genesis 11 in order to reach the conclusion that George Herbert reached in his poem "The Pulley": God withholds complete fulfillment from man so that he has reason to seek the assistance of God.

c. "To a Brown Girl—For Roberta" *(Color)*

The tone of "To a Brown Girl," calling for the enjoyment of the present moment, depends on how the biblical allusions are interpreted. The last stanza can be read in at least two ways. If the word "end" in line 9 is taken literally to mean the end of the life of Jesus, then Cullen is probably referring to Mary Magdalene and the "other Mary" at the cross and the tomb of Jesus (Matt. 27:57-61) and sardonically implying, "What's the use? In the end you'll see your ideals defeated, so why not live it up?" However, if the word "end" is read figuratively to mean "in the long run" or "in the last analysis," then the last stanza becomes less bitter. Magdalen and Mary would then stand for two

217

approaches to life that should be accepted from the start, for eventually they "consort" together anyhow and cannot be separated. In "On Melancholy" Keats concluded that a life of unalloyed beauty and happiness is impossible. Cullen seems to have reached a similar conclusion about the role of Magdalen and Mary in the life of the black woman he is addressing.

d. "Lines to My Father" *(Copper Sun)*

Cullen's father was a successful Methodist minister in Harlem, so it is only natural that Cullen should express his admiration for his father in biblical language. His father deserves the good things that have come to him because he reaps what he has sown (cf. Gal. 6:7-9). He has tilled the soil by the sweat of his brow (cf. Gen. 3:19), and he deserves to be praised as a tree bearing good fruit (cf. Matt. 7:17-19) and as a servant worthy of his hire (cf. Luke 10:7). He has seen his dreams come true because they were built on solid rock rather than on sand (cf. Matt. 7:24-27). The cumulative effect of all these biblical allusions is that his father emerges as a person who has followed closely the teachings of the Bible and is enjoying the rewards of the good life.

e. "Dialogue" *(Color)*

Dialogues between body and soul occur frequently in medieval literature, usually centering on the conflict between spiritual and worldly desires. Cullen has adapted this tradition to point up the difference between the aesthetic and the practical aspects of life, the individual's need for beauty and for physical sustenance. Since Soul is given twice as many lines as Body, we might assume that Cullen is arguing for a greater emphasis on the aesthetic side of life; yet Body has the last word and concludes the poem with an unanswered question. The biblical allusions help to clarify and generalize Soul's message: song is like a Jacob's ladder that opens a new world to the singer (cf. Gen. 28:10-22) and it gives the singer the divine blessings set forth in Psalm 23.

Cullen has three other poems about poetry in which he uses the Bible to illustrate his statement: "Two Poets" (Luke 7:38), "After a Visit" (Matt. 9:20 and 14:36), and "That Bright Chimeric Beast" (Pss. 74:14 and 104:26; Job 41; and Isa. 27:1), the last poem being in some ways a variation on Keats' "Ode on a Grecian Urn." "Dialogue" could be compared with many other poems that deal with the difference between the beautiful and the practical, the ideal and the real, such as Robert Frost's "A Tuft of Flowers" and Keats' "Ode to a Nightingale."

f. "The Black Christ" *(The Black Christ)*

An interesting adaptation and reenactment of the crucifixion and the resurrection. The speaker's brother is lynched for enjoying the rites of spring with a white girl and then appears as Christ to his mother and to his surviving brother. This poem of more than a thousand lines has some dramatic scenes and some effective preaching—the spirit of the lynched man converts his brother from mockery to faith. The references to the Bible include Jacob's vision of the angels, Jacob's wrestling with God, Adam, the exodus from Egypt, Damascus, the washing of hands, and such phrases as "milk and honey," "hem of beauty," "whom seek ye," and "mother, behold thy son." Eleanor Roosevelt was so moved by this poem that she thought it should be required reading in all high schools.

g. "Heritage" *(Color)*

A poem of 128 lines in which the speaker describes the conflict in him between his African heritage and his commitment to the white Christ, who he wishes were black. Some critics consider this Cullen's best poem. One clear reference to the Bible, the Christ of the "twice-turned cheek" (Matt. 5:39), occurs near the end of the poem.

h. "Judas Iscariot" *(Color)*

Like Edgar Lee Masters in a poem with the same title, Cullen is sympathetic to Judas, saying that he was a victim of a divine plan that forced the betrayal on him to enable Jesus to fulfill his mission. Judas is pictured as having a regular place among the twelve disciples at Jesus' table. One of the successful features of this poem is that the strong regular beat running without interruption through 96 lines does not detract from the serious tone.

i. "The Wind Bloweth Where It Listeth" *(Copper Sun)*

A poem in thirteen ballad stanzas telling of a feckless lover who fathers a son out of wedlock and defends his refusal to marry with the words "live like the wind" and don't get tied down to any person. The allusion to John 3:8 in the title seems rather strained, or ironical, because the poem has little connection with Jesus' statement to Nicodemus that the life of the spirit is as mysterious as the blowing of the wind; we hear its sound but cannot tell where it comes from or where it goes. When Bob Dylan says in his song "Blowin' in the Wind" that the answers to many difficult questions are blowing in the wind, he is closer to John 3:8 than Cullen seems to be in this poem.

j. Other Poems with Biblical Allusions

For the sake of completeness, I will list the other poems by Cullen that contain biblical allusions. An asterisk indicates that the poem was reprinted in *On These I Stand*, 1947.

In *Color*, 1925: "For an Anarchist," "For a Skeptic," "Sacrament," "Oh, for a Little While Be Kind," "The Shroud of Color,"* "For a Preacher," and "Bread and Wine."

In *Copper Sun*, 1927: "One Day We Played a Game," "Lines Written in Jerusalem," "In Spite of Death," "Threnody for a Brown Girl,"* "At the Wailing Wall,"* and "Protest."*

In *The Black Christ*, 1929: "Ultima Verba," "The Law That Changeth Not," "Asked and Answered," "Mood,"* "Black Majesty," "By Their Fruits," "Valedictory," and "A Miracle Demanded."

In *The Lost Zoo*, 1940: "The Wakeupworld"* and "The-Snake-That-Walked-Upon-His-Tail,"* two fables for children about animals that didn't quite make it into Noah's ark.

"La Belle, La Douce, La Grande"—General de Gaulle receiving Elijah's mantle from Joan of Arc—was published for the first time in *On These I Stand*.

"Christ Recrucified," first published in *Kelley's Magazine*, October, 1922, was not reprinted until Jean Wagner printed and analyzed it in *Black Poets of the United States* (translated from the French by Kenneth Douglas, University of Illinois Press, 1973). The poem is a bitter denunciation of lynchings in the South.

III A. E. Housman
(1859–1936)*

Alfred Edward Housman was a famous classical scholar and professor of Latin at Cambridge University in England. He published three volumes of poems, *A Shropshire Lad* (1896), *Last Poems* (1922), and *More Poems* (1936). His poems are always concise and usually pessimistic in tone. Readers should be aware that when he refers to the Bible, he seldom preserves the original meaning of the passage. Only a few of Housman's poems have titles; most of them have to be referred to by number.

Poem 45 of *A Shropshire Lad*

If it chance your eye offend you,
  Pluck it out, lad, and be sound:
'Twill hurt, but here are salves to friend you,
  And many a balsam grows on ground.

And if your hand or foot offend you,
  Cut it off, lad, and be whole;
But play the man, stand up and end you,
  When your sickness is your soul.

The first six lines paraphrase the teaching of Jesus concerning the importance of avoiding temptation to sin (Matt. 5:29-30, 18:8-9; Mark 9:43-47). The last two lines, recommending suicide as the manly way to deal with despair, contradict these passages. What is the effect of this unusual juxtaposition, quoting the Bible approvingly and then adding a contradictory thought?

*Commentary by Roland Bartel.

The Carpenter's Son
Poem 47 of *A Shropshire Lad*

"Here the hangman stops his cart:
Now the best of friends must part.
Fare you well, for ill fare I:
Live, lads, and I will die.

"Oh, at home had I but stayed
'Prenticed to my father's trade,
Had I stuck to plane and adze,
I had not been lost, my lads.

"Then I might have built perhaps
Gallow-trees for other chaps,
Never dangled on my own,
Had I but left ill alone.

"Now, you see, they hang me high,
And the people passing by
Stop to shake their fists and curse;
So 'tis come from ill to worse.

"Here hang I, and right and left
Two poor fellows hang for theft:
All the same's the luck we prove,
Though the midmost hangs for love.

"Comrades all, that stand and gaze,
Walk henceforth in other ways;
See my neck and save your own:
Comrades all, leave ill alone.

"Make some day a decent end,
Shrewder fellows than your friend.
Fare you well, for ill fare I:
Live, lads, and I will die."

The speaker in this poem draws several parallels between himself and Jesus: they were both sons of carpenters, they were both ridiculed when they were publicly executed, and they were both executed between thieves. The meaning of these parallels depends upon the interpretation of lines 12 and 24. What does the speaker mean when he says that he should have left "ill alone"? Is he admitting that he did wrong, or is he saying that he tried to correct the ills of society? Is he bitter about his mistakes and urging others not to follow his example, or is he cynical about the fact that society executes both its criminals and its saviors? If the latter interpretation is preferred, then the speaker belittles the sacrifice of Jesus as well as his own and urges his friends not to get involved in trying to help mankind. If the allusion works both ways and makes a comment on the ministry of Jesus as well as on the life of the speaker, then on one level of interpretation the poem should be read as if Jesus were speaking all the lines except the first one.

Poem 2 of *More Poems*

When Israel out of Egypt came
 Safe in the sea they trod;
By day in cloud, by night in flame,
 Went on before them God.

He brought them with a stretched out hand
 Dry-footed through the foam,
Past sword and famine, rock and sand,
 Lust and rebellion, home.

I never over Horeb heard
 The blast of advent blow;
No fire-faced prophet brought me word
 Which way behoved me go.

Ascended is the cloudy flame,
 The mount of thunder dumb;
The tokens that to Israel came,
 To me they have not come.

I see the country far away
 Where I shall never stand;
The heart goes where no footstep may
 Into the promised land.

The realm I look upon and die
 Another man will own;
He shall attain the heaven that I
 Perish and have not known.

But I will go where they are hid
That never were begot,
To my inheritance amid
The nation that is not.

In the first two stanzas the speaker reviews God's guidance of the Israelites during the Exodus, in the third and fourth stanzas he complains that he has never experienced such guidance, in the fifth and sixth stanzas he says that he is like Moses in that he cannot enter the promised land of his dreams, and in the last stanza he resigns himself to the finality of his own death. How do the references to the Bible in the first two stanzas affect the statements in the third and fourth stanzas? How do all the references to the Bible, especially the comparison with Moses, affect the statement in the final stanza?

Poem 22 of *More Poems*

Ho, everyone that thirsteth
And hath the price to give,
Come to the stolen waters,
Drink and your soul shall live.

Come to the stolen waters,
And leap the guarded pale,
And pull the flower in season
Before desire shall fail.

It shall not last for ever,
No more than earth and skies;
But he that drinks in season
Shall live before he dies.

June suns, you cannot store them
To warm the winter's cold,
The lad that hopes for heaven
Shall fill his mouth with mould.

This poem begins by quoting a prophet's call for spiritual rebirth (Isa. 55:1) and then switches to the words of the foolish woman calling for the enjoyment of secret pleasures (Prov. 9:17). After the first two lines, the poem becomes a *carpe diem* poem calling for the enjoyment of the present moment. Line 8 draws support from Proverbs 12:5 for the idea that one should enjoy one's pleasures while one is young. To what extent do the first two lines from Isaiah support the tone of the rest of the poem?

When Adam walked in Eden young

When Adam walked in Eden young,
　　Happy, 'tis writ, was he,
While high the fruit of knowledge hung
　　Unbitten on the tree.

Happy was he the livelong day;
　　I doubt 'tis written wrong:
The heart of man, for all they say,
　　Was never happy long.

And now my feet are tired of rest,
　　And here they will not stay,
And the soul fevers in my breast
　　And aches to be away.

This poem makes sense only if the word "doubt" in line 6 is given the old meaning of "suspect" or "fear." The speaker is saying that he suspects that the Bible is wrong in describing Adam as being completely happy before he partook of the tree of knowledge. He reaches the same conclusion as the speaker in Tennyson's "Ulysses": if life is to be enjoyed it must be regarded as a series of unending experiences and challenges. What are the major differences between the way Housman uses Adam and the way Tennyson uses Ulysses to develop essentially the same theme?

Poem 35 of *More Poems*

Half-way, for one commandment broken,
　　The woman made her endless halt,
And she to-day, a glistering token,
　　Stands in the wilderness of salt.
Behind, the vats of judgment brewing
　　Thundered, and thick the brimstone snowed;
He to the hill of his undoing
　　Pursued his road.

On the surface this poem seems to do nothing more than retell the main events of Genesis 19—the destruction of Sodom and Gomorrah, Lot's wife being turned into a pillar of salt, and Lot's escape into the mountains where he was disgraced by his daughters. Underneath the surface, other things are implied. Is the poet asking, among other things, whether Lot's fate is really very much different from that of his wife?

IV Arna Bontemps
(1902–1973)*

As editor of anthologies, as novelist, short-story writer, teacher, poet, and writer of prose essays, Bontemps was an effective champion of the literature written by black Americans. He was born in Louisiana and lived in California, New York, Illinois, and Kentucky. For twenty-two years he was the librarian at Fisk University. In 1926 "Golgotha Is a Mountain" won the Alexander Pushkin Award for Poetry, given by *Opportunity*, the magazine for which Countee Cullen edited the column "The Dark Tower."

Gethsemane

All that night I walked alone and wept,
I tore a rose and dropped it on the ground.
My heart was lead; all that night I kept
Listening to hear a dreadful sound.

A tree bent down and dew dripped from its hair.
The earth was warm; dawn came solemnly.
I stretched full-length upon the grass and there
I said your name but silence answered me.

The only allusion to the Bible in this poem is in the title. Because of the universal association of Gethsemane with the extreme agony of Jesus before the crucifixion, we can assume from the title that the speaker has suffered a painful loss, probably the death of a friend as implied in the last line.

Nocturne at Bethesda

I thought I saw an angel flying low,
I thought I saw the flicker of a wing

*Commentary by Roland Bartel.

Above the mulberry trees; but not again.
Bethesda sleeps. This ancient pool that healed
A host of bearded Jews does not awake.
This pool that once the angels troubled does not move.
No angel stirs it now, no Saviour comes
With healing in His hands to raise the sick
And bid the lame man leap upon the ground.

The golden days are gone. Why do we wait
So long upon the marble steps, blood
Falling from our open wounds? and why
Do our black faces search the empty sky?
Is there something we have forgotten? some precious
        thing
We have lost, wandering in strange lands?

There was a day, I remember now,
I beat my breast and cried, "Wash me God,
Wash me with a wave of wind upon
The barley; O quiet One, draw near, draw near!
Walk upon the hills with lovely feet
And in the waterfall stand and speak.

"Dip white hands in the lily pool and mourn
Upon the harps still hanging in the trees
Near Babylon along the river's edge,
But oh, remember me, I pray, before
The summer goes and rose leaves lose their red."

The old terror takes my heart, the fear
Of quiet waters and of faint twilights.
There will be better days when I am gone
And healing pools where I cannot be healed.
Fragrant stars will gleam forever and ever
Above the place where I lie desolate.

Yet I hope, still I long to live.
And if there can be returning after death
I shall come back. But it will not be here;
If you want me you must search for me
Beneath the palms of Africa. Or if
I am not there then you may call to me
Across the shining dunes, perhaps I shall
Be following a desert caravan.

I may pass through centuries of death
With quiet eyes, but I'll remember still

A jungle tree with burning scarlet birds.
There is something I have forgotten, some precious
    thing.
I shall be seeking ornaments of ivory,
I shall be dying for a jungle fruit.

       You do not hear, Bethesda.
O still green water in a stagnant pool!
Love abandoned you and me alike.
There was a day you held a rich full moon
Upon your heart and listened to the words
Of men now dead and saw the angels fly.
There is a simple story on your face;
Years have wrinkled you. I know, Bethesda!
You are sad. It is the same with me.

The background for this poem is found in John 5:2-9. The healing pool that has lost its power is an appropriate symbol for a black poet who laments the long wait for racial justice. In the second stanza the speaker identifies the lot of the blacks with that of the helpless man who for thirty-eight years has seen others step ahead of him when the waters of Bethesda possess their healing powers. In the third stanza he strengthens his prayer for healing and direction by invoking a prophet's promise of release from captivity (Isa. 52:7). In the fourth stanza he concludes his prayer by invoking another famous passage concerning the plight of captives, Psalm 137.

Golgotha Is a Mountain

Golgotha is a mountain, a purple mound
Almost out of sight.
One night they hanged two thieves there,
And another man.
Some women wept heavily that night;
Their tears are flowing still. They have made a river;
Once it covered me.
Then the people went away and left Golgotha
Deserted.
Oh, I've seen many mountains:
Pale purple mountains melting in the evening mists and
    blurring on the borders of the sky.

I climbed old Shasta and chilled my hands in its summer
    snows.
I rested in the shadow of Popocatepetl and it whispered
    to me of daring prowess.
I looked upon the Pyrenees and felt the zest of warm
    exotic nights.
I slept at the foot of Fujiyama and dreamed of legend
    and of death.
And I've seen other mountains rising from the wistful
    moors like the breasts of a slender maiden.
Who knows the mystery of mountains!
Some of them are awful, others are just lonely.

*   *   *

Italy has its Rome and California has San Francisco,
All covered with mountains.
Some think these mountains grew
Like ant hills
Or sand dunes.
That might be so—
I wonder what started them all!
Babylon is a mountain
And so is Nineveh,
With grass growing on them;
Palaces and hanging gardens started them.
I wonder what is under the hills
In Mexico
And Japan!
There are mountains in Africa too.
Treasure is buried there:
Gold and precious stones
And moulded glory.
Lush grass is growing there
Sinking before the wind.
Black men are bowing.
Naked in that grass
Digging with their fingers.
I am one of them:
Those mountains should be ours.
It would be great
To touch the pieces of glory with our hands.
These mute unhappy hills,
Bowed down with broken backs,
Speak often one to another:
"A day is as a year," they cry,
"And a thousand years as one day."

We watched the caravan
That bore our queen to the courts of Solomon;
And when the first slave traders came
We bowed our heads.
"Oh, Brothers, it is not long!
Dust shall yet devour the stones
But we shall be here when they are gone."
Mountains are rising all around me.
Some are so small they are not seen;
Others are large.
All of them get big in time and people forget
What started them at first.

Oh the world is covered with mountains!
Beneath each one there is something buried:
Some pile of wreckage that started it there.
Mountains are lonely and some are awful.

*　　*　　*

One day I will crumble.
They'll cover my heap with dirt and that will make a
　　mountain.
I think it will be Golgotha.

The poem begins and ends with the word "Golgotha," the name of the knoll where Jesus was crucified. The first nine lines refer to the suffering and sorrow associated with the crucifixion. Golgotha is not literally a mountain, so we have to look for the symbolic meanings of the term "mountain" as it is used here and elsewhere in the poem. Lines 10 and 11 suggest that mountains will be the basic symbol in the poem.

In lines 12–18 the speaker recalls his romantic associations with four real mountains, but he immediately changes to symbolic mountains which he personifies as "awful" and "lonely." After he refers to the hills of Rome and San Francisco and the cities of Babylon and Nineveh as mountains, the speaker asks what started these symbolic mountains and what lies under the literal mountains of Mexico and Japan. When he shifts to his homeland of Africa, his meditation becomes more personal and more intense. At first the mountains of Africa seem to represent the beauty of nature uncontaminated by civilization, but after a few lines the mountains are "unhappy hills . . . with broken backs," apparently suffering from the exploitation of the mining companies. The speaker telescopes almost thirty centuries into four lines when he recalls that his people saw the caravan of the Queen of Sheba (I Kings 10:1-13) and the coming of the slave traders. The mountains speak out and remind the speaker that the time span he has imagined is of little consequence to them (Ps. 90) and that they will actually outlast the human race. The speaker is depressed and feels mountains closing in on him, prompting him to think that his own grave will be a mountain like Golgotha.

What do the mountains symbolize? When a symbol has as many meanings as the mountains have in this poem, we should start with a general interpretation and narrow it down only as much as the text allows. Are the mountains various kinds of human experience—the suffering at Golgotha, the mystery and excitement of real mountains, the achievements of civilization associated with Rome and San Francisco, the corruption associated with Babylon and Nineveh, the exploitation associated with mining the hills of Africa, etc., etc.? If so, what is the speaker's reaction to the various experiences he surveys? What is gained by using mountains as the basic symbol? Do mountains suggest that some experiences are beyond our control and overwhelm us because we do not understand them? What is suggested by the speaker's questions about what started the mountains or what is under the mountains? Do they indicate the speaker's awareness of the fluctuations in human experience from generation to generation (Babylon and Nineveh began as palaces and hanging gardens)? Do the questions also suggest that surface appearances often conceal the nature of reality? In what sense is Golgotha "almost out of sight" (line 2)? Is the river of tears (line 6) an allusion to the possibilities for redemption associated with Golgotha, or is it a symbol of despair? Which interpretation is most consistent with the rest of the poem? How is the element of time manipulated in various parts of the poem? What is the effect of juxtaposing Rome and San Francisco with Babylon and Nineveh?

This poem might be compared with a poem by another black writer who uses one basic symbol throughout his poem: Langston Hughes' "A Negro Speaks of Rivers." The tone of the two poems is quite different. How are the symbols of mountains and rivers in the two poems used to establish the tone and develop the theme?

V A Brief Interpretation of "Journey of the Magi"*

Elizabeth Drew
(deceased): Scholar and Poetry Critic

Thomas Stearns Eliot (1888–1965), born in St. Louis, Missouri, and educated at Harvard, the Sorbonne, and Oxford, has become one of the most influential poets and critics of our time. In 1913 he took up residence in London, and in 1927 he became a British citizen, subsequently joining the Anglican Church. His thorough knowledge of the Bible is revealed in his play *Murder in the Cathedral* and in such poems as "The Love Song of J. Alfred Prufrock," "Mr. Eliot's Sunday Morning Service," "Ash Wednesday," "A Song for Simeon," and the poem reprinted below, "Journey of the Magi."

The first five lines are based on the following passage written by Lancelot Andrewes, one of the translators of the King James Version of the Bible: "It was no summer progress. A cold coming they had of it at this time of the year, just the worst time of the year to take a journey, and specially a long journey in. The ways deep, the weather sharp, the days short, the sun farthest off, *in solsitio brumali*, 'the very dead of winter.'"—Ed.

Journey of the Magi

'A cold coming we had of it,
Just the worst time of the year
For a journey, and such a long journey:
The ways deep and the weather sharp,
The very dead of winter.'
And the camels galled, sore-footed, refractory,
Lying down in the melting snow.
There were times we regretted
The summer palaces on slopes, the terraces,

*From *Poetry: A Modern Guide to Its Understanding and Enjoyment* (New York: Dell Books, 1959), pp. 239 f. Reprinted by permission of the Office of the Treasurer, Smith College.

And the silken girls bringing sherbet.
Then the camel men cursing and grumbling
And running away, and wanting their liquor and women,
And the night-fires going out, and the lack of shelters,
And the cities hostile and the towns unfriendly
And the villages dirty and charging high prices:
A hard time we had of it.
At the end we preferred to travel all night,
Sleeping in snatches,
With the voices singing in our ears, saying
That this was all folly.

Then at dawn we came down to a temperate valley,
Wet, below the snow line, smelling of vegetation;
With a running stream and a water-mill beating the darkness,
And three trees on the low sky,
And an old white horse galloped away in the meadow.
Then we came to a tavern with vine-leaves over the lintel,
Six hands at an open door dicing for pieces of silver,
And feet kicking the empty wine-skins.
But there was no information, and so we continued
And arrived at evening, not a moment too soon
Finding the place; it was (you may say) satisfactory.

All this was a long time ago, I remember,
And I would do it again, but set down
This set down
This: were we led all that way for
Birth or Death? There was a Birth, certainly,
We had evidence and no doubt. I had seen birth and death,
But had thought they were different; this Birth was
Hard and bitter agony for us, like Death, our death.
We returned to our places, these Kingdoms,
But no longer at ease here, in the old dispensation,
With an alien people clutching their gods.
I should be glad of another death.

The title reminds us of the many medieval and Renaissance paintings of the Adoration, and prepares us for oriental warmth and color, and for the atmosphere of rejoicing "with exceeding great joy" of the Gospels. The insistent bleakness of the opening is therefore unexpected. The first few lines are a direct-quotation from one of the Nativity sermons of the seventeenth century Bishop Lancelot Andrewes, and the method of the poem follows a pattern that Eliot discerns and admires in Andrewes's prose: "Before extracting all the spiritual meaning of a text, Andrewes forces a concrete presence upon us." We hear nothing of the dream or the star of the Gospel story; the cold, the distance, the hardships and the total lack of any quickening presence blot out everything. The moments of regret for the ease and luxury they have left, the summer palaces and the silken girls, are the only personal emotions of the opening paragraph. Everything else is simple enumeration, without comment, of the things to be endured. One after another ("and" is repeated fifteen times in twelve lines), we hear of the obstacles provided by both nature and man to delay, embarrass or obstruct the journey. The adventure wins no support from others; they meet only dishonesty and suspicion, and they have little confidence in themselves as they push on in the darkness, haunted by doubts and with no sight of their goal.

The next paragraph opens with more hope. The rhythm softens and flows more easily. Dawn and dampness and a smell of growing things meets them in the valley, and a sudden intensification of energy, "with a running stream and a water-mill beating the darkness." Running water and the *beating* (suggesting the noise in the ear and the inner triumph of hope over doubt), bring the sense of a vital driving force at work, denying the voices that said it was all folly. These, and the trees and the galloping old horse and the vine-leaves over the tavern door speak of spring and freedom and fruitfulness. But behind the old man's straightforward enumeration of the facts, the reader senses the significance of the "three trees," of the sinister hands "dicing for pieces of silver." The Christian symbolism of the vine, ("I am the true Vine"), is contradicted by the "feet kicking the empty wine-skins." The promise of the "temperate valley" is shot through with ominous ironic signs. The transposing of hints of the crucifixion, of the dicing for Christ's garments and the thirty pieces of silver into the approach to Bethlehem foreshadow the basic ambiguity of the conclusion. Here, as among the mountains, is no clear guide, "no information." The final climax is baldly anti-climactic. The quest ends, not in failure, but in inadequacy. The fulfillment carries no *feeling* of fulfillment, or revelation. "Satisfactory" suggests a tone of flat disappointment, of recognition without illumination.

Instead, all the old man remembers is a bewildering sense of paradox. His faith is firm, "I would do it again," but what was the *purpose* of it all? Was it only to nullify "the old dispensation," and destroy their former ease? What kind of Birth is it that brings only hard and bitter agony of mind, far worse than the earlier physical sufferings of the journey and the nostalgic regrets for the palaces and girls? Now they are alienated forever from their own people and their old beliefs. The old man doesn't doubt the profound importance of the new truth that has been vouchsafed to them. But if it has set them free from the bondage to old idolatries, it has left them adrift in a time-world now empty of significance. It has brought no *creative* change into life. The old man is now so weary and disillusioned that his only longing is to end this time-world altogether.

No "pious insincerity" here; nothing but painful and moving truth of a period of personal spiritual drought skillfully dramatized and distanced into symbolic narrative. It illustrates well too Eliot's comment on the way to *read* religious poetry:

If we learn to read poetry properly, the poet never persuades us to believe anything. . . . What we learn from Dante or the Bhagavadgita or any other religious poetry is what it *feels* like to believe that religion.

VI Karl Shapiro's "Adam and Eve"*

Frederick Eckman

Department of English,
Bowling Green State University (Ohio)

Karl Shapiro (1913–   ) has enjoyed a distinguished career as a poet. In 1946 he received both the Pulitzer Prize and the Shelley Memorial Prize. He was a Guggenheim Fellow in 1944 and 1953, poetry consultant to the Library of Congress 1947–48, and editor of *Poetry* magazine 1950–55. He has taught at Johns Hopkins, Loyola University (Chicago), the University of Nebraska, the University of Wisconsin, and Indiana University.

The author of the following article discusses a series of seven poems that Shapiro published under the title "Adam and Eve." These poems, which will probably appeal to advanced students, may be found in Shapiro's book *Poems of a Jew*, published by Random House in 1958. Shapiro made the following comment about "Adam and Eve":

> These poems were originally printed under the title *Eden Retold*. The poems in this series are not symbolic but literal interpretations. That is, I wrote them according to my own interpretation of the lines in Genesis, where they are first presented. Rilke says that Adam was *determined* to leave the Garden. My argument in the poem is that God determined him to leave it. Much of the imagery of the poems is drawn from the *Zohar* or central work of the cabala, some from the renegade Freudian, Wilhelm Reich. The viewpoint of the sequence, that man is for the world, not for the afterworld, is Jewish.

—Ed.

One might summarize the thesis of "Adam and Eve" as *Cogito, ergo damnatus sum.* Certainly part of the truth resides there. But someone else has observed, "Sentience is

*From "Karl Shapiro's 'Adam and Eve,'" *Texas Studies in English*, 35 (1956):1-10 (3-10). Copyright the University of Texas Press. Reprinted by permission.

suffering"; and both of these characteristically modern attitudes pervade Shapiro's theme. The fall from grace is to him, in any case, something far more complex than mere weakness of the flesh. Nor can the figure of Satan as wily tempter satisfy him. The fate of Adam and Eve must, for contemporary man, relate necessarily and ironically to their emotional and intellectual growth. Selden Rodman's characterization of the poem as "a modern parable of lost innocence" may furnish us with a starting point.

The poem's ideological basis is secular and modern; its guiding metaphor is time, the passing of the seasons—spring and birth to autumn and death; its central metaphor is sexuality as knowledge and suffering. The seven parts make up an episodic narrative which presents Adam's growing consciousness, his morally ambivalent development from superior beast to guilt-ridden man. Shapiro has followed the sequence of Genesis rather than of *Paradise Lost*. Little of Milton's heroic and didactic paraphernalia is present: Satan as a recognizable character nowhere appears, and divine intervention comes always by brief, significant individual action. Shapiro's language is likewise simple and mythic, more Biblical than Miltonic. In tone and structure the poem bears a remarkable resemblance to Rilke's *Marienleben*.

"The Sickness of Adam" is thought, which leads to desire. In the first season of life he is innocent and mindless, but as the Garden becomes familiar

> He lost the lifted almost flower-like gaze
> Of a temple dancer. He began to walk
> Slowly, like one accustomed to be alone.
> He found himself lost in the field of talk;
> Thinking became a garden of its own.

Introspection brings the first powerful emotions ("terrors, and tears shed/Under a tree by him, for some new thought"); desire brings anger ("Once he flung a staff / At softly coupling sheep and struck the ram") and the first punishment (God makes him "lame/And wanderlust").

Later, gazing out at the wastelands beyond Eden, Adam's spirit grows troubled. He has begun to experience suffering, to feel the oppression of thought; and he asks the angel at the gate, "What danger am I in?" To the angel he has become contemptible, "the wingless thing that worried after sin"; and the angel's suddenly-unfurled wings give a sign that "the first season of our life was dead."

Eve's appearance, then, is an event of almost anticlimactic necessity. She comes not as a helpmeet but as the externalized desire that has tortured Adam—less a created being than an object removed by surgery. The first stage of man's lost innocence thus becomes final, as

> Far off, the latent streams began to flow
> And birds flew out of Paradise to nest
> On earth. Sadly the angel watched them go.

"The Recognition of Eve" by Adam begins as animal curiosity ("He hoped she was another of the brutes"), which soon turns to fear as Eve speaks her first word: *thou*. But when she touches the now-healing wound in his side, he is made aware of the reason for her presence:

> He thought the woman had hurt him. Was it she
> Or the same sickness seeking to return;
> Or was there any difference, the pain set free
> And she who seized him now as hard as iron?

Eve wanders away for water and as Adam watches her his sensibility deepens, takes on a new quality—admiration for another: "She found a pool/And there he followed shyly to observe./She was already turning beautiful."

"The Kiss" is a sonnet, a companion-piece to "The Recognition of Eve." Here sexual love is born. First they discover the almost accidental caress of fingertips, then of lips; and finally passion is awakened: "The third kiss was by force." Appropriately enough, their first love-talk is of the Tree—here the "Tree of Guilt," since knowledge of good and evil means, to a contemporary mind, chiefly knowledge of evil; more especially, of man's involvement in evil, hence guilt. Their fourth, all-surrendering kiss is spied upon by "something rustling hideously overhead." The two are made aware simultaneously of love and evil. Terrified by the serpent's presence, they hide.

The fourth and fifth poems of Shapiro's sequence are in all respects central. "The Tree of Guilt" recounts Eve's temptation; "The Confession" presents her subsequent involvement of Adam in sin and is the emotional climax of the suite. Thematically these two poems are the most complex and obscure of the group, yet they are in no real sense inconsistent with the poems that precede and follow them.

With the discovery of sexual love, Eve has reached a stage of emotional development which allows her to act independently of Adam, though less responsibly than he. She sets out to discover the Garden. Ignoring the Tree of Life, whose "whispers of immortality" she is incapable of understanding as yet, she stops at the Tree of Guilt—purposely, it appears, to invoke the Tree's spirit "the oracle of Love":

> So she came breathless to the lowlier one
> And like a priestess of the cult she knelt,
> Holding her breasts in token for a sign,
> And prayed the spirit of the burdened bough
> That the great power of the tree be seen.

Eve, too, is sick with a yearning for knowledge; but unlike Adam, who inquired of the angel at the gate, she has gone directly to the forbidden source. Tantalized by the mystery of sex, "the iridescence of the dove,/Stench of the he-goat, everything that joins," she commits the first act of idolatry. The serpent emerges from the tree and points its head at her loins. Then, out of the tree and rising above it, appears "the oracle of Love":

> it stood
> Straight as a standing-stone, and spilled its seed,
> And all the seed were serpents of the good.
> Again he seized the snake and from its lip
> It spat the venomous evil of the deed.

The poet's interpretative liberties thus consist of substituting for the gustatory symbol of the apple and the theological figure of Satan the phallic symbol of the snake and the Freudian figure of the spirit of guilt. Eve is here almost literally seduced—not by the serpent, who is only the means, but by the spirit of the tree, the oracle of Love. The revelation over, it is Eve whose condition suggests an apple, "fallen from the limb/And rotten." All desire spent, she kicks away the serpent now coiled at her feet and seeks Adam.

Most obscure of all the seven sections is "The Confession." Eve's partially-developed moral sense struggles between the deception she cannot wholly master and the need for forgiveness whose urgency she must obey, though she understands it but dimly. As in "The Kiss" discovery comes to Adam in four stages:

> He waited while she said, "Thou art the tree."
> And while she said, almost accusingly,
> Looking at nothing, "Thou art the fruit I took."
> She seemed smaller by inches as she spoke,
> And Adam wondering touched her hair and shook,
> Half understanding. He answered softly, "How?"
>
> And for the third time, in the third way, Eve:
> "The tree that rises from the middle part
> Of the garden." And almost tenderly, "Thou art
> The garden. *We.*"

Her intention apparently is to deceive and at the same time to implicate Adam in her sin; but she speaks more truth than she intends: for by her symbolism she accurately identifies Adam with the Spirit of Guilt. In the contemporary mind, guilt cannot be attributed to an external force like Satan; it is part and parcel of man's inheritance from God. Man's capacity for sin is as inevitable as his capacity for love or his expulsion from a Paradise he is too complex to inhabit.

On her fourth try at confession Eve attempts the factual

truth but is incapable of it. Instinctively she creates a new myth, one whose implications are less terrifying, though no less final, than the first: "'Under the tree I took the fruit of truth/From an angel. I ate it with my other mouth.'/And saying so, she did not know she lied." She has not, in fact, lied; again symbolically she has described her seduction. Adam, now fully aware of what has happened, weeps

> in the woman's heavy arms,
> Those double serpents, subtly winding forms
> That climb and drop about the manly boughs;
> And dry with weeping, fiery and aroused,
> Fell on her face to slake his terrible thirst
> And bore her body earthward like a beast.

The fall is complete, the cycle rounded out. Adam becomes the tree, Eve the loving, destroying serpent—his personified desire. The act of love evolves to a desperate, bestial struggle.

Part Six, "Shame," is a lyric interlude, dramatically an epilogue to "The Confession," thematically a comment in the poet's own voice on the moral significance of what has happened. Sated with each other, the lovers sleep ("The hard blood falls back in the manly fount,/The soft door closes under Venus' mount"), while the poet gravely meditates their dilemma:

> How to teach shame? How to teach nakedness
> To the already naked? How to express
> Nudity? How to open innocent eyes
> And separate the innocent from the wise?

His answer tells the entire moral history of each of us, as we relive Adam's fall by our painful journey from naked innocence to clothed, guilty manhood:

> By fruits of cloth and by the navel's bud,
> By itching tendrils and by strings of blood,
> By ugliness, by the shadow of our fear,
> By ridicule, by the fig-leaf patch of hair.

Adam and Eve awake to find their sexual nakedness clothed in hair, "the covering that reveals." Terrified by what they think is their metamorphosis into animals, they weep, howl, and hide their eyes. The stigmata of guilt now marks them and their posterity for all time.

The final section of the poem, "Exile," is the only part reminiscent of *Paradise Lost.* Something of the epic grandeur of Books XI and XII is recalled as the angel at the gate—the one whose unfurled wings in Part One had warned Adam against thinking overmuch about sin, and who had again appeared as an omen against the perils of love—now holds the flaming sword to point their way of departure. Somewhat like Milton's pair, who "hand in hand with wandring steps and slow,/Through Eden took their solitarie way," Shapiro's Adam and Eve come "Angrily, slowly by, like exiled kings. . . ./Stare in the distance long and overlong,/And then, like peasants, pitiful and strong,/Take the first step toward earth and hesitate."

As in Milton, Adam calls upon God; but here he speaks gravely, in the tones of a man fully habituated to the wordly condition:

> "My father, who has made the garden pall,
> Giving me all things and then taking all,
> Who with your opposite nature has endowed
>
> Woman, give us your hand for our descent.
> Needing us greatly, even in our disgrace,
> Guide us, for gladly do we leave this place
> For our own land and wished-for banishment."

Adam speaks with the knowledge of good and evil: he sees the fatal dualism as God's, merely personified in himself and Eve, and the fall from grace as as much a product of divine will as the creation. Man's home is not Eden but the outside world. One detects almost a feeling of relief in his words, the sense that things are now in their proper place.

Eve's lamentation here parallels Milton, though it is of course much briefer: "Guide us to Paradise," she prays. But there can be no return to innocence: the act of love is for

Eve a commitment to the world. Ahead of them the animals and birds move into the wasteland of earth, "the wild abyss." When Adam and Eve have passed beyond the gate of Paradise the angel, for a fourth and final time, signals them—this time by name:

> They turned in dark amazement and beheld
> Eden ablaze with fires of red and gold,
> The garden dressed for dying in cold flame.

And it was autumn, and the present world.

Autumn, the season of death, has come to man. His flourishing has been brief and troubled; the rest is to be a slow decline from innocence to guilt and dying. The poem's last line foreshadows all the tragic consequences of the Fall, stating in the seasonal metaphor what Milton more explicitly announced in his famous opening lines: "Of Man's first Disobedience and the Fruit/. . . whose mortal tast/ Brought Death into the World, and all our woe." But the secular modern mind will not accept Milton's assurance that "one greater Man" will come to "Restore us, and regain the blissful seat." The act of disobedience, because divinely willed, is final: the tendrils of love, knowledge, and guilt twine inextricably about us; they compose the human condition. Shapiro, in his melancholy summation, is the spokesman not only for a contemporary Christian society whose belief has been irrevocably damaged but also for the Jew, who (as he has told us earlier in "Synagogue")

> has no bedecked magnificat
> But sits in stricken ashes after death,
> Refusing grace; his grave is flowerless,
> He gutters in the tallow of his name.

Eve too is unforgiven by Judaism, which "womanless refuses grace/To the first woman as to Magdalene," and "doubts/Either full harlotry or the faultless birth." Though it refers specifically to the Jews, this closing passage from "Synagogue" can be read as a postscript to "Adam and Eve" which applies to all contemporary mankind:

We live by virtue of philosophy,
Past love, and have our devious reward.
For faith he gave us land and took the land,
Thinking us exiles of all humankind.
Our name is yet the identity of God
That storms the falling altar of the world.

In the kind of analysis I have made here many of the poem's uniquely poetic excellences—for instance, its rich metaphor, its exquisite rhythms, and its simple but powerful diction—have not been given the praise they deserve. I hope that the frequent quotations will help to compensate for this necessary neglect and to affirm my belief that the poem is also a triumph of artistry.

An equally misleading notion might be that "Adam and Eve" is a didactic poem, upon whose slender narrative thread Shapiro has strung the beads of his theology. Again I must caution against any such inference. I have said that the poem is mythic; and by this I mean no more or less than that Shapiro has retold, with surpassing skill and in terms of the modern consciousness, one of the great seminal myths of Western culture.

The poet forever writes with the past over his shoulder; he is not obliged to write *about* it, but he must write with an awareness of its omnipresence. And when he does choose to turn and face it, he must attempt to account for it—explain it to himself and his age; for otherwise it will remain a dark abyss of terror and he only a tiny, frightened contemporary. Myth, the accumulated wisdom of the collective imagination, must forever be reinterpreted to succeeding ages if it is to remain more than a quaint historic survival. Every age, it is true, creates its own myths; but the artists of every age have an equal obligation to preserve the mythic past. The artist does not accomplish this, of course, by superimposing his culture on the past—in the case of Adam and Eve, by making them moderns in an ancient setting. Such a result can only be comic—deliberately, as in Twain's "Extracts From Adam's Diary," or unconsciously, as in a Hollywood Biblical "epic." Nor can he redeem myth by archaeological restoration: scale-model dummies and fake ruins. The poet must—as Milton did and as, I believe, Shapiro has done—look at the past through his own contemporary eyes, the only eyes he *can* see with. Shapiro's poem interprets for his age the Judaic-Christian myth of man's creation and fall in much the same way that Rilke's *Marienleben* illuminates the life and character of the Blessed Virgin, Pound's "Canto I" the story of Odysseus' descent into Hell, Yeats's "Leda and the Swan" the ominous, terrifying conception of Helen. With the appearance of "Adam and Eve" Shapiro has placed himself in the succession of these great modern poets, whose artistry joins past and present with the golden cord of myth. All of which is a way of saying something that a more seasoned critic might not care to risk: that a poem scarcely six years published and still to be subjected to the erosions of time is a distinguished work of art, possibly a great one.

VII Henry Wadsworth Longfellow (1807–1882)

Biblical allusions are almost a commonplace in the poetry of Longfellow. In most poems the allusions serve to suggest a brief comparison, but in a few, as in "The Chamber over the Gate," the allusion is basic to the structure of the entire poem. Another poet whose use of the Bible is similar to that of Longfellow's is John Greenleaf Whittier.

The Chamber over the Gate[1]

Written October 30, 1878. Suggested to the poet when writing a letter of condolence to the Bishop of Mississippi, whose son, the Rev. Duncan C. Green, had died at his post at Greenville, Mississippi, September 15, during the prevalence of yellow fever.

> Is it so far from thee
> Thou canst no longer see,
> In the Chamber over the Gate,
> That old man desolate,
> Weeping and wailing sore
> For his son, who is no more?
>   O Absalom, my son!
>
> Is it so long ago
> That cry of human woe
> From the walled city came,
> Calling on his dear name,
> That it has died away
> In the distance of to-day?
>   O Absalom, my son!
>
> There is no far or near,
> There is neither there nor here,

[1] II Sam. 18:33.

There is neither soon nor late,
In that Chamber over the Gate,
Nor any long ago
To that cry of human woe,
    O Absalom, my son!

From the ages that are past
The voice sounds like a blast,
Over seas that wreck and drown,
Over tumult of traffic and town;
And from ages yet to be
Come the echoes back to me,
    O Absalom, my son!

Somewhere at every hour
The watchman on the tower
Looks forth, and sees the fleet
Approach of the hurrying feet
Of messengers, that bear
The tidings of despair.
    O Absalom, my son!

He goes forth from the door,
Who shall return no more.
With him our joy departs;
The light goes out in our hearts;
In the Chamber over the Gate
We sit disconsolate.
    O Absalom, my son!

That 't is a common grief
Bringeth but slight relief;
Ours is the bitterest loss,
Ours is the heaviest cross;
And forever the cry will be
"Would God I had died for thee,
    O Absalom, my son!"

The Jewish Cemetery at Newport

How strange it seems! These Hebrews
    in their graves,
  Close by the street of this fair seaport
    town,
Silent beside the never-silent waves,
  At rest in all this moving up and
    down!

The trees are white with dust, that o'er
    their sleep
  Wave their broad curtains in the south-
    wind's breath,
While underneath these leafy tents they
    keep
  The long, mysterious Exodus of Death.

And these sepulchral stones, so old and
    brown,
  That pave with level flags their burial-
    place,
Seem like the tablets of the Law,[2] thrown
    down
  And broken by Moses at the mountain's
    base.

The very names recorded here are strange,
  Of foreign accent, and of different
    climes;
Alvares and Rivera interchange
  With Abraham and Jacob of old times.

"Blessed be God, for he created Death!"
  The mourners said, "and Death is rest
    and peace;"
Then added, in the certainty of faith,
  "And giveth Life that nevermore shall
    cease."

Closed are the portals of their Synagogue,
  No Psalms of David now the silence
    break,
No Rabbi reads the ancient Decalogue
  In the grand dialect the Prophets spake.

Gone are the living, but the dead remain,
  And not neglected; for a hand unseen,
Scattering its bounty, like a summer rain,
  Still keeps their graves and their remembrance
    green.

How came they here? What burst of
    Christian hate,
  What persecution, merciless and blind,

[2] Exod. 32:19.

Drove o'er the sea—that desert desolate—
    These Ishmaels and Hagars of mankind?[3]

They lived in narrow streets and lanes obscure,
    Ghetto and Judenstrass, in mirk and mire;
Taught in the school of patience to endure
    The life of anguish and the death of fire.

All their lives long, with the unleavened
        bread
    And bitter herbs of exile and its fears,
The wasting famine of the heart they fed,
    And slaked its thirst with marah of their
        tears.

Anathema maranatha! was the cry
    That rang from town to town, from
        street to street:
At every gate the accursed Mordecai[4]
    Was mocked and jeered, and spurned by
        Christian feet.

Pride and humiliation hand in hand
    Walked with them through the world
        where'er they went;
Trampled and beaten were they as the
        sand,
    And yet unshaken as the continent.

For in the background figures vague and
        vast
    Of patriarchs and of prophets rose sublime,
And all the great traditions of the Past
    They saw reflected in the coming time.

And thus forever with reverted look
    The mystic volume of the world they
        read,
Spelling it backward, like a Hebrew book,
    Till life became a Legend of the Dead.

But ah! what once has been shall be no
        more!
    The groaning earth in travail and in pain
Brings forth its races, but does not restore,
    And the dead nations never rise again.

---

[3] Gen. 16, 21:8-21.
[4] The book of Esther.

Sand of the Desert in an Hour-Glass

A handful of red sand, from the hot
    clime
  Of Arab deserts brought,
Within this glass becomes the spy of Time,
  The minister of Thought.

How many weary centuries has it been
  About those deserts blown!
How many strange vicissitudes has seen,
  How many histories known!

Perhaps the camels of the Ishmaelite[5]
  Trampled and passed it o'er,
When into Egypt from the patriarch's sight
  His favorite son they bore.

Perhaps the feet of Moses, burnt and bare,
  Crushed it beneath their tread,
Or Pharaoh's flashing wheels into the air
  Scattered it as they sped;

Or Mary, with the Christ of Nazareth
  Held close in her caress,
Whose pilgrimage of hope and love and
    faith
  Illumed the wilderness;

Or anchorites beneath Engaddi's palms
  Pacing the Dead Sea beach,
And singing slow their old Armenian psalms
  In half-articulate speech;

Or caravans, that from Bassora's gate
  With westward steps depart;
Or Mecca's pilgrims, confident of Fate,
  And resolute in heart!

These have passed over it, or may have
    passed!
  Now in this crystal tower
Imprisoned by some curious hand at last,
  It counts the passing hour.

[5] Gen. 37:25-36.

And as I gaze, these narrow walls expand;—
  Before my dreamy eye
Stretches the desert with its shifting sand,
  Its unimpeded sky.

And borne aloft by the sustaining blast,
  This little golden thread
Dilates into a column high and vast,
  A form of fear and dread.

And onward, and across the setting sun,
  Across the boundless plain,
The column and its broader shadow run,
  Till thought pursues in vain.

The vision vanishes! These walls again
  Shut out the lurid sun,
Shut out the hot, immeasurable plain;
  The half-hour's sand is run!

The Slave in the Dismal Swamp

In dark fens of the Dismal Swamp
  The hunted Negro lay;
He saw the fire of the midnight camp,
And heard at times a horse's tramp
  And a bloodhound's distant bay.

Where will-o'-the-wisps and glow-worms
    shine,
  In bulrush and in brake;
Where waving mosses shroud the pine,
And the cedar grows, and the poisonous
    vine
  Is spotted like the snake;

Where hardly a human foot could pass,
  Or a human heart would dare,
On the quaking turf of the green morass
He crouched in the rank and tangled grass,
  Like a wild beast in his lair.

A poor old slave, infirm and lame,
  Great scars deformed his face;
On his forehead he bore the brand of
    shame,
And the rags, that hid his mangled frame,
  Were the livery of disgrace.

All things above were bright and fair,
　All things were glad and free;
Lithe squirrels darted here and there,
And wild birds filled the echoing air
　With songs of Liberty!

On him alone was the doom of pain,
　From the morning of his birth;
On him alone the curse of Cain[6]
Fell, like a flail on the garnered grain,
　And struck him to the earth!

The Warning

Beware! The Israelite of old,[7] who tore
　The lion in his path,—when, poor and
　　blind,
He saw the blessed light of heaven no more,
　Shorn of his noble strength and forced to
　　grind
In prison, and at last led forth to be
A pander to Philistine revelry,—

Upon the pillars of the temple laid
　His desperate hands, and in its overthrow
Destroyed himself, and with him those who
　made
　A cruel mockery of his sightless woe;
The poor, blind Slave, the scoff and jest of
　all,
Expired, and thousands perished in the fall!

There is a poor, blind Samson in this land,
　Shorn of his strength and bound in bonds
　　of steel,
Who may, in some grim revel, raise his hand,
　And shake the pillars of this Common-
　　weal,
Till the vast Temple of our liberties
A shapeless mass of wreck and rubbish lies.

[6] Gen. 4:11-16.
[7] Judg. 14–16.

To William E. Channing

The pages of thy book I read,
　　And as I closed each one,
My heart, responding, ever said,
　　"Servant of God! well done!"[8]

Well done! Thy words are great and bold;
　　At times they seem to me,
Like Luther's, in the days of old,
　　Half-battles for the free.

Go on, until this land revokes
　　The old and chartered Lie,
The feudal curse, whose whips and yokes
　　Insult humanity.

A voice is ever at thy side
　　Speaking in tones of might,
Like the prophetic voice, that cried
　　To John in Patmos, "Write!"[9]

Write! and tell out this bloody tale;
　　Record this dire eclipse,
This Day of Wrath, this Endless Wail,
　　This dread Apocalypse!

[8] Matt. 25:21.
[9] Rev. 1:9-11.

VIII Vachel Lindsay
(1879–1931)

[Nicholas] Vachel Lindsay wrote many of his poems for oral recitation and public performance. He made several walking tours through various parts of the United States, trading his verses and verse readings for room and board. "Daniel," "John Brown," "King Solomon and the Queen of Sheba," and "How Samson Bore Away the Gates of Gaza" are among the poems suitable for choral reading and dramatization. Looking up the biblical allusions in these poems will help the reader decide what kind of oral interpretation is most appropriate for each poem.

The two poems reprinted below use the Bible to praise President Theodore Roosevelt and his four sons. What is the effect of the allusions and how successful are they?

In Which Roosevelt Is Compared to Saul

(Written and published in 1913, and republished five years later, in the Boston *Transcript*, on the death of Roosevelt)

Where is David? . . . Oh God's people
Saul has passed, the good and great.
Mourn for Saul, the first anointed,
Head and shoulders o'er the state.

He was found among the prophets:
Judge and monarch, merged in one.
But the wars of Saul are ended,
And the works of Saul are done.

Where is David, ruddy shepherd,
God's boy-king for Israel?
Mystic, ardent, dowered with beauty,
Singing where still waters dwell?

Prophet, find that destined minstrel
Wandering on the range today,

Driving sheep, and crooning softly
Psalms that cannot pass away.

"David waits," the prophet answers,
"In a black, notorious den,
In a cave upon the border,
With four hundred outlaw men.

"He is fair and loved of women,
Mighty-hearted, born to sing:
Thieving, weeping, erring, praying,
Radiant royal rebel-king.

"He will come with harp and psaltry,
Quell his troop of convict swine,
Quell his mad-dog roaring rascals,
Witching them with tunes divine.

"They will ram the walls of Zion.
They will win us Salem hill,
All for David, shepherd David,
Singing like a mountain rill."

Hail to the Sons of Roosevelt

"Out of the eater came forth meat, and out of the strong came
forth sweetness."—Samson's riddle.

There is no name for brother
Like the name of Jonathan
The son of Saul.
And so we greet you all:
The sons of Roosevelt—
The sons of Saul.

Four brother Jonathans went out to battle.
Let every Yankee poet sing their praise
Through all the days—
What David sang of Saul
And Jonathan, beloved more than all.

God grant such sons, begot of our young men,
To make each generation glad again.
Let sons of Saul be springing up again:

Out of the eater, fire and power again.
From the lost lion, honey for all men.

I hear the sacred Rocky Mountains call,
I hear the Mississippi Jordan call:
*"Stand up, America, and praise them all,
Living and dead, the fine young sons of Saul!"*

IX Edgar Lee Masters (1869–1950)

Masters' poems on minor biblical figures have several things in common with his well known *Spoon River Anthology* (1915). In both groups of poems he speculates about the private lives of the people he is describing and freely adds confessions and revelations to make them more human. When he retells biblical episodes, he likewise embellishes his subject with realistic details not found in the Bible or in Bible commentaries.

"The Wedding Feast" is one of several poems in which Masters adds interesting details to a biblical story without disturbing its original tone. Other poems of a similar nature are "Simon Surnamed Peter" (see below, pp. 289-91) "Delilah," "Gabriel and Zacharias," "Tribute Money," and "John in Prison." "Business Reverses" represents another group of poems, those in which Masters adds some droll humor to well-known biblical stories. Others of this kind are "At Decapolis," "The Apology of Demetrius," "The Fig Tree," and "First Entrants." In his largest group of biblical poems, Masters adapts biblical material to social criticism, ranging in tone from cynicism to hostility. This group includes "The Two Malefactors," "The Single Standard," "The Great Merger," "Oh You Sabbatarians," "Cities of the Plain," and "Ananias and Sapphira."

Masters' *Selected Poems* (New York: Macmillan, 1925) contains all the poems mentioned above except "Delilah," first published in *Toward the Gulf* (1918), and "Oh You Sabbatarians," first published in *Starved Rock* (1919).

The Wedding Feast

(St. John, Chap. II)

Said the chief of the marriage feast to the groom,
Whence is this blood of the vine?

Men serve at first the best, he said,
   And at the last, poor wine.

Said the chief of the marriage feast to the groom,
   When the guests have drunk their fill
They drink whatever wine you serve,
   Nor know the good from the ill.

How have you kept the good till now
   When our hearts nor care nor see?
Said the chief of the marriage feast to the groom,
   Whence may this good wine be?

Said the chief of the marriage feast, this wine
   Is the best of all by far.
Said the groom, there stand six jars without
   And the wine fills up each jar.

Said the chief of the marriage feast, we lacked
   Wine for the wedding feast.
How comes it now one jar of wine
   To six jars is increased?

Who makes our cup to overflow?
   And who has the wedding blest?
Said the groom to the chief of the feast, a stranger
   Is here as a wedding guest.

Said the groom to the chief of the wedding feast,
   Moses by power divine
Smote water at Meribah from the rock,
   But this man makes us wine.

Said the groom to the chief of the wedding feast,
   Elisha by power divine
Made oil for the widow to sell for bread,
   But this man, wedding wine.

He changed the use of the jars, he said,
   From an outward rite and sign:
Where water stood for the washing of feet,
   For heart's delight there's wine.

So then 'tis he, said the chief of the feast,
   Who the wedding feast has blest?
Said the groom to the chief of the feast, the stranger
   Is the merriest wedding guest.

He laughs and jests with the wedding guests,
   He drinks with the happy bride.
Said the chief of the wedding feast to the groom,
   Go bring him to my side.

Jesus of Nazareth came up,
   And his body was fair and slim.
Jesus of Nazareth came up,
   And his mother came with him.

Jesus of Nazareth stands with the dancers
   And his mother by him stands.
The bride kneels down to Jesus of Nazareth
   And kisses his rosy hands.

The bridegroom kneels to Jesus of Nazareth
   And Jesus blesses the twain.
I go a way, said Jesus of Nazareth,
   Of darkness, sorrow and pain.

After the wedding feast is labor,
   Suffering, sickness, death,
And so I make you wine for the wedding,
   Said Jesus of Nazareth.

My heart is with you, said Jesus of Nazareth,
   As the grape is one with the vine.
Your bliss is mine, said Jesus of Nazareth,
   And so I make you wine.

Youth and love I bless, said Jesus,
   Song and the cup that cheers.
The rosy hands of Jesus of Nazareth
   Are wet with the young bride's tears.

Love one another, said Jesus of Nazareth,
   Ere cometh the evil of years.
The rosy hands of Jesus of Nazareth
   Are wet with the bridegroom's tears.

Jesus of Nazareth goes with his mother,
   The dancers are dancing again.
There's a woman who pauses without to listen,
   'Tis Mary Magdalen.

Forth to the street a Scribe from the wedding
   Goes with a Sadducee.
Said the Scribe, this shows how loose a fellow
   Can come out of Galilee!

Business Reverses

(St. Mark, Chap. VI)

Everything! Counter and scales—
    I'll take whatever you give.
I'm through, and off to Athens,
    Where a man like me can live.

And Hipparch, the baker, is going;
    My chum, who came with me
To follow the crowds who follow
    The prophet of Galilee.

We two were there at Damascus
    Dealing in figs and wine.
Nice little business! Some one
    Said: "Here, I'll give you a line!

"Buy fish, and set up a booth,
    Get a tent and make your bread.
There are thousands who come to listen,
    They are hungry and must be fed."

And so we went. Believe me,
    There were crowds, and hungry, too.
Five thousand stood in the desert
    And listened the whole day through.

Famished? Well, yes. The disciples
    Were saying to send them away
To buy their bread in the village,
    But the prophet went on to say:

"Feed them yourselves, O you
    Of little faith." But they said:
"We have just two little fishes
    And five little loaves of bread."

We heard it, me and Hipparch,
    And rubbed our hands. You see
We were there to make some money
    In the land of Galilee.

We had stock in plenty. We waited.
    I wiped the scales, and my chum
Re-stacked the loaves. We bellowed,
    But no one seemed to come.

"Fresh fish!" I bawled my lungs out:
    "Nice bread!" poor Hipparch cried,
But what did they do? Sat down there
    In fifties, side by side,

In ranks, the whole five thousand.
    Then—well, the prophet spoke,
And broke the two little fishes,
    And the five little loaves he broke,

And fed the whole five thousand.
    Why, yes! So gorged they slept.
And we stood beaten and bankrupt.
    Poor Hipparch swore and wept.

They gathered up twelve baskets
    Full from the loaves of bread;
    Two fishes made twelve baskets
    Of fragments after they fed.

And we—what was there to do
    But dump our stock on the sand?
That's what we got for our labor
    And thrift, in such a land.

We met a man near Damascus
    Who had joined the mystagogues.
He said: "I was wicked as you men
    Until I lost my hogs."

Now Hipparch and I are going
    To Athens, beautiful, free.
No more adventures for us two
    In the land of Galilee.

X Edwin Muir (1887–1959)

The poems of Edwin Muir have an intellectual quality that makes them seem a bit obscure at first, but they all repay careful reading. Anyone willing to read them thoughtfully and sympathetically finds them interesting and meaningful.

"The Heroes" is an Italian sonnet on one of the paradoxes of life: why is it that the fame of heroes increases after they have turned to dust in their graves? They did not have the advantage of a spectacular departure from this life, as did Elijah (II Kings 2:11). Why does their glory increase after they have lost their material identity? "Abraham" successfully evokes the spirit of the trusting Abraham, comparing his wanderings with the meandering of water. "The Succession" traces the passing of the faith from Abraham to Isaac to Jacob to succeeding generations down to our time and comments on the risks one is willing to take if one is guided by faith and hope. "The Killing" is a realistic account of the crucifixion as seen by a stranger who happened to be in Jerusalem and was deeply affected by what he saw. (This poem might be compared with another poem spoken by an observer of the crucifixion, Ezra Pound's "Ballad of the Goodly Fere.") "One Foot in Eden" raises the basic questions that keep recurring in all of Muir's poems: What are the consequences of the fall? Can Eden be recovered in our own lives? What is the connection between evil and love? "The Horses" reverses the process of creation as described in Genesis and merges this allusion with classical allusions—the fall of Icarus and the ferrying of the dead across the river in Hades—to describe the world after a nuclear war. Once man's technological world has destroyed itself, he is receptive to the values represented by the horses that come to him as emissaries from Eden. (George MacBeth's poem "Bedtime Story," spoken by a super-insect that has emerged after a nuclear war, would make an interesting comparison with "The Horses.")

Several other poems, all published in Muir's *Collected Poems* (New York: Oxford University Press, 1965), might be studied for their use of biblical material: "The Fall," "The Solitary Place," "Moses," "The Transfiguration," "The Toy Horse," "The Animals," "The Days," "Adam's Dream," "Outside Eden," "The Annunciation."

The Heroes

When these in all their bravery took the knock
And like obedient children swaddled and bound
Were borne to sleep within the chambered rock,
A splendour broke from that impervious ground,
Which they would never know. Whence came that greatness?
No fiery chariot whirled them heavenwards, they
Saw no Elysium opening, but the straitness
Of full submission bound them where they lay.

What could that greatness be? It was not fame.
Yet now they seemed to grow as they grew less,
And where they lay were more than where they had stood.
They did not go to any beatitude.
They were stripped clean of feature, presence, name,
When that strange glory broke from namelessness.

Abraham

The rivulet-loving wanderer Abraham
Through waterless wastes tracing his fields of pasture
Led his Chaldean herds and fattening flocks
With the meandering art of wavering water
That seeks and finds, yet does not know its way.
He came, rested and prospered, and went on,
Scattering behind him little pastoral kingdoms,
And over each one its own particular sky,
Not the great rounded sky through which he journeyed,
That went with him but when he rested changed.
His mind was full of names
Learned from strange peoples speaking alien tongues,
And all that was theirs one day he would inherit.
He died content and full of years, though still
The Promise had not come, and left his bones,
Far from his father's house, in alien Canaan.

The Succession

Legendary Abraham,
The old Chaldean wanderer,
First among these peoples came,
Cruising above them like a star
That is in love with distances
And has through age to calmness grown,
Patient in the wilderness
And untarrying in the sown.
At last approached his setting mark.
Thence he sent his twin star out,
Isaac, to revolve alone.
For two great stars that through an age
Play in their corner of the sky,
Separate go into the dark,
And ere they end their roundabout
One must live and one must die.

Isaac in his tutelage
Wheeled around the father light.
Then began his pilgrimage
Through another day and night,
Other peoples, other lands.
Where the father could not go
There is gone the careless son.
He can never miss his way.
By strangers' hands to strangers' hands
He is carried where he will.
Free, he must the powers obey,
Serve, be served by good and ill,
Safe through all the hazards run.
All shall watch him come and go
Until his quittance he has won;
And Jacob wheels into the day.

We through the generations came
Here by a way we do not know
From the fields of Abraham,
And still the road is scarce begun.
To hazard and to danger go
The sallying generations all
Where the imperial highways run.
And our songs and legends call
The hazard and the danger good;

For our fathers understood
That danger was by hope begot
And hazard by revolving chance
Since first we drew the enormous lot.

The Killing

That was the day they killed the Son of God
On a squat hill-top by Jerusalem.
Zion was bare, her children from their maze
Sucked by the demon curiosity
Clean through the gates. The very halt and blind
Had somehow got themselves up to the hill.

After the ceremonial preparation,
The scourging, nailing, nailing against the wood,
Erection of the main-trees with their burden,
While from the hill rose an orchestral wailing,
They were there at last, high up in the soft spring day.

We watched the writhings, heard the moanings, saw
The three heads turning on their separate axles
Like broken wheels left spinning. Round *his* head
Was loosely bound a crown of plaited thorn
That hurt at random, stinging temple and brow
As the pain swung into its envious circle.
In front the wreath was gathered in a knot
That as he gazed looked like the last stump left
Of a death-wounded deer's great antlers. Some
Who came to stare grew silent as they looked,
Indignant or sorry. But the hardened old
And the hard-hearted young, although at odds
From the first morning, cursed him with one curse,
Having prayed for a Rabbi or an armed Messiah
And found the Son of God. What use to them
Was a God or a Son of God? Of what avail
For purposes such as theirs? Beside the cross-foot,
Alone, four women stood and did not move
All day. The sun revolved, the shadow wheeled,
The evening fell. His head lay on his breast,
But in his breast they watched his heart move on
By itself alone, accomplishing its journey.
Their taunts grew louder, sharpened by the knowledge
That he was walking in the park of death,
Far from their rage. Yet all grew stale at last,
Spite, curiosity, envy, hate itself.

They waited only for death and death was slow
And came so quietly they scarce could mark it.
They were angry then with death and death's deceit.

I was a stranger, could not read these people
Or this outlandish deity. Did a God
Indeed in dying cross my life that day
By chance, he on his road and I on mine?

One Foot in Eden

One foot in Eden still, I stand
And look across the other land.
The world's great day is growing late,
Yet strange these fields that we have planted
So long with crops of love and hate.
Time's handiworks by time are haunted,
And nothing now can separate
The corn and tares compactly grown.
The armorial weed in stillness bound
About the stalk; these are our own.
Evil and good stand thick around
In the fields of charity and sin
Where we shall lead our harvest in.

Yet still from Eden springs the root
As clean as on the starting day.
Time takes the foliage and the fruit
And burns the archetypal leaf
To shapes of terror and of grief
Scattered along the winter way.
But famished field and blackened tree
Bear flowers in Eden never known.
Blossoms of grief and charity
Bloom in these darkened fields alone.
What had Eden ever to say
Of hope and faith and pity and love
Until was buried all its day
And memory found its treasure trove?
Strange blessings never in Paradise
Fall from these beclouded skies.

The Horses

Barely a twelvemonth after
The seven days war that put the world to sleep,
Late in the evening the strange horses came.

By then we had made our covenant with silence,
But in the first few days it was so still
We listened to our breathing and were afraid.
On the second day
The radios failed; we turned the knobs; no answer.
On the third day a warship passed us, heading north,
Dead bodies piled on the deck. On the sixth day
A plane plunged over us into the sea. Thereafter
Nothing. The radios dumb;
And still they stand in corners of our kitchens,
And stand, perhaps, turned on, in a million rooms
All over the world. But now if they should speak,
If on a sudden they should speak again,
If on the stroke of noon a voice should speak,
We would not listen, we would not let it bring
That old bad world that swallowed its children quick
At one great gulp. We would not have it again.
Sometimes we think of the nations lying asleep,
Curled blindly in impenetrable sorrow,
And then the thought confounds us with its strangeness.

The tractors lie about our fields; at evening
They look like dank sea-monsters couched and waiting.
We leave them where they are and let them rust:
"They'll moulder away and be like other loam."
We make our oxen drag our rusty ploughs,
Long laid aside. We have gone back
Far past our fathers' land.
                                        And then, that evening
Late in the summer the strange horses came.
We heard a distant tapping on the road,
A deepening drumming; it stopped, went on again
And at the corner changed to hollow thunder.
We saw the heads
Like a wild wave charging and were afraid.
We had sold our horses in our fathers' time
To buy new tractors. Now they were strange to us
As fabulous steeds set on an ancient shield
Or illustrations in a book of knights.
We did not dare go near them. Yet they waited,
Stubborn and shy, as if they had been sent
By an old command to find our whereabouts
And that long-lost archaic companionship.
In the first moment we had never a thought
That they were creatures to be owned and used.
Among them were some half-a-dozen colts

Dropped in some wilderness of the broken world,
Yet new as if they had come from their own Eden.
Since then they have pulled our ploughs and borne our loads,
But that free servitude still can pierce our hearts.
Our life is changed; their coming our beginning.

XI D. H. Lawrence
(1885–1930)

Although David Herbert Lawrence is known primarily as an English novelist, his poetry has in recent years received an increasing amount of attention. Both his novels and his poems contain frequent biblical allusions. The poems printed below are only a few of those in which Lawrence alludes to the Bible. You will observe that Lawrence is fairly consistent in the way he uses the Bible. How would you describe his dominant tone? What are his primary themes?

Lord's Prayer [1]

For thine is the kingdom
the power, and the glory.

Hallowed be thy name, then
Thou who art nameless—

Give me, Oh give me
besides my daily bread
my kingdom, my power, and my glory.

All things that turn to thee
have their kingdom, their power, and their glory.

Like the kingdom of the nightingale at twilight
whose power and glory I have often heard and felt.

Like the kingdom of the fox in the dark
yapping in his power and his glory
which is death to the goose.

Like the power and the glory of the goose in the mist
honking over the lake.

[1] Matt. 6:9-13

And I, a naked man, calling
calling to thee for my mana,
my kingdom, my power, and my glory.

Fatality [2]

No one, not even God, can put back a leaf on to a tree
once it has fallen off.

And no one, not God nor Christ nor any other
can put back a human life into connection with the living
    cosmos
once the connection has been broken
and the person has become finally self-centred.

Death alone, through the long process of disintegration
can melt the detached life back
through the dark Hades at the roots of the tree
into the circulating sap, once more, of the tree of life.

Vengeance Is Mine [3]

Vengeance is mine, saith the Lord, I will repay.
And the stiff-necked people, and the self-willed people, and
    self-important ones, the self-righteous, self-absorbed
all of them who wind their energy round the idea of themselves
and so strangle off their connection with the ceaseless tree of life,
and fall into sharp, self-centred self-assertion, sharp or soft,
they fall victim at once to the vengeance of the unforgiving god
as their nerves are stretched till they twangle and snap
and irritation seethes secretly through their guts, as their tissue
    disintegrates
and flames of katabolistic energy alternate
with ashes of utter boredom, ennui, and disgust.

It is the vengeance of the Lord, long and unremitting
till the soul of the stiff-necked is ground to dust, to fertilising meal
with which to manure afresh the roots of the tree of life.
And so the Lord of Vengeance pays back, repays life
for the defection of the self-centred ones.

[2] Gen. 2:9.
[3] Rom. 12:19; Exod. 32:9-10.

But I Say unto You:
Love One Another [4]

Oh I have loved my fellow-men—
and lived to learn they are neither fellow nor men
but machine-robots.

Oh I have loved the working class
where I was born,
and lived to see them spawn into machine-robots
in the hot-beds of the board-schools and the film.

Oh how I loved the thought of thoughtful people
gentle and refined,
and lived to find out
that their last thought was money
and their last refinement bluff, a hate disguised,
and one trapped one's fingers in their brassy, polished
     works!

Love Thy Neighbour [5]

I love my neighbour
but
are these things my neighbours?
these two-legged things that walk and talk
and eat and cachinnate, and even seem to smile
seem to smile, ye gods!

Am I told that these things are my neighbours?

All I can say then is Nay! nay! nay! nay! nay!

As Thyself! [6]

Supposing I say: dogs are my neighbours
I will love dogs as myself!

Then gradually I approximate to the dog,
wriggle and wag and slaver, and get the mentality of a dog!
This I call a shocking humiliation.

The same with my robot neighbours.
If I try loving them, I fall into their robot jig-jig-jig,
their robot cachinnation comes rattling out of my throat—
and I had better even have approximated to the dog.

[4] John 13:34.
[5] Luke 10:27.
[6] *Ibid.*

Who then, O Jesus, is my neighbour?[7]
If you point me to that fat money-smelling man in a motor-
        car,
or that hard-boiled young woman beside him
I shall have to refuse entirely to accept either of them.

My neighbour is not the man in the street, and never was:
he jigs along in the imbecile cruelty of the machine
and is implacable.

My neighbour, O my neighbour!
Occasionally I see him, silent, a little wondering
with his ears pricked and his body wincing
threading his way among the robot machine-people.

O my neighbour
sometimes I see her, like a flower, nodding her way and
        shrinking
from the robot contact on every hand!

How can that be my neighbour
which I shrink from!

Dark Satanic Mills[8]

The dark, satanic mills of Blake
how much darker and more satanic they are now!
But oh, the streams that stream white-faced, in and out
in and out when the hooter hoots, white-faced, with a
        dreadful gush
of multitudinous ignominy,
what shall we think of these?
They are millions to my one!

They are millions to my one! But oh
what have they done to you, white-faced millions
mewed and mangled in the mills of man?
What have they done to you, what have they done to you,
what is this awful aspect of man?

Oh Jesus, didn't you see, when you talked of service
this would be the result!
When you said: Retro me, Satanas![9]
this is what you gave him leave to do
behind your back!

[7] Luke 10:29.
[8] The title is from Blake's poem "Milton."
[9] Matt. 16:23.

And now, the iron has entered into the soul
and the machine has entangled the brain, and got it fast,
and steel has twisted the loins of man, electricity has
    exploded the heart
and out of the lips of people jerk strange mechanical noises
    in place of speech.

What is man, that thou art no longer mindful of him![10]
and the son of man, that thou pitiest him not?
Are these no longer men, these millions, millions?
What are they then?

Solomon's Baby[11]

Property is now Solomon's baby
and whoever gets it, it'll be a dead baby
a corpse, even of property.

Neither Moth Nor Rust[12]

God, only God is eternally.
God is forever, and only He.
Where, white maid, are the men you have loved?
They are dead, so God was between you, you see.

Many Mansions[13]

When a bird flips his tail in getting his balance on a tree
he feels much gayer than if somebody had left him a fortune
or than if he'd just built himself a nest with a bathroom—
Why can't people be gay like that?

Grasshopper Is a Burden[14]

Desire has failed, desire has failed
and the critical grasshopper
has come down on the heart in a burden of locusts
and stripped it bare.

Basta[15]

When a man can love no more
and feel no more
and desire has failed
and the heart is numb

[10] Ps. 8:4.
[11] I Kings 3:16-27.
[12] Matt. 6:19.
[13] John 14:2.
[14] Eccles. 12:5.
[15] *Ibid.*

then all he can do
is to say: It is so!
I've got to put up with it
and wait.
This is a pause, how long a pause I know not,
in my very being.

Man's Image[16]

What a pity, when a man looks at himself in a glass
he doesn't bark at himself, like a dog does,
or fluff up in indignant fury, like a cat!

What a pity he sees himself so wonderful,
a little lower than the angels!
and so interesting!

There Are Too Many People[17]

There are too many people on earth
insipid, unsalted, rabbity, endlessly hopping.
They nibble the face of the earth to a desert.

Souls To Save[18]

You tell me every man has a soul to save?
I tell you, not one man in a thousand has even a soul to lose.
The automat has no soul to lose.
so it can't have one to save.

Retort to Whitman[19]

And whoever walks a mile full of false sympathy
walks to the funeral of the whole human race.

Retort to Jesus[20]

And whoever forces himself to love anybody
begets a murderer in his own body.

[16] Ps. 8:5.
[17] Matt. 5:13.
[18] Matt. 16:26.
[19] Matt. 5:41.
[20] Matt. 5:44.

Commandments[21]

When Jesus commanded us to love our neighbour
he forced us to live a great lie, or to disobey:
for we can't love anybody, neighbour or no neighbour, to order,
and faked love has rotted our marrow.

Race and Battle[22]

The race is not to the swift
but to those that can sit still
and let the waves go over them.

The battle is not to the strong
but to the frail, who know best
how to efface themselves
to save the streaked pansy of the heart from being trampled to
　　mud.

The Hills[23]

I lift up mine eyes unto the hills
and there they are, but no strength comes from them to me.

Only from darkness
and ceasing to see
strength comes.

[21] Matt. 19:19.
[22] Eccles. 9:11.
[23] Ps. 121:1.

XII The Bible in Negro Spirituals
Roland Bartel

A detailed discussion of all aspects of Negro spirituals may be found in John Lovell's interesting book, *Black Song: The Forge and the Flame,* published by Macmillan in 1972. This comprehensive study is the primary source for most of the comments that follow. All the numbers in parentheses refer to page numbers in this book.

According to Lovell, the slave poets used the Bible more than any other source because they found in the Bible repeated demands for improvement of the social order (223). They put into their songs the biblical heroes "involved in upheaval and revolution (Moses, Daniel, the Hebrew children, Samson, Elijah, Gideon, Jesus, Paul)," (228). They also chose biblical heroes whose character traits they admired: "Noah for his goodness, manhood, and concern for peace. Jacob because he showed how a man could rise step by step. Moses for his leadership and preoccupation with freedom. Samson for his strength, but not for his folly. Daniel for his courage and wisdom. Shadrach, Meshach, Abednego for courage that defied flames and a king's anger. Lazarus because he built a home in the rock" (289).

The slave poets were selective in their use of the Bible. They concentrated on those parts that dealt with deliverance from oppression and confinement, with achievement against overwhelming odds, and with the rewards of faith. They used these parts repeatedly and adapted them to their own purposes. They were not evangelists but poets who regarded the Bible as a sourcebook for materials they needed for their songs of freedom (255).

Many spirituals can be understood only if we recognize that their primary theme is the slaves' desire for freedom. Those that deal with death, judgment day, crossing the Jordan river, entering camp ground, entering Canaan, and entering the New Jerusalem in most instances refer to deliverance from slavery in this world as well as to the better life beyond the grave (239, 307, 330). The walls of Jericho became symbolic of obstacles that stood between the slaves and their promised land of freedom (229). In a similar vein, the songs about the healing power of the troubled waters (John 5:2-9) and the hem of Jesus' garment (Matt. 9:20-22, 14:36) suggested that what could be done for individuals could also be done for groups of slaves.

Negro spirituals have several distinctive literary qualities. They rely heavily on refrains and other forms of repetition to emphasize their basic message and to aid the memory of the singers. Their language is precise and direct. Of special importance are the first lines, which often sum up the essence of the songs. "First lines are the creative explosion of wisdom, sentiment, and beauty on which the originality and appeal of the song rest. First lines get the song off the ground and into the air where its full development takes place" (214). The spirituals make frequent use of personal pronouns, which gives them a sense of immediacy. They treat biblical events and heroes with respectful familiarity rather than with objectivity and distance. All of these qualities should become apparent as we look at some of the spirituals that rely heavily on the Bible.

"We Are Climbing Jacob's Ladder" is a good example of the slave poet's ability to adapt a memorable scene to his own purpose. Jacob's vision of the ladder extending to heaven (Gen. 28:12) provides the basic symbol for a song that has nothing at all to do with Jacob himself. As the poet sings about self-improvement that takes place as he advances from one round to the next, he uses another device that occurs frequently in spirituals: he merges in one song the episodes from several parts of the Bible without regard to chronology. The most popular version of the song ends with a call to follow Jesus; a lesser known version begins with Jacob's ladder and then moves on to Paul and Silas praying in jail (Acts 16:25), the angels singing in heaven and in the New Jerusalem (Rev. 14:3, 21:2), and finally to God's bleeding lamb (Rev. 7:14) and a sheet of blood all mingled with fire (Rev. 15:2).

"Wrestle on, Jacob" combines Jacob's wrestling with God (Gen. 32:24) with Peter's becoming a fisher of men (Luke 5:10) as examples of the value of perseverance for a worthwhile cause. The "tremblin' han'" in the first stanza and the "tremblin' limb" in the sixth stanza probably do not suggest nervousness or uncertainty but rather an awareness of the importance of the occasion as in the line "O sometimes it causes me to tremble, tremble" from the song "Were You There When They Crucified My Lord?"

H. L. Mencken, American journalist and critic of the 1920s and 1930s, believed that "Swing Low, Sweet Chariot," "Deep River," and "Roll, Jordan, Roll" were all written by one black poet who "left a heritage to his country that few white men have ever surpassed. He was one of the greatest poets we have ever produced, and he came so near to being our greatest musician that I hesitate to look for a match for him" *(Mencken on Music* [New York: Knopf, 1961], p. 154). All three of these songs illustrate the point made earlier that words referring to life after death can also be code words referring to freedom in this life. Concerning the images in songs like these Lovell says, "Constant references . . . to chariots, trains, ships, rivers, the sea, the promised land are a trend for escaping slavery" (124) and "if one were choosing the outstanding occupation for singing spirituals and other songs it would have to be that associated with boats, the ships, the rivers and the sea" (161). "Swing Low, Sweet Chariot" is based on Elijah's ascension into heaven (II Kings 2:11) and refers also to the angels that carried Lazarus to the bosom of Abraham (Luke 16:22). "Deep River" and "Roll, Jordan, Roll" are based on the passages in the Bible in which the realization of a better life is dependent on crossing a river, as in Joshua 3, Daniel 12, and Revelation 22.

"Go Down Moses" is the most direct and probably the best-known of the many songs that call for freedom for the oppressed. It does not rely on subtle symbolism but rather on the power of direct statement. No one can miss the obvious analogy: what Moses did for the Hebrew children (Exod. 1–20) should be done for slaves everywhere. Lovell says about this song: "When it is spoken or sung in anything close to the way it was conceived and composed, it leaves an indelible impression. The listener cannot be casual about slavery or freedom ever again" (327). He says that the leader should sing the first and third line of each stanza, the chorus the second and fourth line, and the leader and the chorus should join in the refrain.

"Steal Away," another effective freedom song, has been the subject of much scholarly comment. It has been suggested that when the opening phrases alarmed the plantation owner who feared that his slaves were singing about stealing away to freedom, the poet quickly added the words "to Jesus" to make the song sound like a harmless Christian hymn. The vivid imagery in this song is drawn from Revelation 8:5 and Matthew 27:51.

Lovell says that in his research for his book he discovered six thousand spirituals, five hundred of which he refers to in his book. Since most of the spirituals are rooted in the Bible, we cannot possibly deal with all of them. Listed below are some of the better-known spirituals that have strong echoes from the Bible. The best source for these spirituals are the two books edited by James Weldon Johnson and J. Rosamond Johnson which were published as one book by Viking in 1942 with the title *Books of American Negro Spirituals*, and Christa Dixon's *Wesen und Wandel*, published in Wuppertal, Germany, in 1967. Miss Dixon lists fifty-five biblical spirituals, each with several variations, and identifies all the biblical allusions.

In the list that follows, the references to the Bible are given in the order in which they appear in each song.

"Joshua Fit de Battle of Jericho"
    (Josh. 6; Judg. 7; I Sam. 16)
"Lit'l David, Play on Yo' Harp"
    (I Sam. 16:23; Ps. 137:2; II Kings 2:11)

"Didn't My Lord Deliver Daniel"
  (Dan. 6; Jon. 1; Dan. 3; Joel 2:30; Rev. 7:1-3)
"Gambler, You Got to Plumb the Line"
  (Amos 7:7; Dan. 3)
"Weeping Mary, Weep-a-no More"
  (John 20:11, 24; 12:6; Matt. 14:25)
"My God Is a Rock in a Weary Land"
  (Isa. 32:1; Luke 23:33, 4:18; Matt. 11:5; Rev. 21:21;
  John 2:7)
"I Got a Home in-a Dat Rock, Don't You See?"
  (John 14:2; Luke 16:19; Gen. 9:11; Luke 17:26)
"Jesus Blood Done Mek Me Whole"
  (Matt. 9:20; Rev. 1:5)
"Were You There When They Crucified My Lord?"
  (John 19 and 20; Acts 5; Matt. 27)
"I Got a Robe, You Got a Robe"
  (Rev. 6:11; Matt. 7:21; Isa. 40:31; Rev.
  5:8; Luke 15:22; Rev. 14:3; Luke 14:27)
"Dese Bones Gwine to Rise Again" (found only in Lovell,
  256-57) (Gen. 2 and 3)

See the discussion above for the biblical allusions in
"We Are Climbing Jacob's Ladder"
"Wrestle On, Jacob"
"Swing Low, Sweet Chariot"
"Deep River"
"Roll, Jordan, Roll"
"Go Down Moses"
"Steal Away"

At the conclusion of his study, Lovell says that the Afro-Americans are developing a new respect for spirituals, now that scholars have demonstrated that the spirituals were not slavish songs but were rather the work of gifted poets with an intense desire for freedom and self-respect. The recognition that the use of religious imagery does not limit the spirituals to a narrow religious interpretation has made it possible to adapt them to present needs and problems (584).

XIII Two Biblical Passages That Have Appealed to Poets

Roland Bartel

A. Simon the Cyrenian

And as they led him away, they laid hold upon one Simon, a Cyrenian, coming out of the country, and on him they laid the cross, that he might bear it after Jesus.
—Luke 23:26. (See also Matt. 27:32 and Mark 15:21.)

Simon the Cyrenean

"And as they came out they found a man of Cyrene, Simon by name; him they compelled to bear his cross."

This is the tale from first to last;—
　Outside Jerusalem
I saw them lead a prisoner past
　With thorns for diadem.
Broken and weak and driven fast
　He fell at my garment's hem.

There stood no other stranger by
　On me they laid his load.
The Cross whereon he was to die
　I bore along the road,
I saw him nailed, I heard him cry
　Forsaken of his God.

Now I am dead as well as he,
　And, marvel strange to tell,
But him they nailed upon the tree
　Is Lord of Heaven and Hell,
And judgeth who doth wickedly,
　Rewardeth who doth well.

He has given to me the beacons four,
　A Cross in the southern sky,
In token that his Cross I bore
　In his extremity;
For one I never knew before
　The day he came to die.

Lucy Lyttleton

Simon of Cyrene

I walked that day out to the death-marked hill—
They call the place "the skull"—and saw him bear
His cross until he fell. It was not fair,
I thought, to place it on him. Strength and skill
Were mine from country toil. I bore it till
We came to Golgotha. I did not dare
To speak my grief; I only thought to spare
Him pain—his grateful look lives with me still.

And as we walked along, some women wept.
I could not censure them—my eyes were dim.
But know ye what he said? His words I've kept
Within my heart these years for love of him:
"Weep not for me. Dark days await you too.
Forgive these men: they know not what they do."

Georgia Harkness

Simon the Cyrenian Speaks

Look not on me with scorn because
    My skin's of darker hue—
Remember once these shoulders bore
    The cross he bore for you.

Glen Baker

Men Follow Simon

They spat in his face and hewed him a cross
On that dark day.
The cross was heavy; Simon bore it
Golgotha way.
    O Master, the cross is heavy!

They ripped his hands with driven nails
And flayed him with whips.
They pressed the sponge of vinegar
To his parched lips.
    O Master, Thy dear blood drips!

Men follow Simon, three and three,
And one and one,
Down through valleys and up long hills
Into the sun.
    O Master, Master—into the sun!

Raymond Kresensky

Lyttleton's poem divides into two parts, the first two stanzas dealing with Simon's experience with the crucifixion in this life, and the last two stanzas dealing with the rewards in the next life. It is a narrative poem and adds the kind of supernatural details often found in old ballads. In the sonnet by Harkness, Simon implies that he volunteered to carry the cross out of a sense of fairness and pity. He remembers Jesus' look of gratitude and his generous spirit in asking his followers not to weep and in forgiving those who were executing him. Baker assumes that Simon was black and has him plead for equality and respect as a recompense for the service he rendered. Kresensky's poem is the most didactic of the four. The author reviews the events of the crucifixion and concludes that we have much to learn from Simon.

The poems by Lyttleton, Harkness, and Baker are written in the first person with Simon as the speaker. Their juxtaposition invites students to consider these questions: What kind of person is Simon in each poem? What are his main concerns? How does Kresensky's poem, which is written in the third person, compare with the other three? Finally, how do these poems compare with the two that Countee Cullen wrote on the same subject? (See above, pp. 210-12.)

B. Peter's Denial of Jesus

References to this episode are found in Matthew 26:57-58, 69-75; Mark 14:54, 66:72; Luke 22:54-62; John 18:15-18, 25-27.

In the Servants' Quarters

"Man, you too, aren't you, one of these rough followers of
    the criminal?
All hanging hereabout to gather how he's going to bear
Examination in the hall." She flung disdainful glances on
The shabby figure standing at the fire with others there,
    Who warmed them by its flare.

"No indeed, my skipping maiden: I know nothing of the
    trial here,
Or criminal, if so he be.—I chanced to come this way,
And the fire shone out into the dawn, and morning airs
    are cold now;
I, too, was drawn in part by charms I see before me play,
    That I see not every day."

"Ha, ha!" then laughed the constables who also stood to
    warm themselves,
The while another maiden scrutinized his features hard,
As the blaze threw into contrast every line and knot that
    wrinkled them,
Exclaiming, "Why, last night when he was brought in by
    the guard,
    You were with him in the yard!"

"Nay, nay, you teasing wench, I say! You know you
    speak mistakenly,
Cannot a tired pedestrian who has legged it long and far
Here on his way from northern parts, engrossed in
    humble marketings,
Come in and rest awhile, although judicial doings are
    Afoot by morning star?"

"O, come, come!" laughed the constables. "Why, man,
    you speak the dialect
He uses in his answers; you can hear him up the stairs.
So own it. We sha'n't hurt ye. There he's speaking now!
    His syllables
And those you sound yourself when you are talking
    unawares,
    As the pretty girl declares."

"And you shudder when his chain clinks!" she rejoined.
    "O yes, I noticed it.
And you winced, too, when those cuffs they gave him
    echoed to us here.
They'll soon be coming down, and you may then have to
    defend yourself
Unless you hold your tongue, or go away and keep you
    clear
    When he's led to judgment near!"

"No, I'll be damned in hell if I know anything about the
    man!
No single thing about him more than everybody knows.
Must not I even warm my hands but I am charged with
    blasphemies?" . . .
—His face convulses as the morning cock that moment
    crows,
    And he droops, and turns, and goes.

Thomas Hardy

The Look

The Saviour looked on Peter. Ay, no word,
No gesture of reproach; the Heavens serene
Though heavy with armed justice, did not lean
Their thunders that way: the forsaken Lord
Looked only, on the traitor. None record
What that look was, none guess; for those who have seen
Wronged lovers loving through a death-pang keen,
Or pale-cheeked martyrs smiling to a sword,
Have missed Jehovah at the judgment-call.
And Peter, from the height of blasphemy—
"I never knew this man"—did quail and fall
As knowing straight THAT GOD; and turnèd free
And went out speechless from the face of all,
And filled the silence, weeping bitterly.

Elizabeth Barrett Browning

The Meaning of the Look

I think that look of Christ might seem to say—
"Thou Peter! art thou then a common stone
Which I at last must break my heart upon,
For all God's charge to his high angels may
Guard my foot better? Did I yesterday
Wash *thy* feet, my beloved, that they should run
Quick to deny me 'neath the morning sun?
And do thy kisses, like the rest, betray?
The cock crows coldly.—Go, and manifest
A late contrition, but no bootless fear!
For when thy final need is dreariest,
Thou shalt not be denied, as I am here;
My voice to God and angels shall attest,
Because I KNOW *this man, let him be clear.*"

Elizabeth Barrett Browning

The Two Sayings

Two sayings of the Holy Scriptures beat
Like pulses in the Church's brow and breast;
And by them we find rest in our unrest
And, heart deep in salt-tears, do yet entreat
God's fellowship as if on heavenly seat.
The first is JESUS WEPT,—whereon is prest
Full many a sobbing face that drops its best
And sweetest waters on the record sweet:
And one is where the Christ, denied and scorned,
LOOKED UPON PETER. Oh, to render plain,
By help of having loved a little and mourned,
That look of sovran love and sovran pain
Which HE, who could not sin yet suffered, turned
On him who could reject but not sustain!

Elizabeth Barrett Browning

Simon Surnamed Peter

Time that has lifted you over them all—
O'er John and o'er Paul;
Writ you in capitals, made you the chief
Word on the leaf—
How did you, Peter, when ne'er on His breast
You leaned and were blest—
And none except Judas and you broke the faith
To the day of His death,—
You, Peter, the fisherman, worthy of blame,
Arise to this fame?

'Twas you in the garden who fell into sleep
And the watch failed to keep,
When Jesus was praying and pressed with the weight
Of the oncoming fate.
'Twas you in the court of the palace who warmed
Your hands as you stormed
At the damsel, denying Him thrice, when she cried:
"He walked at his side!"
"You, Peter, a wave, a star among clouds, a reed in
the wind,
A guide of the blind,
Both smiter and flyer, but human alway, I protest,
Beyond all the rest.

When at night by the boat on the sea He appeared
Did you wait till he neared?

You leaped in the water, not dreading the worst
In your joy to be first
To greet Him and tell Him of all that had passed
Since you saw Him the last.
You had slept while He watched, but fierce were you,
    fierce and awake
When they sought Him to take,
And cursing, no doubt, as you smote off, as one of the
    least,
The ear of the priest.
Then Andrew and all of them fled, but you followed
    Him, hoping for strength
To save him at length
Till you lied to the damsel, oh penitent Peter, and
    crept,
Into hiding and wept.

Oh well! But he asked all the twelve, "Who am I?"
And who made reply?
As you leaped in the sea, so you spoke as you smote
    with the sword;
"Thou art Christ, even Lord!"
John leaned on His breast, but he asked you, your
    strength to foresee,
"Nay, lovest thou me?"
Thrice over, as thrice you denied Him, and chose you
    to lead
His sheep and to feed;
And gave you, He said, the keys of the den and the fold
To have and to hold.
You were a poor jailer, oh Peter, the dreamer, who saw
The death of the law
In the dream of the vessel that held all the four-footed
    beasts,
Unclean for the priests;
And heard in the vision a trumpet that all men are
    worth
The peace of the earth
And rapture of heaven hereafter,—oh Peter, what
    power
Was yours in that hour:
You warder and jailer and sealer of fates and decrees,
To use the big keys
With which to reveal and fling wide all the soul and
    the scheme
Of the Galilee dream,

When you flashed in a trice, as later you smote with
     the sword:
"Thou art Christ, even Lord!"

We men, Simon Peter, we men also give you the crown
O'er Paul and o'er John.
We write you in capitals, make you the chief
Word on the leaf.
We know you as one of our flesh, and 'tis well
You are warder of hell,
And heaven's gatekeeper forever to bind and to
          loose—
Keep the keys if you choose.
Not rock of you, fire of you make you sublime
In the annals of time.
You were called by Him, Peter, a rock, but we give
          you the name
Of Peter the Flame.
For you struck a spark, as the spark from the shock
Of steel upon rock.
The rock has his use but the flame gives the light
In the way in the night:—
Oh Peter, the dreamer, impetuous, human, divine,
Gnarled branch of the vine!

Edgar Lee Masters

Peter

Lifted by the teaching of a Master
From the pallid shores of a lake
To the azure heights it mirrored,
He fell before a woman's scorn:
Three times he denied his Lord;
And immediately the cock crew.

He was crucified head-downward
Because he thought himself unworthy
To die the death of Jesus.

Denial,
Cock-crow,
Crucifixion—
His was a sacred way
That only the strong dare follow.

Earl Marlatt

> He forgot—and I—remembered—
> 'Twas an everyday affair—
> Long ago as Christ and Peter—
> "Warmed them" at the "Temple fire."
>
> "Thou wert with him"—quoth "the Damsel"?
> "*No*"—said Peter, 'twasn't me—
> Jesus merely "looked" at Peter—
> Could I do aught else—to Thee?
> *Emily Dickinson*

Hardy follows the account in Matthew 26:57-75, in which Peter denies his connection with Jesus to two maids and the men standing around the fire before he hears the cock crow. Consider the effect of the following changes that Hardy makes in the biblical narrative:

That Peter was tired after a long walk from the north to the markets in the south.

Peter's excuses that he entered the hall where the trial was taking place because he was attracted by the warm fire and the charms of the maiden.

The assurance of the constables that they won't hurt him if he admits his connection with Jesus.

The observation of the maiden that Peter shudders when he hears the chain clink and winces when he hears the sound of handcuffs.

Changing the biblical statement that Peter wept bitterly to "His face convulses . . . and he droops, and turns, and goes."

The cumulative effect of all these changes.

Elizabeth Barrett Browning's three sonnets are based on Luke 22:61-62. While Peter was denying his connection with Jesus a third time, he heard the cock crow. "And the Lord turned, and looked upon Peter. And Peter remembered the word of the Lord, how he had said unto him, Before the cock crow, thou shalt deny me thrice. And Peter went out, and wept bitterly."

In "The Look" Mrs. Browning is fascinated by the power of Jesus' look that caused Peter to break down. The look was not accompanied by words or natural disturbances and was unlike any look mortal man has ever seen on the faces of wronged lovers or martyrs. This poem might be compared with Cullen's "Simon the Cyrenian Speaks" (page 210), where the speaker's life is also changed by the force of Jesus' look.

In "The Meaning of the Look" Mrs. Browning tries to imagine what was communicated by the look. Did Jesus recall the divine protection that kept him from dashing his foot against a stone (Matt. 4:6) and then ask himself whether Peter would be the stone to make him stumble? This may be an ironic reference to Matthew 16:18, "Thou art Peter, and upon this rock I will build my church." Did Jesus recall the Last Supper and Judas' betrayal when he looked at Peter? Mrs. Browning concludes that Peter will be forgiven and allowed to enter heaven.

In "The Two Sayings" Mrs. Browning stresses the significance of two phrases, "Jesus wept" (John 11:35) and "looked upon Peter" (Luke 22:61). Instead of probing for implied meanings, she simply asserts their importance.

Edgar Lee Masters, in "Simon Surnamed Peter," looks at Peter's denial in the perspective of his entire career. He reviews the events in Peter's life to find the answer to this question: Why has the disciple who made so many mistakes achieved such elevation over the others? Masters closes his poem with a tribute to Peter's humanity and his divinity.

Marlatt praises Peter for having risen to such great heights from his origins as a fisherman and for having risen from his denial to new heights of loyalty and humility. That Peter requested that he be crucified head downward is a strong extrabiblical tradition and is used in this poem as evidence of Peter's strength of character.

Emily Dickinson compares one of her personal experiences with Peter's denial of Jesus, and that is about all the information we get from the poem.

Part Three:
The Bible in Drama

I Biblical Angels and English Shepherds: The Gospel Tradition in *The Second Shepherds' Play*

C. Clifford Flanigan

Comparative Literature Program, Indiana University

A casual reading of the first 189 lines of *The Second Shepherds' Play*[1] might suggest that the playwright used an inordinate amount of space to introduce his chief characters. On closer examination, however, we can see that he has developed the biblical and theological themes of the play with great care and economy. By temporarily frustrating his audience's expectation of a Christmas play, he has forced its members to experience that waiting for the coming of the Messiah which medieval man believed characterized the entire Old Testament period. More important, he has confronted the audience with the need for the Incarnation, both from the perspective of salvation history and from its own experience of the fallen world. Rather than present a straightforward account of the events of the first Christmas, he has chosen to stress first the significance of the events. One of the ways he does this is by linking the shepherds of the first century with the people of England in the fifteenth century. What may seem like anachronisms at first—the use of fifteenth-century

[1] The standard edition of *The Second Shepherds' Play* is in *The Wakefield Pageants in the Towneley Cycle*, ed. A. C. Cawley (Manchester: The University Press, 1958). Line numbers will be cited from this text. The number of critical studies on *The Second Shepherds' Play* is very great; especially helpful are William A. Manly, "Shepherds and Prophets: Religious Unity in the Towneley *Secunda Pastorum*," *PMLA*, 78 (1963), 151-55, and Lawrence J. Ross, "Symbol and Structure in the *Secunda Pastorum*," *Comparative Drama*, 1 (1967), 122-49. Two important recent book-length studies on the medieval English drama are V. A. Kolve, *The Play Called Corpus Christi* (Stanford: Stanford University Press, 1966), and Rosemary Woolf, *The English Mystery Plays* (Berkeley: University of California Press, 1972). I have freely borrowed from these and earlier studies of the play.

expressions, the references to places in England, and the allusion to social and domestic problems in fifteenth-century England—is actually a method of suggesting that the needs of the people of both centuries are similar: they both live in a fallen world, and they both stand sorely in need of the coming of God in Christ. There is a distinction, of course; the Wakefield Master (the anonymous author of the play) and his audience live in the new dispensation of God's grace, while the first-century shepherds lived at the end of the old. Yet by accenting the fact that the world of his contemporaries shares in the fallenness of the Old Testament world, and by giving his biblical world a specifically fifteenth-century English coloring, the playwright has stressed the significance of the Incarnation for his own time. The world of his shepherds with its perverted human and sexual relationships needs to experience anew the once-for-all event of the birth of Christ. The same purpose is served by the allusions to the winter weather which realistically are more appropriate to December in England than in Palestine; but, like the other apparent anachronisms, they serve to emphasize the need for salvation in a world which is touched by evil at every turn.

The figures of Mak and Gyll have their origins in the English folk tradition. What is of interest to us, however, is not so much the sources from which the Wakefield Master inherited them as the way in which he used them in his play. On first consideration we might be tempted to consider Mak just another inhabitant of the fallen world in which the shepherds live. Yet, as the shepherds immediately recognize, he is different. He enters the play with a false claim, that he is the yeoman of a great king. His pretentious airs, his feigned city accent, and his demand that he have respect anger the others so much that they almost physically assault him; they know that, despite his claims and his phony costumes, Mak is a liar and a thief. His tunic and cloak are apparently in sharp contrast to the poor clothing of the other shepherds, and although he complains, like the others, that he isn't getting enough to eat, there is every indication that he and Gyll eat well—at least when there is food to be stolen. Even his complaints against women and sex seem at least partially belied by what we see of his relationship with his wife, although Gyll does seem a bit shrewish when Mak comes home with the stolen sheep.

From the moment Mak enters the play, much is made of the contrast between Mak's lies and the truth that the shepherds know. On seeing Mak, Daw warns the others to be on guard against theft, and a little later Gyb tells Mak directly that he has a reputation for stealing sheep. Thus Mak appears less a victim of the fall into sin than the agent of that continuing catastrophe. According to the Christian understanding of the fall, sin entered the world through the devil, who, since he was not satisfied with his original crime, continues to tempt men and inflict evil on them. It is important in this connection to note the numerous associations made between Mak and the devil. On seven occasions the shepherds slip in references to the devil when they are talking to or about Mak. These connections between Mak, whom we know to be a liar, and the devil seem natural when we remember that, according to the author of the Fourth Gospel, Jesus said that the devil "has nothing to do with truth, because there is no truth in him. When he lies, he speaks according to his own nature, for he is a liar and the father of lies" (John 8:44).

It would· be a mistake, however, to allow the text's frequent association of Mak with the demonic to encourage us to see him as an allegorical representation of Satan; he is obviously a humorous character who populates the biblical world and the English world of the play. Nevertheless, once we realize that the author has drawn Mak as a thief and an agent of sin, it is important to remember that "he who commits sin is of the devil; for the devil has sinned from the beginning" (I John 3:8).

If Mak's activities are broadly demonic, they are specifically directed toward sheep-stealing. In this way too he stands in contrast to the shepherds, who are keepers and protectors of sheep. Mak himself says that he has never been a shepherd (l. 288), and Daw dreams that he saw Mak dressed in a wolfskin (l. 368). Here the playwright is clearly calling on his audience's knowledge of the biblical tradition, for this line is an ironic reference to Jesus' warning "Beware of false prophets, who come to you in sheep's clothing, but inwardly are ravenous wolves" (Matt. 7:15). This saying seems relevant because Mak, like the false prophets in Jesus' warning, attempts to disguise what he really is. This suggests that just as on a literal level Mak stands in opposition to the shepherds, on a metaphorical level he stands in contrast to the true prophet and the true shepherd. This contrast in turn suggests another one which would never be far from the minds of a Christian audience watching a shepherds' play, namely, Jesus' description of himself as the Good Shepherd who saves his sheep from wolves and thieves (John 10:1-12).

With this saying of Jesus in mind, we can define Mak's role in the play more specifically. As an agent of the devil, a thief, and a liar, he is like the robber described by Jesus. The play's biblical shepherds live in Bethlehem in a time before the birth of the Good Shepherd; their world is full of the works of the false shepherd and therefore stands desperately in need of God's Good Shepherd, who will be born at the end of the play.

Thus we can see that with stunning originality the Wakefield Master has converted a comic figure of folklore into an agent of his chief thematic concerns. But the analogies are pressed even further. Just as underlying the dramatic action there is an implicit connection between Mak, the false shepherd, and the Christ Child, the Good Shepherd, so there is also a contrast between the lamb who is falsely represented as a baby boy and the baby boy who, according to the Christian tradition, was the true Lamb of God. This opposition gives theological import to the humorous scene in Mak's cottage. The parallels are indeed striking. Aligned with Mak and his lie, Gyll claims to have given birth to a child; she is thus contrasted with the Virgin, who appears at the end of the play and whose motherhood is genuine, for she has actually given birth to him who is truth personified. Gyll's "child" bears a striking similarity to Mary's boy. When Daw pulls the blanket off the sheep in the cradle he says they will see how the four feet were swaddled in the middle; according to Luke's Gospel the baby Jesus was "wrapped . . . in swaddling clothes" (KJV). And in contrast to Mak's son's cradle, a bed intended for a child rather than a beast, Mary's son, the true Lamb, is found lying in a manger, between the beasts.

The text of the play points to yet other parallels between the stolen sheep and the baby Jesus. The Christ Child's birth was universally regarded by the fifteenth century as miraculous, for the Bible describes Jesus as virginally conceived and born. Gyll likewise puts forth the claim of miraculous intervention in the events surrounding her "son's" birth (ll. 616-19); this claim, unlike Mary's, is, however, false. There is also an implicit contrast in Mak's and Gyll's repeated ironic promise to eat their own child if Mak has stolen the sheep; the true Lamb born at the play's end will, of course, give himself as food to his followers in the Eucharist. So complete is the parallelism between the two births that each child is called a day-star (ll. 577, 727), a common christological title derived from II Peter 1:19. Their true identities are, of course, quite different.

The Mak episode is unquestionably one of the highpoints in early English comedy. We should not restrain our laughter at it; surely its original audience did not. While they were chuckling, however, they, like us, must have raised the question of the relevance of this unexpected portion of the play for the Nativity drama which they were awaiting. As was the case for the first part of the play, the playwright has frustrated their expectations. Just as the initial speeches of Coll, Gyb, and Daw caused the audience to reflect on the fact that it was living in a fallen world which, like the world of the first century, stood in need of the coming of Christ, so the Mak episode forces the audience to see that its world is one where the false shepherd is already at work, aping the good deeds of Christ for perverse ends. This insight in turn suggests a perspective from which the Nativity, when it is finally enacted, may be understood—not only as a past event, but as an assurance offered to us that God will come again into this sinful world and set all things right. Once we understand this fact—and only then—we are ready to see that part of the play that we, as audience, have long been anticipating. By frustrating the audience's expectations, and our expectations as readers of the play, with a comic "prelude" which extends for more than two-thirds of the entire play, the author has related the old stories to the present needs and concerns of a specific community living at a clearly delineated time in history. And yet, since the fifteenth-century English elements are in fact only historical accidents which from a medieval Christian perspective express the underlying universal truth about man's need for divine help, the initial episodes of the drama have nearly the same effect on our understanding of the story of the Nativity as they had on the play's original audience. Once Mak is tossed in the blanket—an act which may foreshadow the justice tempered with mercy which comes with the birth of Jesus at the end of the play—we are finally ready to see the Christ Child. By now the heightened sense of our need for the Incarnation moves us to hope with Coll that God will turn everything to good.

With the conclusion of the Mak episode the play seems to begin anew; the three shepherds return to their fields and begin to complain and act as if the Mak episode had never taken place. At long last we actually see the Nativity play that we have been anticipating. Yet the playwright will not allow either his shepherds or his audience to forget the lessons that the earlier parts of the play have taught. Once again we are repeatedly reminded by his skillful use of parallelisms. For the second time in the play the shepherds join in the singing of a song, lie down to sleep, and awake to the announcement of a birth. And again the shepherds make a journey to seek out a newborn child and present him with gifts. For a second time also they encounter the woman who claims to be the child's mother. As we have already seen, however, Mary stands in sharp contrast to Gyll, for she is indeed a mother who has supernaturally borne a child and she speaks not lies but words of grace and comfort. Yet it is the Child of Bethlehem who represents the sharpest antithesis to his counterpart in the earlier part of the play. Of him Coll says that he has *cursed* the devil, the author of evil, thus accenting the difference between the first and the second child, a difference made all the more vivid because of our prolonged experience of the Mak episode.

These differences are also accented by the nature of the shepherds' language in the final portion of the play. Kneeling before the manger, they speak with a lyricism which to modern sensibilities may seem out of character, but which is especially appropriate to the mood of a Nativity play. It is as if the audience is finally allowed to hear the level of language conventionally associated with the expected plot of the play. These lyrical pieces express the joy of fallen nature at the birth of the Savior and at the same time stress the theological significance of the events of Christmas. Thus Coll's remark points to the underlying theme of the entire play (ll. 712-15), while Daw's expression of joy stresses the paradox of the Incarnation which is at the heart of the drama both formally and thematically.

The gifts of cherries, a bird, and a tennis ball which the shepherds bring to the Christ Child invariably charm modern readers of the play. As we might expect by now, however, they add more than local coloring to the final scene of adoration.[2] There is no biblical parallel for the shepherds' gifts. This tradition has undoubtedly developed

[2] On the iconography of the shepherds' gifts see Eugene N. Cantelupe and Richard Griffith, "The Gifts of the Shepherds in the Wakefield *'Secunda Pastorum'*: An Iconographical Interpretation," *Mediaeval Studies*, 28 (1966), 328-445; John P. Cutts, "The Shepherds' Gifts in *The Second Shepherds' Play* and Bosch's 'Adoration of the Magi,'" *Comparative Drama* 4 (1970), 120-24; and especially the article by Ross (see n. 1, above).

out of the gospel accounts of the three Magi who brought presents to the baby Jesus. Although our shepherds are patterned after these kings from the East, in some ways they stand in sharp contrast to them. The Magi offered expensive gifts of gold, frankincense, and myrrh. On the other hand, the shepherds, typifying, perhaps, a world spiritually as well as materially poor, present gifts of little apparent value. But once again the Wakefield Master is employing seemingly insignificant details to enhance his thematic emphasis. Coll presents the Christ Child with a bunch of cherries, a perfectly normal rustic gift except for the fact that cherries do not grow in the cold English winter described at the play's beginning. But Coll's cherries are more than real fruit. Their very existence in the midst of the winter weather, which, as we saw earlier, is used as a metaphor for the fallenness of the world, suggests the rebirth of life in the midst of the chill of sin and death. The birth of the Christ Child means new life for men of every age. The gift of cherries points to the coming of spiritual and physical salvation which, as the play has shown us, the English world of the fifteenth century desperately needed.

The cherries may also stand as a testimony of the miracle of the Incarnation. A significant literary link between Christmas and cherries is attested in the tradition embodied in the well-known "Cherry Tree Carol." According to this ballad, cherries are emblems of the virginal conception of Jesus. They are symbols, frequently encountered in the visual arts of the late Middle Ages and the Renaissance, of the fact that the Christ Child is true God and true man, "begotten of his Father before all worlds," yet taking human flesh from the body of the Virgin Mary. Thus Coll's gift has symbolic overtones which point to the nature and task of the child whom he worships. They are, in fact, the visual counterpart of his own oral confession (ll. 710-13).

Much the same might be said of Gib's gift of a bird; it needs to be understood both on a realistic pastoral level and in terms of Christian symbolism. Like the bob of cherries, it refers to the nature of the Christ Child and to his work for the sake of the fallen world, but the traditions invoked are complicated and far from monolithic. Although the text does not designate the species of the bird, late medieval and Renaissance depictions of the Nativity frequently include a dove, and we can assume that Gib's bird is such also. In the biblical tradition the dove is frequently characterized as a beautiful, innocent bird (cf. Matt. 10:16) whose flight sometimes symbolizes man's desire to return to Paradise. Thus, for example, the dove becomes an image of escape in Psalm 55:4-8. Hosea uses similar imagery in his prophecy of a new exodus (11:11), a promise which medieval Christians believed was fulfilled in the birth of Christ. Thus Gyb's gift becomes a sign of the newborn child's role as a restorer of the lost salvation so much lamented earlier in the drama.

The dove also has more specific associations with Christmas. According to the four Gospels, at the time of Jesus' baptism the Holy Spirit descended on him in the form of a dove. Luke describes this event and explains its significance thus: "The Holy Spirit descended upon him in bodily form, as a dove, and a voice came from heaven, 'Thou art my beloved Son; with thee I am well pleased'" (Luke 3:22). Medieval Bibles added to this passage a disputed textual reading which has its ultimate source in the Second Psalm: "Today I have begotten you." Such passages designating the dove as a symbol of Jesus' divinity were assimilated in the history of Christian art to Luke's account of the Annunciation. There Gabriel tells the woman who is about to be the human mother of Jesus that "the Holy Spirit will come upon you, and the power of the Most High will overshadow you; therefore the child to be born will be called holy, the Son of God" (Luke 1:35). These associations partially account for the frequent inclusion of a symbolic dove hovering in the background in paintings of the Annunciation scene. Thus the second shepherd's gift is an emblem of Jesus' divinity, a visual testimony that the child is, as Gyb says, a suffering savior.

As we might expect, Daw's simple tennis ball also has

symbolic as well as literal significance. A common feature of many of the visual arts in these periods was the depiction of the infant Jesus holding a symbolic world in his hand; this motif is an expression of the central paradox of the Incarnation. Until recently, this same motif was common in Roman Catholic churches in statuary figures of the so-called Divine Child of Prague. Perhaps it is best known today through the spiritual "He's Got the Whole World in His Hands." In any case, Daw's gift of a tennis ball, like the presents of the other shepherds, points to the theological significance of the Christ Child's identity. Still the gift need lose nothing of its simple charm. The genius of the Wakefield Master is expressed in such a way that the simple world of the biblical shepherds, the fallen world of fifteenth-century England, and the iconic world of divine activity are fused into an artistic whole.

With the shepherds' presentation of their gifts the play has come full course. We have moved from the fifteenth-century world burdened by sin and its effects, to a presentation of a figure of the false shepherd actively at work in that world, to a presentation of the Nativity which partakes of both the comic world of the earlier part of the play and the more sublime theological world of biblical events. It remains only for the Virgin to summarize the meaning of all that we have seen and heard. In the most elevated speech in the entire play she formally states the theological significance of the Christmas events (ll. 737-45). Here at last is the message and the tone that the audience which has been awaiting a Nativity play has expected all along.

For the shepherds the movement of the play has been from misery to relief, from darkness to light. But since the shepherds are English shepherds as well as biblical ones, the audience's own experience of the play has likewise been one moving from sorrow to joy. It is, in fact, in the design of this pattern that much of the play's artistry is revealed. We, as audience, anticipated only a happy Christmas play; the playwright has first made us experience the tragedy of sin in our world and then has offered us the comedy of the Nativity. The birth of Christ is presented as a past event, but one that sets in motion the conquest of evil and provides an earnest promise that the evil which touches on the audience's life will ultimately be resolved by God's second coming. By the play's end the biblical world and the world of the audience have merged; the first person plural pronouns in the drama's final lines refer to both the shepherds and the audience. The Wakefield Master has made the members of his audience experience the need for redemption and the reality of the coming of God into their own times and lives. In reaction to what they have experienced, the only fitting ending is the joyous Christmas song which the final rubrics require.

II Shakespeare's Use of Scripture*

Edna Moore Robinson

*(deceased): Department of English,
Taylor University (Upland, Indiana)*

Strange as it may seem, one of the most helpful discussions of Shakespeare's use of the Bible appears in the book on Tennyson excerpted below. Dozens of books and articles have been written on Shakespeare's use of the Bible, but most of them catalogue the biblical allusions without discussing their function in the plays. The most complete list of all the allusions, arranged first by the plays and then in the order of their appearance in the Bible, is found in Richmond Noble's *Shakespeare's Biblical Knowledge*, published by Macmillan in 1935.

In the discussion reprinted below the comparisons with Tennyson may be ignored. They could not be removed without destroying the coherence of the article.—Ed.

Shakespeare uses Scripture in its primary, literal, and natural sense. But he never enters into a scripture scene or story with imaginative and elaborative delight, as Tennyson did in his first period. He uses one passage at a time for direct and immediate effect. This is true even where he employs two citations in close connection. Carlisle tells the assembled lords that if they give the crown to Hereford,

> Disorder, horror, fear and mutiny
> Shall here inhabit, and this land be call'd
> The field of Golgotha and dead men's skulls.
> Oh! if you rear this house against this house,
> It will the woefullest division prove
> That ever fell upon this cursed earth.[1]

*From *Tennyson's Use of the Bible* (Baltimore: Johns Hopkins Press, 1917), pp. 74-84. Reprinted by permission of Gordian Press. (Footnotes renumbered.)

[1]*Richard Second*, IV, i, 142-147; *Matthew*, XXVII, 33; XII, 25.

But the reference to Golgotha vivifies the conception of disorder and death, and the reference to the divided house enforces another and different idea, the evil of family conflict and civil war. Again, Richard urges, against giving up the crown, the fact that Northumberland's own record is

> Mark'd with a blot, damn'd in the book of heaven.[2]

and then in a moment adds

> Though some of you with Pilate wash your hands,
> Showing an outward pity; yet you Pilates
> Have here deliver'd me to my sour cross.
> And water cannot wash away your sins.[3]

But the book of heaven is connected with Northumberland's inconsistency, and Pilate's washing his hands with the fact that mere outward pity and ceremony cannot excuse an accompanying and deliberate sin. Combinations like those just cited are rare in Shakespeare.

The fact that Shakespeare cites only one passage at a time of course precludes his fashioning and altering a set of scripture phrases into the forms necessary to build them into an allegory unified by some extra-scriptural conception. . . . His simplicity and directness in making biblical allusions render such complex moulding still more impossible than piecing Scripture together into mosaics. In fact he seems never consciously and purposely to use scripture expressions, as Tennyson so often does, simply for the sake of their forceful idiom, their general biblical flavor, or their mere homogeneity with some general figure he happens to be using. It is the essential meaning, the straightforward, commonly accepted meaning, that he always has in mind. Even his satire makes more direct and obvious thrusts, tho sometimes less powerful ones, than Tennyson's. Occasionally . . . Tennyson's reference is doubtful. Shakespeare's on

---

[2] *Richard Second*, IV, i, 236; *Psalms*, LIX, 28.
[3] *Richard Second*, IV, i, 239-242; *Matthew*, XXVII, 24.

the other hand is always unquestionable. It is never necessary to look it up or study its context.

It is not to be inferred from what has been said of Shakespeare's simplicity that he does not sometimes handle single passages of Scripture with great imaginative power. It is only contended that he uses but one passage at a time. Fairness perhaps requires that some illustrations of his genius in employing biblical citations be given at this point. The following are taken from *Macbeth* and *Hamlet* as examples from the tragedies and from *Measure for Measure* as from one of the comedies. Macduff knows that Duncan, as a King, is the Lord's anointed and that man's body is a sacred temple and says of the murdered King:

> Most sacrilegious murder hath broke ope
> The Lord's anointed temple, and stole thence
> The life o' the building.[4]

When Macbeth falls into his last, fierce pessimism, he sees life as a place for fools, unrealities, and stage effects. The Psalmist said, "Our days on the earth are as a shadow" and again, "We spend our years as a tale that is told." Macbeth makes the shadow walk and puts the tale into the mouth of an imbecile:

> Life's but a walking shadow, a poor player
> That struts and frets his hour upon the stage,
> And then is heard no more; it is a tale
> Told by idiot, full of sound and fury,
> Signifying nothing.[5]

In the mature and finished *Hamlet* the scripture allusions are more numerous and of wider range. Two citations illustrate the extremes. The king's guilt forces him to say

> It hath the primal eldest curse upon't;
> A brother's murder.[6]

[4] *Macbeth*, II, iii, 67-69: *1 Corinthians*, III, 16, 17.
[5] *Macbeth*, V, v, 24-28; *Psalms*, CXLIV, 4 and XC, 9.
[6] *Hamlet*, III, iii, 37 f.; *Genesis*, IV, 11.

The First Clown can prove that Adam belonged to the nobility.

> *First Clown.* There is no ancient gentlemen but gardeners, ditchers, and grave-makers; they hold up Adam's profession.
> *Second Clown.* Was he a gentleman?
> *First Clown.* A' was the first that ever bore arms.
> *Second Clown.* Why he had none.
> *First Clown.* What! art a heathen? How dost thou understand the Scripture? The Scripture says, Adam digged; could he dig without arms?[7]

In *Measure for Measure* there is a reference to letting our light shine.

> Heaven doth with us as we with torches do.
> Not light them for ourselves; for if our virtues
> Did not go forth of us, 'twere all alike
> As if we had them not. Spirits are not finely touched
> But to fine issues.[8]

The commandment scraped out of the table which the pirate took with him when he went to sea may also be cited.[9] A complete examination of Shakespeare's dramas yields the conclusion that his rhetorical and literary power with Scripture is exercised upon isolated passages as distinguished from Tennyson's artistic blendings of many passages. Thruout his career Shakespeare's method was essentially the same; but Tennyson's was varied because of the stages of development thru which it passed. Shakespeare always touched a passage briefly, naturally, and livingly; Tennyson often wrought one out more elaborately, and sometimes left upon it the mark of the chisel or the smell of the lamp.

There are at least four plays of Shakespeare which point a contrast of another kind. In each of these four the scripture citations are nearly all put into the mouth of the principal

---

[7] *Hamlet,* v, i, 30-38; *Genesis,* II, 15.
[8] *Measure for Measure,* I, i, 32-36; *Matthew,* v, 14, 16.
[9] *Measure for Measure,* I, ii, 7-14; *Exodus,* xx, 15.

character in the play, or into the mouths of those who describe the qualities or career of that character. The citations are in close sympathy with the movement of the play and as a whole have an ethical intent. They point the moral as it were of the successive situations and, as already intimated, reach at the close of the drama a climax which pronounces a final moral judgment on the whole action, or on the fate of the leading character.

The four plays referred to above are *Richard Second, Henry Fourth, Richard Third,* and *Merchant of Venice.* Richard II was fashioned for failure, for speech-making rather than action. By contrast, Bolingbroke was forceful and successful even if unlovable. The sequence of scripture allusions shows the progress of the contrasted success and failure together with Shakespeare's special sympathy for Richard, the principal character portrayed. In Gloucester's death Bolingbroke hears a summons to active vengeance. His blood

> like sacrificing Abel's, cries
> Even from the tongueless caverns of the earth
> To me for justice and rough chastisement;
> And, by the glorious worth of my descent,
> This arm shall do it or this life be spent.[10]

Bolingbroke and Mowbray insist upon a bloody conflict with each other. Richard seeks to stop the deadly quarrel. He and Mowbray make out of Jeremiah's simile a piece of rhetoric that illustrates Richard's speechmaking inefficiency at the very outset.

> King Richard.   Rage must be withstood
>   Give me his gage: lions make leopards tame.
> *Mowbray.* Yea, but not change his spots.[11]

In the second act Isaiah furnishes Salisbury with the image of Richard's ruin.

---

[10]*Richard Second,* I, i, 104-108; *Genesis,* IV, 4, 10.
[11]*Richard Second,* I, i, 173-175; *Jeremiah,* XIII, 23.

> Ah, Richard, with the eyes of heavy mind
> I see thy glory like a shooting star
> Fall to the base earth from the firmament.[12]

From this point onward Richard himself describes the treacheries and hypocrisies that work his ruin. He hears that Bagot, Bushy, and Green have made peace with Bolingbroke and cries:

> O villains, vipers, damn'd without redemption,
> Dogs, easily won to fawn on any man!
> Snakes in my heart-blood warm'd, that sting my heart!
>   Three Judases, each one thrice worse than Judas!
> Would they make peace? terrible hell make war
> Upon their spotted souls for this offence.[13]

In a passage already quoted Carlisle likens the land to Golgotha and the kingdom to a divided house.[14] A little further on Richard's sense of treachery makes bitter capital out of the betrayal of Jesus.

> I well remember
> The favors of these men; were they not mine?
> Did they not sometime cry, 'all hail' to me?
> So Judas did to Christ: but he, in twelve,
> Found truth in all but one; I in twelve thousand, none.[15]

Again the action progresses from the betrayal to the self-excusing, seeming-pitiful but selfish and murderous judgment Richard's energetic enemies pronounce upon him. They are like the cold unscrupulous Roman governor in the gospel.[16] Still later Richard is required to read the accusing paper before he is deposed and exclaims

> Fiend, thou torment'st me ere I come to hell.[17]

---

[12]*Richard Second*, II, iv, 18-20; *Isaiah*, XIV, 12.
[13]*Richard Second*, III, ii, 129-134; *Matthew*, XXVI, 14-16.
[14]See page 308.
[15]*Richard Second*, IV, i, 167-171; *Matthew*, XXVI, 49; *John*, XVII, 12.
[16]For the passage see page 309.
[17]*Richard Second*, IV, i, 270; *Matthew*, VIII, 29.

His sentimental double-mindedness sets the Bible itself in antithesis to the Bible.

> As thus: 'come, little ones'; and then again,
> 'It is as hard to come as for a camel
> To thread the postern of a needle's eye.'[18]

At the prison-assassination Shakespeare's sympathy assigns the king the fierce and powerful courage of despair. He kills two of his murderers and as a scripture counterpart assigns them to the fire that is not quenched, and then gives a grand turn to the ancient verse regarding the return of the dust to earth and of the spirit to God who gave it:

> That hand shall burn in never quenching fire
> That staggers thus my person. Exton, thy fierce hand
> Hath with the king's blood stain'd the king's own land,
> Mount, mount my soul! thy seat is up on high,
> Whilst my gross flesh sinks downward, here to die.[19]

Then comes the final scripture judgment upon the murderers of Richard and, by implication, upon Bolingbroke himself:

> Though I did wish him dead,
> I hate the murderer, love him murdered.
> The guilt of conscience take thou for thy labor,
> But neither my good word not princely favor:
> With Cain go wander through the shade of night.[20]

In both parts of *Henry Fourth* and in *The Merry Wives of Windsor* it is Falstaff who knows his Bible. He is poor as Job but not so patient.[21] He is not afraid of Goliath with a weaver's beam because life itself is a swift-moving shuttle.[22] He surely knows by experience the story of the prodigal.[23] If Adam fell in the state of innocency, what should poor Jack Falstaff do in the days of villainy? He has

[18]*Richard Second*, V, v, 15-17; *Matthew*, XI, 28; XIX, 24.
[19]*Richard Second*, V, v. 108-112; *Mark*, IX, 44; *Eccl.* XII, 7.
[20]*Richard Second*, V, vi, 39-43; *1 John*, III, 15; *Genesis*, V, 14.
[21]*Second Part Henry Fourth*, I, ii, 127; *James*, V, 11.
[22]*Merry Wives of Windsor*, V, i, 23, 24; *1 Samuel*, XVII, 7.
[23]*Second Part Henry Fourth*, II, i, 146; *Luke*, XV, 11 seq.

more flesh than other men and therefore more frailty.[24] Sometimes he is guilty of leaving the fear of God on the left hand.[25] If however mere fat makes a man hated, Pharoah's lean kine are to be loved.[26] He and Harry may repent, but it will not be in ashes and sackcloth, but in new silk and old sack.[27] He has irreverent knowledge of Lazarus and the dogs that licked his sores,[28] and of Dives burning in hell.[29] He understands that as he that handles pitch is defiled, so the company a man keeps affects his morals.[30] Henry's goodness comes from his association with him, for a tree is known by its fruit.[31] It is God who gives men a spirit of persuasion.[32] Men themselves, however, must rouse up fear and trembling.[33] If he has an enemy the man is an Ahitophel.[34] If men are saved by merit, no hole in hell is hot enough for him.[35] A man who has plenty of gold-pieces is possessed of a legion of "angels."[36] Falstaff can even make sport of Paul's lofty injunction to owe no man anything but love.[37] Sometimes, in fine, his scripture quotations are themselves, like Mrs. Ford's scriptural remark about him, quite unquotable.[38] Falstaffs whole character may be known by the Scripture he uses and by the way he uses it. But, once more, in the closing scripture citation Shakespeare passes an unrelenting judgment upon the profane and

---

[24]*First Part Henry Fourth,* III, iii, 172-174; *Genesis,* III, 6; *Romans,* VII, 18.

[25]*Merry Wives of Windsor,* II, ii, 23; *Romans,* III, 18.

[26]*First Part Henry Fourth,* II, iv, 481-483; *Genesis,* XLI, 19 f.

[27]*Second Part Henry Fourth,* I, ii, 198-199; *Jonah,* III, 6.

[28]*First Part Henry Fourth,* IV, ii, 25, 26; *Luke,* XVI, 20 f.

[29]*First Part Henry Fourth,* III, iii, 33, 34; *Luke,* XVI, 23 f.

[30]*First Part Henry Fourth,* II, iv, 421-423; *Ecclesiasticus,* XIII, 1.

[31]*First Part Henry Fourth,* II, iv, 436-438; *Matthew,* XII, 33.

[32]*First Part Henry Fourth,* I, ii, 152; *1 Kings,* XXII, 21.

[33]*Second Part Henry Fourth,* IV, iii, 14; *Philippians,* II, 12.

[34]*Second Part Henry Fourth,* I, ii, 35; *2 Samuel,* XV, 31.

[35]*First Part Henry Fourth,* I, ii, 109 f.; *James,* II, 24; *Luke,* XVI, 23 f.

[36]*Merry Wives of Windsor,* I, iii, 54; *Mark,* V, 9.

[37]*First Part Henry Fourth,* III, iii, 54; *Mark,* V, 9.

[37]*First Part Henry Fourth,* III, iii, 144; *Romans,* XIII, 8.

[38]*Merry Wives of Windsor,* II, i, 60-67; *Jonah,* II, 10.

surfeited fool and jester whose character he has created. Falstaff comes before the bar of a single passage and is found guilty. What was his wild and wanton story, and what had Henry's protracted association with him been but a long light-headed dream? Falstaff's tongue had most certainly walked thru the earth, and his eyes had stood out with fatness. But of such the Psalmist had already said, "As a dream when one awaketh, so, O Lord, when thou awakest thou wilt despise their image."

> I have long dreamed of such a kind of man,
> So surfeit-swell'd, so old, and so profane;
> But, being awaked, I do despise my dream.[39]

So Henry feels, and as Falstaff's unlimited wit at the expense of Scripture is preceded by Shakespeare's most heartfelt reference to Jesus and his cross,[40] so it is also followed by this vision of judgment.

Richard III is a man of fixed craftiness, unconquerable force, and consistent devotion to the most satanic evil. His murders and his own words show that he is "determined to prove a villain." His use of Scripture constitutes equally cogent evidence. It is as perverted as that of the amended Vivien and far more extended and varied. Perversion of the Bible is in fact an integral part of his adopted profession of evil. He prays for God's pardon for Clarence's persecutors. It is the Christian's part to pray for the wrong-doer, not to curse him. To have cursed the prospective murderer, morever, would have been to curse himself.[41] He tells how men urge him to be revenged on Rivers, Grey, and Vaughan and then soliloquizes:

[39]*Second Part Henry Fourth*, V, v, 51-53; *Psalms*, LXXIII, 7-9 and esp. 20.

[40]*First Part Henry Fourth*, I, i, 24-27.

[41]*Richard Third*, I, iii, 315-319; *Luke*, VI, 27 f.

> But then I sigh, and, with a piece of scripture,
> Tell them that God bids us do good for evil:
> And thus I clothe my naked villainy
> With odd old ends stolen forth of holy writ,
> And seem a saint when most I play the devil.[42]

There is nothing like this in all the vast bulk of Scripture in Tennyson's dramas. His evil characters pervert the sacred words incidentally and temporarily. Perversion is not their profession as it is with Richard. Of the two children smothered to death in the tower he says,

> The Sons of Edward sleep in Abraham's bosom.[43]

When Queen Elizabeth and the Duchess of York upbraid him for his murders he calls for music to drown out such blasphemy.

> A flourish, trumpets! strike alarum, drums!
> Let not the heavens hear these tell-tale women
> Rail on the Lord's anointed. Strike, I say.[44]

He asks Elizabeth to press his suit upon her daughter. His heart is pure, immaculate, devoted. Elizabeth replies and he retorts:

> *Queen Elizabeth.* Shall I be tempted of the devil thus?
> *King Richard.* Aye, if the devil tempt thee to do good.[45]

And finally, . . . he perverts the shining of the sun of God's universal love in favor of his evil life. Does not God cause his light to fall on the evil as well as the good?

> Not shine today! Why, what is that to me
> More than to Richmond? For the selfsame heaven
> That frowns on me looks sadly upon him.[46]

---

[42]*Richard Third*, I, iii, 334-338; *Romans*, XII, 17, 21; *2 Corinthians*, XI, 14 f.
[43]*Richard Third*, IV, iii, 38; *Luke*, XVI, 22.
[44]*Richard Third*, IV, iv, 149-151; *Psalms*, II, 2.
[45]*Richard Third*, IV, iv, 419 f.; *Matthew*, IV, 1 seq.
[46]*Richard Third*, V, iii, 286-288; *Matthew*, V, 45.

Just before the end comes the one unperverted allusion. The thousand-tongued witness of a self-accusing and self-condemning conscience pronounces its sentence upon Richard's whole career.

> My conscience hath a thousand several tongues,
> And every tongue brings in a several tale
> And every tale condemns me for a villain.[47]

In the *Merchant of Venice* a very different biblical vein is worked. Shylock is familiar with the *New Testament* as well as with the *Old*. He will not dine with Bassanio lest there be pork on the table. He recalls the swine of Gadara and will not "eat of the habitation which your prophet the Nazarite conjured the devil into."[48] Any Christian looks to him like a fawning publican.[49] He defends his usury by a full account of Jacob's methods with Laban's flocks.[50] He appeals to Father Abram[51] and swears by Jacob's staff[52] and by the holy Sabbath.[53] He calls Launcelot a fool of Hagar's offspring.[54] He is aware of God's curse upon his nation but never really felt it till he lost the costly diamond.[55] Then comes the resolving incident of the "Daniel come to judgment," the "second Daniel," and "still the Second Daniel."[56] Then, once more, at the end, as in *Richard Second*, occurs a double scripture climax which sets the silent music of the spheres[57] against the noisy disharmonies of earth, and sets Shylock's greed and murderous hate against the kindly deeds of those who let their good light shine forth among men.

[47]*Richard Third*, V, iii, 194-196; *Romans*, II, 15.
[48]*Merchant of Venice*, I, iii, 32 f.; *Matthew*, VIII, 31 f.
[49]*Merchant of Venice*, I, iii, 39; *Luke*, XVIII, 11.
[50]*Merchant of Venice*, I, iii, 75-88; *Genesis*, XXX, 31-43.
[51]*Merchant of Venice*, I, iii, 158; *John*, VIII, 53.
[52]*Merchant of Venice*, II, v, 36; *Genesis*, XXXII, 10.
[53]*Merchant of Venice*, IV, i, 36; *Exodus*, XX, 8.
[54]*Merchant of Venice*, II, v, 43; *Genesis*, XVI, 16.
[55]*Merchant of Venice*, III, i, 82-84; *Malachi*, III, 9.
[56]*Merchant of Venice*, IV, i, 221, 332, 339; *Daniel*, IV, 8.
[57]*Merchant of Venice*, V, i, 60-65; *Psalms*, XIX, 2-4.

That light you see is burning in my hall,
How far that little candle throws his beams!
So shines a good deed in a naughty world.[58]

In Shakespeare, then, the scripture passages are employed in the interest of manifest destiny, dramatic development, or the verdict of conscience. Taken all together and in their climax the citations give the moral of the play. They are for the most part connected with a single character and progress to a final ethical judgment upon him.

[58]*Merchant of Venice*, V, i, 89-91; *Matthew*, V, 16.

III Christopher Fry's Use of the Bible in *A Sleep of Prisoners*

John H. Hafner

Department of English,
Spring Hill College (Mobile, Alabama)

Christopher Fry, a contemporary British dramatist, has written two plays on biblical subjects, *The First Born*, the story of Moses and his attempt to free the Israelites from Egypt, and *A Sleep of Prisoners*, the play discussed below. *A Sleep of Prisoners* mingles four familiar stories from the Old Testament to raise some questions about the connection between dreams and reality in our lives. In the discussion that follows, the four dream sequences are compared with their sources in the Bible.—Ed.

A Sleep of Prisoners uses four biblical stories explicitly and echoes the way the Bible uses them. The stories of Cain and Abel, David and Absalom, Abraham and Isaac are presented through dreams within a frame story that is based on the experience of the men in the fiery furnace of the book of Daniel. Fry connects these stories by suggesting similarities in theme and characterization. In doing so, he imitates the typological technique of the Bible. For example, the Cain-Abel relationship is similar to other brother relationships in the Bible. The story is also related to the problem, thematic in the Bible, of understanding man's capacity for evil. Cain and Abel become representatives of the opposing forces of good and evil in all men. Fry is certainly dealing with this latter aspect of the story he retells, just as the Bible presents variations on so many of its central stories as it explores certain attributes of man's nature.

A Sleep of Prisoners is a frame play containing three other plays. The frame is the story of four men who are prisoners of war, imprisoned in a chapel. Their situation is presented as parallel to that of the three men in the fiery furnace; the fourth man is the angel who joins them. In the Bible story, King Nebuchadnezzar orders all his people to worship a particular idol; failure to do so will result in death by fire. Shadrach, Meshach, and Abednego refuse to worship the idol and are thrown into a furnace. They are miraculously saved from death and are joined in the fire by an angel (who, in the Septuagint version, leads them in chanting a hymn of praise to the Lord). When Nebuchadnezzar releases them and hears their story, he converts to belief in their God. In Fry's frame we are aware of the imprisonment at the beginning of the play; the connection of this imprisonment with the fiery furnace story is emphasized at the end of the play—in the last of the four dreams, that of Corporal Adams. Within the frame story we have the other three prisoners, one after the other, dreaming their own dreams, each of which parallels another biblical story.

Fry first establishes the frame and the character of each of the four men. We learn a great number of things about the men, especially about Peter Able and David King. David is domineering, authoritarian. He is sarcastic, blatantly so. Fry emphasizes David's physical qualities, suggesting that he is ruled by his physical nature. Peter even refers to him as "an example of the bestial passions that beset mankind." He gets angry and violent easily. In the opening scene he attacks Peter violently without seeming to intend to do so. After the attack he is contrite, very much concerned about Peter's welfare, so that he seems to have acted spontaneously, almost unconsciously. By way of apology, he asks Peter,

> Why don't
> You do some slaughtering sometimes? Why always
> Leave it to me?

Peter is just the opposite. He is loose, casual, takes things easily, doesn't get upset. We are told that he feels at home anywhere and is a kind of peacemaker. Fry shows him playing the church organ, reading the Bible. He even has to be reminded that he is at war, that he is a prisoner of war. He and David are close friends, set up as contrasts to each other: David, the physical man; Peter, the man who attempts to transcend the physical, to rise above the restrictions of physical nature. David says to him, "You don't deserve to inherit the earth."

The other two characters, Tim Meadows and Joe Adams, are authority figures. Joe Adams outranks the other three as a corporal. Tim Meadows is old enough to be the father of the other three.

Having established the frame story of the four men imprisoned in a chapel during a war, Fry now begins his sequence of dream plays. The first dream is dreamed by Tim Meadows. His role in the dream is set when he comments, "I didn't ask to be God." In this first dream, Corporal Joe Adams plays Adam; David King is Cain; Peter Able, Abel. The dream story is obviously biblical at the same time that it extends the militaristic setting of the frame story. In the dream David/Cain and Peter/Abel shoot dice. David gets worked up over it; Peter is relaxed, just playing a game. Peter wins. David gets angry and kills him. Meadows then judges and banishes David, promising that he will never be killed.

The second dream is David's. Its story is based on the David-Absalom relationship in II Samuel, which Fry simplifies. Again the main characters are David King and Peter Able. Corporal Adams plays the military figure parallel to Joab. The David-Absalom dream continues the characterization from the previous dream and the frame story. Again we have a killing, but with a crucial difference from the murder in the Cain-Abel story. This time the violence is once-removed. Cain killed Abel. But Absalom is killed by Joab, who misreads King David's orders. David mourns deeply over Absalom's death in the Bible story, another progression, for in the Genesis account Cain showed very little concern for Abel's death.

This movement is carried farther still in the third dream.

Peter's dream is based on the Abraham-Isaac story. In Fry's version David/Abraham leads Peter/Isaac to be sacrificed. The killing is prevented by Corporal Adams as the dream angel. The movement in the play has been from Cain killing Abel, to David accidentally causing Absalom's death, to no death at all. In all three dreams David King's role has been forceful and physical, but it has become less irrationally violent. David/Abraham is ready to sacrifice Peter/Isaac because God has ordered him to do so. But he would not have initiated the violence.

In the fourth dream, Corporal Adam's dream, we are brought back into the frame story. Adams begins his dream and is joined in the dream by the other three prisoners; then all four awake from their collective dream and continue, awake, the activities they had been dreaming about. In the final dream, which becomes the closing frame, the four men have moved beyond violent confrontation, have established a peaceful, harmonious relationship. There is still violence, but now it comes from outside, from the enemy without.

The four men have not been radically changed; they have been refined, civilized, pacified. David can still pray,

> Let me, dear God, be active
> And seem to do right, whatever damned result.
> Let me have some part in what goes on
> Or I shall go mad!

And several lines later he says,

> I've got to know which side I'm on.
> I've got to be on a side.

He has to commit himself, take a stand, do something. But he has reached a point where he can control what before was irrational violence. Peter is still the calm peacemaker who not only doesn't have to take sides but has to be reminded that there are sides to be taken. Corporal Adams is still an authority figure, but not merely in his previously assured, military way. Now he answers David's questions of whose side they are on by asking his own question:

> Who are we, Dave, who
> Are we?

In doing so, he attempts to get at basic issues, to get a larger, higher view. Later he finds he must change, from ordering the men to stand at attention to ordering the men to fall on their knees. This change occurs when the men change from a dream of specific and personal military interrogation and punishment to a more awakened state, in which the suffering and threat of fire are related to the more general human condition of pain and suffering. According to Meadows the men will survive their suffering in the fiery furnace if they have patience, love, honesty. Fry's play ends with an echo of the biblical story of the three men in the fiery furnace, with a hymn of praise, a statement of hope. These last words, "Hope so. Hope so," not only refer to the specific dramatic situation at the end of the play but are also a general comment on the theme of the nature of man developed within the play.

That theme is developed in the three plays within the play. It is also developed through the ways in which the stories relate to each other, lead to each other. Fry ignores the biblical chronology in order to allow for a dramatic chronology of a greater movement toward hope, toward some kind of peace. In the Bible the Abraham-Isaac story comes before David and Absalom. But Fry's arrangement allows a different movement: Abel is killed in the first dream; Absalom is killed in the second, but accidentally; Isaac is saved in the third dream; and in the frame story the men cooperate in a declaration of hope in the nature and future of man. The play moves from a view of man which is close to hopeless because of his senseless violence to a view that man's better nature has the ability to prevail and to find peace, community, love.

A speech by David as Abraham in the third dream illustrates how the theme can be reflected in the language as well as in the action:

> Keep close to me,
> It may not be for long. Time huddles round us,

> A little place to be in. And we're already
> Up the heavy hill. The singing birds
> Drop down and down to the bed of the trees,
> To the hay-silver evening, O
> Lying gentleness, a thin veil over
> The long scars from the nails of the warring hearts.
> Come up, son, and see the world.
> God dips his hand in death to wash the wound,
> Takes evil to inoculate our lives
> Against infectious evil. We'll go on.
> I am history's wish and must come true,
> And I shall hate so long as hate
> Is history, though, God, it drives
> My life away like a beaten dog. Here
> Is the stone where we have to sacrifice.
> Make my heart like it. It still is beating
> Unhappily the human time.

This is a fine passage. David/Abraham is leading his son to the sacrifice. His speech contains all the strength and sorrow appropriate to a man of power reluctantly obeying a command. The image of evening in the first lines, the "hay-silver evening," provides a veil that hides, falsifies, lies gently. The beauty of the singing birds bedding down misrepresents the harsh reality of the sacrifice that must be made. And the father bitterly invites his son to view the world where death and evil are the agents that cleanse and cure. The bitterness and the hatred lead to a desire that his heart be turned to stone instead of remaining human. The rhythm is slow, stately; the language is direct and harsh. The bitter tone is brilliantly conveyed through the image of the deceptive beauty of the evening. And the heart-turned-to-stone metaphor is saved from triteness, made effective by its appropriate connection with the stone altar of sacrifice. The stone heart will also be a site of sacrifice for the human emotions which must be killed before the son is killed.

Another example of Fry's careful artistry is the "Three Blind Mice" motif. At the beginning of the play Peter plays "Three Blind Mice" on the organ. It is a corny thing to do—only funny, if it is funny, because of the incongruity of playing a nursery rhyme on a church organ. At the end of the play Corporal Adams refers to "Three Blind Mice" again. But this time he names the mice Shadrach, Meshach, and Abednego. "Three Blind Mice" is no longer just an irreverent nursery rhyme; it has become a comment on the question of faith and hope that the play is raising: blind faith is the answer to the human questions. Violence, war, hatred all exist: the mice are threatened by the farmer's wife with a carving knife; Shadrach, Meshach, Abednego are put into the furnace by the king; David, Peter, Adams, Meadows are imprisoned and threatened by the enemy. Men can eliminate some of these evils, but it is only faith that allows men to prevail. Fry's playing with words, his punning, his self-conscious use of sounds might have been silly or, at best, precious if he did not carry that word play to the point where it becomes meaningful in the context of everything else that is happening in his play.

A Sleep of Prisoners is fine poetic drama, whose craftsmanship we have here only begun to examine. It is also an example of the way a writer can use the Bible to achieve a depth, a universality. Fry's use of the Bible stories is all-pervading: the entire play, its plot, structure, characters, and themes are built on both the specific stories from the Bible and the literary methodology of the Bible, with meaning and to great effect.

IV Biblical Perversions in *Desire Under the Elms**

Peter L. Hays

*Department of English,
University of California at Davis*

Eugene O'Neill (1888–1953) won Pulitzer prizes for his plays in 1920, 1922, 1928, and 1937 and the Nobel Prize in 1936. *Desire Under the Elms*, as the following article points out, uses the Bible not to achieve universality but to reinforce a dual perspective through the ironic use of a series of biblical allusions.—Ed.

While O'Neill's plays are noted primarily for the dramatic force with which they express his tragic view of life, many of them—*The Hairy Ape, All God's Chillun Got Wings, Marco Millions, Iceman Cometh,* and others—contain a great deal of social criticism. So does his early tragedy *Desire Under the Elms,* which has been critically examined for its use of the Hippolytus and Medea myths, its Freudian elements, its relation to O'Neill's early plays (e.g., *The Rope*) and own biography,[1] but there has been little close attention to the way in which religious references inform the play, and the way religion both causes the tragedy and comments upon it.

Eben's first word in the play is "God!" His first line of dialogue is "Honor thy father!"—his sarcastic reply to his brothers' statement that they must wait for their father's death before they can hope to own the farm—which Eben follows with, "I pray he's died."[2] This ironic use of the Biblical commandment and the perverse form of Eben's

---

*From *Modern Drama,* 11 (February, 1969): 423-28. Reprinted by permission.

[1] Cf. Arthur and Barbara Gelb, *O'Neill* (New York, 1960, 1962), pp. 378, 538-541.

[2] *The Plays of Eugene O'Neill* (New York: Random House, n.d.), I, 203, 205. All subsequent quotations will be from this edition and paginated in my text.

prayer set the tone of the play and forewarn us to note how almost all expressions of religious origin are similarly twisted. In fact, they help us appreciate the harsh and equally twisted religion practiced on this farm, a loveless religion largely responsible for the play's tragedy.

The reaction of Eben's brothers to his wish that Ephraim Cabot, their father, were dead is typical of the hypocrisy in religious and other matters.

> SIMEON. . . . Looky here! Ye'd oughtn't t' said that, Eben.
> PETER. Twa'n't righteous.
> EBEN. What?
> SIMEON. Ye prayed he'd died.
> EBEN. Waal—don't yew pray it? (p. 206)

For it is Simeon himself who says that they must wait for the farm until Ephraim dies. Their denunciation of Eben is perfunctory and conventional rather than an expression either of filial or Christian piety. Later in the play even this sanctimonious facade is dropped, though the dialogue still is couched in canonical terms. Speaking of their new step-mother, Simeon says:

> Waal—I hope she's a she-devil that'll make him wish he was dead an' livin' in the pit o' hell fur comfort.
> PETER. (fervently) Amen! (p. 215)

Similarly, the townspeople in Part III, Scene 1, suspecting that the baby is Eben's and not Ephraim's, express themselves in terms of ribaldry, concealed envy, or mockery for Ephraim—whose physical strength they respect too much for them to ridicule to his face, but whose cuckoldry makes them feel superior to him. They come to eat, drink, and have fun behind the Cabots' backs:

> MAN. Listen, Abbie—if ye ever git tired o Eben, remember me. (p. 248)
> CABOT. . . . [Eben] kin do a day's work a' most up t'what I kin.
> . . .
> FIDDLER. An' he kin do a good night's work, too! (A roar of laughter.) (p. 249)
> FIDDLER. . . . Let's celebrate the old skunk gittin' fooled! We kin have some fun now he's went. (p. 253)

No one sympathizes or expresses genuine moral concern. And they too pervert scripture for their own ends. The fiddler says that Eben is in church offering prayers of thanksgiving, "'Cause unto him a—*(He hesitates just long enough)* brother is born!" (p. 248).

It is Ephraim, though, more than any other character in the play who makes religious statements apply to irreligious acts. He tells Simeon: "I been hearin' the hens cluckin' an' the roosters crowin' all the durn day. I been listenin' t' the cows lowin' an' everythin' else kickin' up till I can't stand it no more. It's spring an' I feel damned. . . . An' now I'm ridin' out t' learn God's message t' me in the spring, like the prophets done" (p. 210). Then he drives off in the buggy, singing a hymn. In spite of his seventy-five years, what Ephraim feels is need—for a woman, almost any woman. And as Simeon says when he hears that the elder Cabot has remarried for the third time:

"I'm ridin' out t' learn God's message t' me in the spring like the prophets done," he says. "I'll bet right then an' thar he knew plumb well he was going whorin', the stinkin' old hypocrite! (p. 215)

But Ephraim is not a hypocrite if we insist that hypocrisy be conscious dissembling. Ephraim is cruel, harsh, and devoid of charity, but knows himself to be so, desires to be so, and feels that he has Divine sanction for his ruthlessness. He practices a harsh and loveless Puritanical religion that worships toil, scorns ease and sentiment or even the expression of honest sentiment. As he says to Abbie in a rare burst of self-expression which she does not hear—like the soliloquies of Chekov's characters, spoken at but rarely to a listener:

When ye kin make corn sprout out o' stones, God's livin' in yew! . . . God hain't easy. . . . I growed hard. Folks allus sayin' he's a hard man like 'twas sinful t' be hard. . . . God's hard, not easy! God's in the stones! . . . Stones. I picked 'em up an' piled 'em into walls. Ye kin read the years of my life in them walls, every day a hefted stone, . . . fencin' in the fields that was mine, whar I made thin's grow out of nothin'—like the will o' God, like the servant o' His hand. It wa'n't easy. It was hard an' He made me hard fur it. (pp. 236-237)

The whole rambling passage emphasizes possession, hardness, the sinfulness of easy wealth, the equation of virtue with hard work, and Ephraim's loneliness. The "objective correlative" of the passage is *stone:*[3] hard, unyielding, impenetrable. Piled one on top of another, they wall the farm like a prison, as Ephraim's values imprison him, his successive wives, and his sons, creating their mutual lack of contact; for stones piled to make a wall are individual objects, not a unit, without some sort of bond or mortar. And on the Cabot farm there is no such agent until Abbie and Eben realize their love late in the play. Instead there are the worst distortions of the Protestant ethic: greed, vengeance, incessant toil, and individual isolation. Even Ephraim, so insensitive to the real feelings of Eben's mother, Eben, or Abbie, feels this chill sense of loneliness—"It's cold in this house [though at midsummer]. It's oneasy. They's thin's pokin' about in the dark—in the corners" (p. 238). And so for comfort, Ephraim goes down to the barn where it is warm and peaceful, largely because the animals do not covet one another's possessions, and because their behavior doesn't suffer from the restrictions and inhibitions of Ephraim's Christianity. Edwin Arlington Robinson summed up the situation well in his famous sonnet "New England":

> Passion is here a soilure of the wits,
> We're told, and Love a cross for them to bear;
> Joy shivers in the corner where she knits
> And conscience always has the rocking chair. . . .
>
> (ll. 9-12)

Thus, though each of the characters has his own desires, each pharisaically condemns the others' as lusts. Abbie,

---

[3] It is not without significance that not only does Peter's name mean stone, but so does Eben's, in Greek and Hebrew, respectively.

who has married Ephraim for the security of a home, tries to seduce Eben, and when she fails, when Eben goes off to see the town whore instead, screams, "Git out o' my sight! Go on t' yer slut—disgracin' yer Paw 'n' me!" (p. 230). Though her motive is jealousy, not piety, she denounces Eben to his father in these terms: "[Eben's gone] t' see that harlot, Min! . . . Disgracin' yew an' me—on the Sabbath, too!" (p. 233). As if the day mattered to Abbie. And Cabot replies, *"(rather guiltily)* He's a sinner—nateral-born. It's lust eatin' his heart" (p. 233). Ephraim's guilt is two-fold, for Min was his mistress long before she was Eben's, and he has his own lusts: the one which drove him away from the farm months before to seek a wife, the same one for which he "stares at her [Abbie] desirously" and addresses her in terms of that ancient fertility chant, The Song of Songs; and the lust for a new son, proof of his virility, and worthy heir to the farm. Though Ephraim condemns Eben for lust, he himself calls Abbie his "Rose o' Sharon! Behold, yew air fair; yer eyes air doves; yer lips air like scarlet; yer two breasts air like two fawns. . . . *(He covers her hand with kisses . . .)*" (p. 232). Though he denounces Simeon and Peter's desire to visit the California goldfields as "Lust fur gold—fur the sinful, easy gold o' Californi-a" (p. 223), he desperately covets a son as an extension of his own right of ownership:[4]

. . . What son o' mine'll keep on here t' the farm—when the Lord does call me? Simeon an' Peter air gone t'hell—an' Eben's follerin' 'em.

. . . A son is me—my blood—mine. Mine ought t' git mine. An' then it's still mine—even though I be six foot under. (p. 234)

For good or for bad, Ephraim and even Abbie use prayer. When Abbie sees that her only real security lies in providing Cabot a son, she suggests to him that "mebbe the Lord'll give *us* a son" (p. 234); she emphasizes "us" because a new son will disinherit Eben, even though Eben is his

[4]That a man's blood line descends through his sons is, of course, a common folk belief that finds expression in the Bible, Gen. 48:16 and Deut. 25:6.

father—which is what we, at this point in the play, suspect, and what Abbie plans. She says to Ephraim, ". . . I been prayin' it'd happen . . . ," and he responds:

> It'd be the blessin' o' God, Abbie—the blessin' o' God A'mighty on me—in my old age—in my lonesomeness! . . .
>
> Pray t' the Lord agen, Abbie. It's the Sabbath! I'll jine ye! Two prayers air better nor one. "An' God hearkened unto Rachel"! An' God harkened unto Abbie! Pray fur him to hearken' *(He bows his head, mumbling. She pretends to do likewise but gives him a side glance of scorn and triumph.)* (p. 234-235)

God does not hear the prayer, for the son Abbie bears is Eben's, even though Ephraim thinks it is his, and when Abbie suffocates the infant and is jailed for the crime with Eben, Cabot is even more alone—without any wife or son. And so this "good" prayer, for a son, is frustrated. But Ephraim prays for evil, too. When Simeon and Peter desert the farm, *his* farm, he prays to God to curse them:

> CABOT. . . . Lord God o' Hosts, smite the undutiful sons with Thy wust cuss!
>
> EBEN. . . . Yew 'n' yewr God! Allus cussin' folks—allus naggin' 'em!
>
> CABOT. *(oblivious to him—summoningly)* God o' the old! God o' the lonesome!
>
> EBEN. *(mockingly)* Naggin' His sheep t' sin! T' hell with yewr God. (p. 227)

Cabot's God is indeed the God of the old—He is the harsh, avenging God of the Old Testament, as popularly conceived of, distinct from the more loving, more forgiving and charitable God of the New Testament. But of course, this is not so—the God of the Old Testament, the same God, is merciful, forgiving, and loving; but Ephraim's perverse belief in Him as a hard and lonesome God (pp. 227, 268) has caused Cabot to value hardness and isolation, to work his first two wives to death, to drive off his two elder sons, to instill as values in his sons craftiness, vengeance, and suspicion instead of love, and to wall himself up and prevent any warm, personal, truly communicative relationship with any of his wives or sons. And so Eben seeks vengeance for himself and his mother's death through Abbie; Ephraim seeks to dispossess Eben and hand the farm on to a still younger son; and Abbie—at first—seeks to cheat them both, loving neither. Whatever tendencies of character Ephraim may have inherited that caused him to be as he is, undoubtedly his harsh religion—the same religion as Hawthorne's John Endicott and O'Neill's own Mannons—has developed and confirmed these traits. And by purposeful use of Biblical language or quotations in debased contexts, O'Neill has underscored this perversion of religion for us. He has also provided, by allusion, an analogue for comment and contrast.

For if one believes that Ephraim Cabot does ride from the farm to learn God's message as the prophets did, then one must assume that the message was to marry. And, indeed, God did instruct the first of the so-called Minor Prophets, Hosea, to marry—to marry, in fact, a harlot, which is what Eben calls Abbie for marrying Cabot in order to have a home. Hosea is commanded to wed a prostitute, and, even though she is unfaithful to him and deserts him, he is told to buy her back and to reaffirm his devotion—all as an allegory of the Lord's relation to Israel, which had broken its covenant with God and was prostituting itself both figuratively, with false gods, and literally: "the prophet's personal life is an incarnation of God's redeeming love."[5] And significantly, Hosea addresses Israel, the nation's eponymous name after Jacob, by the name of Joseph's younger son, eponymous founder of one of the twelve tribes (Gen. 48), Ephraim. And like Ephraim Cabot,

> E'phraim is oppressed, cursed in judgment,
>> because he was determined to go after vanity.
>>> (Hos. 5:11)
>
> . . . E'phraim has hired lovers. (8:9)
>
> E'phraim has said, "Ah, but I am rich,
>> I have gained wealth for myself:"

[5] *The Oxford Annotated Bible with the Apocrypha* (New York, 1965), p. 1088.

> but all his riches can never offset
> the guilt he has incurred. (12:8)

By denying Hosea's message of love and forgiveness, by perverting the message of the Bible, Ephraim Cabot has taught "Bloody instructions, which, being taught, returns to plague the inventor." He has freed his animals before he learns that Eben has taken his savings, and all his relations are gone—"It's a-goin' t' be lonesomer now than ever it war afore—an' I'm gittin' old, Lord—ripe on the bough" (p. 268). In the words of Hosea, he has sown the wind and reaped the whirlwind (8:7).

In his review of *Desire Under the Elms*,[6] Joseph Wood Krutch said that "the meaning and unity of his work lies not in any controlling intellectual idea and certainly not in a 'message,' but merely in the fact that each play is an experience of extraordinary intensity." Certainly this is as true for *Desire* as it is for O'Neill's other plays, but it is no less true that *Desire* is, if not controlled, then at least shaped, by an intellectual idea and a message: that the harsh, loveless, and covetous Puritanical religion practiced by Ephraim Cabot is a perversion of religion that cripples love and destroys men.

[6] *The Nation*, CXIX (Nov. 26, 1924), 578; quoted by the Gelbs, p. 571.

V How Genuine Is *The Green Pastures?* *

Nick Aaron Ford

Department of English,
Morgan State College (Baltimore)

Marc Connelly (1890–   ) received the Pulitzer Prize in 1930 for *The Green Pastures*, a play based on Roark Bradford's *Ol' Man Adam an' His Chillun*, published in 1928. The following exchange between two college teachers raises questions about Connelly's purpose and achievement, especially in his interpretation of the God of the Old Testament.—Ed.

Commenting on the television debut of *The Green Pastures*, over the NBC-TV network, October 17, 1957, John Crosby, well-known radio and television critic, said in his newspaper column, *"Green Pastures*, which I feared might seem a little naive and precious at this late date, was fresh and endearing and moving as ever."

I propose in this brief discussion to re-examine *The Green Pastures* to see how genuine it is and to see whether or not it deserves the amazing veneration it has enjoyed in some quarters for approximately twenty-eight years. It is conceivable that the judges might have grievously erred in awarding it the once coveted Pulitzer Prize.

A critic may ask himself three basic questions in respect to any litarary work he proposes to criticize. (1) What has the author attempted to do? (2) How well has he achieved his purpose? (3) How significant is the objective he has set for himself? Despite sincere efforts of the critic, criticism can hardly escape entirely from the taint of subjectivism. Nevertheless, every critic worth his salt must strive continually to achieve objectivity. The first two questions I have posed can be answered fairly objectively by any critic who takes his task seriously. Only the third by its very nature involves varying degrees of subjectivity.

*From *Phylon*, 20 (March, 1959): 67-70. Copyright Atlanta University. Reprinted by permission.

However, if the second question is answered in the negative, there is little need to proceed to the third. Only if the author has achieved what he set out to accomplish does the significance of his achievement deserve evaluation in so far as the greatness of a literary work is concerned. In other words, if the author fails to achieve his objective, or if he achieves it badly, his work may lay claim to greatness as a philosophic treatise or as a historical document, but not as a literary masterpiece.

What has Mr. Connelly attempted to do in *The Green Pastures?* According to columnist John Crosby he has attempted to present a "view of the Old Testament as seen through the imagination of a bunch of Negro kids in Bible school." Donald Kirkley, another radio and television critic, says the author has attempted to present a story of the Bible "as it appeared to an imaginative child in a Sunday school in Louisiana." According to another commentator who hailed the play as one of the greatest, it is a presentation of the highlights of the Old Testament as seen through the eyes of an unlettered Negro. These comments clearly indicate that there is some misunderstanding of the author's purpose among those who speak with assurance of the greatness of the work.

In the "Author's Note" in the printed version, published by Farrar and Rinehart, 1930, Mr. Connelly himself states what he has attempted to do. He says:

"The Green Pastures" is an attempt to present certain aspects of a living religion in the terms of its believers. The religion is that of thousands of Negroes in the deep South. With terrific spiritual hunger and the greatest humility these untutored black Christians—many of whom cannot even read the book which is the treasure house of their faith—have adapted the contents of the Bible to the consistencies of their everyday lives. . . .

One need not blame a hazy memory of the Bible for the failure to recall the characters of Hezdrel, Zeba and others in the play. They are the author's apocrypha, but he believes persons much like them have figured in the meditations of some of the old Negro preachers, whose simple faith he has tried to translate into a play.

In the first place, we are immediately impressed with an inconsistency in the author's purpose as he states it himself. He says he is attempting to translate the religious conceptions of thousands of untutored Negroes as they have adapted the Bible stories to suit the experiences of their everyday lives. Yet in the last paragraph he admits that he has used certain characters in his dramatization which are not in the Bible at all. His only justification for using such counterfeit characters is his belief that "persons like them have figured in the meditations of some of the old Negro preachers."

However, let us not hold this inconsistency against Mr. Connelly. Let us see whether or not he has achieved his main purpose, which is to present a genuine representation of the religious beliefs of thousands of untutored Negroes in the deep South.

I charge that Mr. Connelly has utterly failed to accomplish this purpose and that his representation is counterfeit.

First, he has misrepresented the unlettered Negro's conception of the physical features of God. Because of religious indoctrination during slavery, the Negro cannot imagine a black God. In all of his testimony concerning his visions and dreams about God, he pictures God and the angels as white. He is sure that the color of his skin is only a sign of his mortality, and that when he dies and goes to Heaven he will be transformed into a white angel.

If Mr. Connelly had followed the tradition of all good writers who attempt to deal with unfamiliar folk material, he would have done a little research in the religious literature of colored people, or he would have sat at the feet of some of these "old Negro preachers" and sought the truth. If he had done any one of these things, he would have learned that of all the spirits of the other world, so far as unlettered Negroes are concerned, only the devil is black. God, the angels, and all the heavenly creatures are as white as the drifting snow.

Secondly, he has misrepresented the Negro Christian's

conception of the personal habits of God. Under no circumstances would God be expected to smoke a cigar or to utter such ungodly expression as "I be doggone."

Thirdly, he has misrepresented the Negro Christian's conception of God's moral sensitivity. The colored man's God will not allow himself to be personally taunted and insulted by fresh girls and wicked men as is done in the play. There are thousands of old untutored Negroes today who still warn their grandchildren that they must not play or even talk during a thunder storm. For God will smash them down with a bolt of lightning if they talk while He is talking. (Thunder is God talking.)

There is hardly a Negro community in the deep South that does not have several examples in its religious lore of neighbors or acquaintances who were dramatically struck down by God while they were in the act of blasphemy either directly against God or against the church.

Furthermore, no untutored Negro Christian would believe that God would be so wishy-washy as to say to Cain after he had killed Abel: "Well, I ain't sayin' you right an' I ain't sayin' you wrong. But I do say was I you I'd jest git myself down de road." Nor would they believe that God would stoop to argue with Noah about Noah's desire to take two "kags of likker" in the Ark with him.

Fourthly, he has misrepresented the Negro Christian's conception of Heaven. There is no such person alive as one who thinks of Heaven as one eternal fish-fry. Heaven, in the eyes of the Negro Christian, is different from anything he has ever known or seen on earth. All of his everyday experiences are so tied up with poverty and inadequacy and second-class quality that he conceives of Heaven as an entirely new experience. The Indian and the rich white man may think of Heaven as a continuation of their everyday activities, but not the Negro.

I could go on indefinitely presenting evidence to show the failure of Mr. Connelly to do what he said he intended to do in *The Green Pastures*. But I think I have said enough to prove my case.

Even though the facts I have presented cannot be denied, there are some who may say that the dignity with which "de Lawd" is portrayed offsets the lack of genuineness of all the rest. This I deny. In fact, I cannot accept as dignified the portrayal of de Lawd in Act I, Scene 2, when he complains that the custard he is eating at the heavenly fish-fry is not seasoned just right, for it "needs jest a little bit mo' firmament" in it. After the custard maker tells Him that he used all the firmament he had and that "Dey ain't a drop in de jug," God says, "Dat's all right. I'll jest r'ar back an' pass a miracle. Let it be some firmament! An' when I say let it be some firmament, I don't want jest a little bitty dab o' firmament caize I'm sick an' tired òf runnin' out of it when we need it. Let it be a whole mess of firmament."

To anyone who wishes to understand what a genuine interpretation of the untutored Negro Christian's conception of God and the Bible might be, I suggest that he read the seven sermons and the prayer in *God's Trombones* by James Weldon Johnson.

Now, of course, the legitimate question arises as to the validity of my assertions concerning what the devout Negro Bible reader believes. A random sampling of opinions of Negroes from any stratum of the population will support my assertions. The day after the televised version of *The Green Pastures* was presented I took an informal random poll of approximately one hundred students, teachers, ministers, and untutored citizens, and found that at least nine out of every ten who had seen or read the play protested vehemently against the author's failure to accomplish what he said he intended to do.

In conclusion, let me clearly state that it has not been my purpose to criticize Mr. Connelly's craftsmanship as a playwright, nor to deny him the right to use his imagination in any way he might choose in the creation of drama. I have sought to show only that he failed to achieve the purpose he set for himself and that in his failure he has forfeited for his work any claim to literary greatness.

VI *The Green Pastures Again**

Doris B. Garey
*(Emeritus), Department of English,
North Manchester College (Indiana)*

Mr. Nick Aaron Ford's "How Genuine Is *The Green Pastures?*"[1] raises some complex and fascinating problems of literary criticism. As a fellow English teacher who had often used Mr. Ford's "three basic questions," I began reading the article with a comfortable feeling of being quite at home. By the time I had finished it, however, I was feeling somewhat at sea. The issues involved here go so far beyond *The Green Pastures* as an isolated phenomenon that they brought into sharp focus several questions about which my previous thinking had been far too cursory.

But I shall have to approach these questions indirectly, by the meandering path of personal reminiscence. My first acquaintance with *The Green Pastures* was made through seeing a performance of the play in the 1930's, with Richard B. Harrison as "de Lawd." Few experiences in my life have been so moving; and probably my evaluation of the play is in part due to the accidental influence of this remarkable interpretation. I have never wanted to see anyone else's interpretation, but in rereading the play from time to time I have continued to be deeply moved.

Not until a while after the initial experience did I begin to have certain qualms. These were first induced through the ecstasies voiced by some white spectators over the "quaintness" of the cleaning-lady angels and the fish fry. The sudden realization that one effect of the play might be to perpetuate racial stereotypes destroyed my original innocence. And the fact that a class of Negro college students fiercely resented this danger increased my realization that the difficulty was a real one. Yet my

---

*From *Phylon*, 20 (June, 1959): 193-94. Copyright Atlanta University. Reprinted by permission.
[1] See pp. 335-39 above.—Ed.

emotional response to the play remained—and remains—almost unaltered.

Coming now to Mr. Ford's commentary—it undoubtedly makes a convincing case for the thesis that Mr. Connelly has failed to achieve his professed purpose. And insofar as this professed purpose may help to establish misleading stereotypes in the minds of ill-informed people, one could certainly object to it on what might be called sociological grounds. But from the literary standpoint, the most interesting questions to me are questions that could be raised not only about *The Green Pastures* but about other works of many types. To what extent can we assume an author's own statement of purpose to be valid and adequate? Are the author as creative artist and the author as critical interpreter of his own work always necessarily the same person? And if these questions must sometimes be answered negatively, as I think they must, does a disparity between the author's professed purpose and his actual performance necessarily condemn his work?

To introduce a bizarre comparison: almost all critics today seem agreed that Poe could not possibly have composed "The Raven" according to the principles and methods which he later professed to have employed. But if some of us take a dim view of "The Raven," our reason would not, and should not, be that there is a disparity between Poe the poet and Poe the theorist. Rather—to put the matter crudely—the main reason would probably be that whereas we sense Poe's intention to be impressively somber, we feel that his methods are too transparent, one might almost say too childish, to induce in us the intended mood.

Of course these reflections do place us at times in an awkward situation, for they suggest that we are arrogating to ourselves the ability to understand an author's creative "purpose" better than he himself does. We should doubtless be cautious about making this bland assumption, and yet on the whole I see no escape from the dilemma. There is a bit of comfort in the remark once made, apparently without irony, by Thomas Mann in a public lecture. Mann cited an interpretation which had been made of one of his works, and said he had sometimes been asked whether this interpretation was correct. His answer was, in effect: "Very likely—I don't remember any longer just how I felt when I wrote it. It is outside of me now, and belongs to you."

At any rate—to return to *The Green Pastures* once more—I have often been puzzled by the fact that in most discussions of this play, little or nothing is said about what seems to me its most impressive element, namely, its portrayal of the "growth" of God. I know of no other imaginative work that re-creates so strikingly what we find in the Bible itself—the development of man's conception of God from a tribal deity with almost-human weaknesses to a universal deity loving, and suffering for, all mankind.[2] In the play, of course, this development is expressed in terms of God's own successive stages of learning. The God who—frivolously, if you like—calls for "mo' firmament" is very different from the God at the end of the play.

Needless to say, a paradox here is that this growth in man's conception of God is not consciously understood by most untutored folk, either Negro or white. Hence we have one more evidence for Mr. Ford's thesis that Mr. Connelly is not literally reflecting the thought processes of an untutored group as he professes to do. Can we, then, guess what may have unconsciously influenced his choice of a medium? My own guess would be that he was searching for what one might term a sort of idealized naivete through which to view an extremely complex subject. In the Bible itself, this blend of surface naivete and underlying maturity is perhaps most strikingly represented by the Book of Jonah.

To make such an interpretation is not necessarily to deny what many people would doubtless suspect, namely, that the author may have depended on superficial quaintnesses and stereotyping to insure the popularity of the play.

---

[2] Most biblical scholars would disagree with this characterization of the "developing" view of God found in the Bible.—Ed.

Shakespeare himself, as we all know, was quite deliberate about courting popularity, about producing "good theatre." But if this had been his only aim, he would not have done many of the things that he actually did do, and we would not reverence him today.

I have not been trying to establish the "greatness" of *The Green Pastures*, though I have confessed to being personally moved by it. Rather, I have tried to suggest (1) that judging a work on sociological and on literary grounds may produce quite different results, and (2) that an author's own professed purpose may not always give us an adequate insight into the underlying motives of his creation.

VII MacLeish's *J.B.**

Murray Roston

Department of English,
Bar Ilan University, Tel Aviv, Israel

The four essays that follow provide a variety of approaches to the study of *J.B.* Murray Roston examines the play in the context of twentieth-century views about God and the meaning of suffering and guilt. W. D. White makes a detailed comparison between the play and the book of Job. Ruth Hallman reports on classroom procedures that have made both the play and the book of Job come to life for her students. In the final essay, MacLeish himself discusses the relation between his play and the Bible and then comments on their relevance to our times.

A short story that might well be taught in connection with *J.B.* and the book of Job is Bernard Malamud's "Angel Levine." It isn't until the central character in the story learns to transcend the narrow boundaries of his faith that the black angel Levine is able to give him any relief from his Job-like tribulations. When he exclaims at the end of the story "there are Jews everywhere," he as much as admits that suffering and salvation are not restricted to any one racial or ethnic group.—Ed.

The play itself begins with the most effective device yet for avoiding the credulous dramatizations of the supernatural so distasteful to the twentieth century. The device consists of a gradual transition from the phenomenal world to the symbolic and, through the symbolic, to the supernatural—a move calculated to pacify the atheists within the audience and perhaps to satisfy MacLeish's own objection to complacent pietism. Had God and Satan begun conversing in the booming voices of a Sunday School play, the drama would disintegrate into mere religious propaganda. Instead, two broken-down actors, now reduced to selling

*Reprinted by permission of Faber and Faber Ltd. from *Biblical Drama in England* by Murray Roston, pp. 314-21.

balloons and popcorn, enter the huge circus tent, pathetic
human failures dwarfed by their surroundings, yet betraying faint traces of their previous dignity. Their names, Mr.
Zuss and Nickles, suggest their symbolic representation of
God (Zeus) and Satan (Old Nick), but nothing in their
speech or behaviour as yet confirms the suspicion. Curi-
ously they examine the stage-setting for a performance of
Job and casually finger the masks worn by their namesakes
in the play. As each handles the mask, he seems to catch
something of its quality, and their discussion of Job's
courage or impertinence foreshadows the argument of the
play. From a tersely colloquial dialogue they lapse into a
more poetic, yet still colloquial, verse which creates an
atmosphere more suited to symbolism.

> Nickles: But this is God in *Job* you're playing:
> God the Maker: God Himself!
> Remember what He says?—the hawk
> Flies by His wisdom! And the goats—
> Remember the goats?

They try on the masks and at once their voices are, as the
stage directions inform us, "so magnified and hollowed by
the masks that they scarcely seem their own." The masks
begin to speak as though of their own volition, and as the
actors tear them off, horrified at what they have seen
through the eye-holes, Nickles questions whether he is
really playing Satan. Zuss's answer marks the penultimate
stage of the merger:

> Maybe Satan's playing you.

They replace their masks in readiness to begin the play,
but the opening line is uttered by neither of them. A
mysterious Distant Voice intones the biblical lines, and
from then on God and Satan speak, as it were, through the
mouths of Zuss and Nickles. The transition from realism to
the supernatural has been achieved through the contemporary symbolist technique of the stage so that the effect is

one of dramatic sophistication instead of pious gullibility. An equally valuable achievement is a deliberate ambiguity which leaves us unsure throughout the play when God is speaking through Zuss and when Zuss is interjecting his own human objections.

As his name J.B. suggests, MacLeish's Job is a successful American executive, thankful in a slightly complacent way for the blessings of life. He denies formally that the blessings are deserved, but knows instinctively that God is with him. In this twentieth-century form of postfiguration, MacLeish has injected his own religious problems into the ancient story, adapting the specific details of the original without altering the ultimate lesson. As calamities overwhelm the modern Job—two children killed in a crash, a toddler murdered by a sex-maniac, a daughter crushed in the collapse of his own bank, a son destroyed by war—J.B. is faced by the horror of an inexplicable and ruthless injustice. But at this stage, it is not J.B.'s answer which interests us so much as the comments of Zuss and Nickles. For MacLeish has still to work at removing the instinctive antipathy of a predominantly disbelieving generation, and he achieves his purpose largely by forestalling these objections himself. Into Nickles' mouth he puts all the cynicism of the nihilist, jeering at J.B.'s "ham" acting, his "insufferable" rich man's piety, the "poisonous" doctrines he instils into his children. Even Zuss is hesitant in defending J.B. But Nickles' cynicism is just sufficiently overdrawn to alienate the audience's sympathy.

> Best thing you can teach your children
> Next to never drawing breath
> Is choking on it.

This is too vicious a philosophy even for the iconoclast, and Zuss dismisses it as a product of rancid intellectualism. The same technique is effective in discrediting Nickles immediately after the calamity. Where the biblical Job at once answers "The Lord giveth, the Lord taketh away. Blessed

be the name of the Lord," MacLeish's J.B. can only utter
the first half. Zuss urgently whispers:

> Go on!
> Go on! Finish it! Finish it!

but J.B. remains silent. Nickles exults in his victory; why
should J.B. go on, he asks:

> To what? To where? He's got there, hasn't he?
> Now he's said it, now he knows.
> He knows Who gives, he knows Who takes now.

At last J.B., mastering his rebelliousness, murmurs
brokenly the conclusion of the verse—"Blessed be the name
of the Lord." It is, perhaps, only a verbal affirmation of
faith at this stage, but it is sufficient to discredit Nickles
who believed that no man in his senses could even play the
part of an accepting Job. . . .

By the time of the comforters' scene MacLeish can afford
to be less generous to his inner atheist and to begin his
rejection of that viewpoint; although even at this point the
presence of the formal Church among the false comforters
continues his rebellious unorthodoxy. The three comforters
consist of Zophar the seedy cleric, Eliphaz the disillusioned
scientist, and Bildad the communist. The first two are
discredited on entry by their filthy clothing; and since the
communist uses his rags as a badge of class-distinction,
MacLeish takes care to denigrate him by means of the
women's caustic comments. In a deliberate caricature of
religious, scientific and communist jargon, MacLeish puts
into their mouths the modern tendency to exonerate the
criminal on the grounds of heredity, psychological impulse,
class struggles, and original sin. The communist argues that
historical necessity and the concept of the State make
nonsense of the so-called sins of the individual:

> Innocent! Innocent!
> Nations shall perish in their innocence.
> Classes shall perish in their innocence.

> Young men in slaughtered cities
> Offering their silly throats
> Against the tanks in innocence shall perish.
> What's your innocence to theirs?
> God is history. If you offend Him
> Will not History dispense with you?
> History has no time for innocence.

Eliphaz offers the supposedly soothing explanation of the quack psychiatrist:

> Come! Come! Come! Guilt is a
> Psychophenomenal situation—
> An illusion, a disease, a sickness:
> That filthy feeling at the fingers,
> Scent of dung beneath the nails . . .

and Zophar, the cleric, insists categorically:

> All mankind are guilty always!

But in lone obstinacy, deserted even by his wife, J.B. proclaims as the corner-stone of his faith that without responsibility for his own actions man is a worthless statistic:

> I'd rather suffer
> Every unspeakable suffering God sends,
> Knowing it was I that suffered,
> I that earned the need to suffer,
> I that acted, I that chose,
> Than wash my hands with yours in that
> Defiling innocence.

To argue as some critics have that MacLeish has merely acted out Job in modern dress is to miss this central point. In fact, he has reoriented the story to meet an attack from the opposite direction. The biblical Job rejected the neat contemporary belief in a retaliatory God by insisting that his own punishment was undeserved, while the comforters, representing the conventional view, insisted on his guilt. In the twentieth century the roles are reversed: the comforters come to assure J.B. of his innocence, and it is he who insists on his guilt. Where Job and J.B. are at one is in their conviction of the individual's moral responsibility in a universe intimately concerned with his actions. But in defending that position, the modern Job must of necessity redirect his defensive fire, and therein lay the basic originality of MacLeish's play.

With the climactic scene of J.B.'s insistence on his guilt, the *peripeteia* begins. The Distant Voice (not Zuss) speaks from the whirlwind in the original words of the Bible, intoning what MacLeish described elsewhere as some of the greatest lines in all literature, the recounting of the might, majesty, and magnificence of creation, whose immense workings puny men cannot begin to comprehend.[1]

> Who is this that darkeneth counsel
> By words without knowledge? . . .
>
> Where wast thou
> When I laid the foundations of the earth . . .
> When the morning stars sang together
> And all the sons of God shouted for
> Joy? . . .
>
> Wilt thou condemn
> Me that thou mayest be righteous?

J.B. is silenced not by logic, for the answer is meaningless to an atheist rejecting the existence of God. But for J.B., convinced that creation is purposive and ordered, the reply is fraught with meaning. It does not prove that justice exists; it questions whether man possesses sufficient knowledge of the master-plan and of its intricate workings to pronounce finally on its merits. As a Christian and perhaps also in response to existentialist parallels, Mac-Leish concludes with the theme of love. In a discussion of the biblical *Job* published in the *Christian Century* he argued that a primary message of the book is God's need to

[1] In "About a Trespass on a Monument." [Reprinted below, pp. 373-78.]

prove that man can love him for love's own sake and not as a *quid pro quo*.

"Without man's love God does not exist as God, only as creator, and love is the one thing no one, not even God himself, can command."[2]

With this in mind, the close of his drama takes on a deeper meaning. J.B. submissively bows his head before the divine reproof, admits his error, and repents. At once both Nickles and Zuss tear off their masks and begin cynically to sneer at his "arrogant, smiling, supercilious humility" in giving in to God. Again the author puts into their mouths the arguments of the sceptics, and having already discredited Nickles earlier in the play, now exploits Zuss in the part of the scoffer. The carpings and cavillings of Nickles and Zuss, despite their contrast with the stirring lines that have preceded them, are persuasive. Nickles, horrified to learn that God "pays up" by restoring the wife and children, inquires cynically whether they are the same children or merely substitutes. Most of all, he cannot conceive how J.B. could be willing to accept life after such an experience. He attempts to persuade him to suicide, but J.B. turns away with humble dignity to welcome his wife back in love. In the midst of the darkness, resembling symbolically the desolation of Hiroshima and the empty blackness of MacLeish's earlier sonnet, Sarah whispers the closing message of the play:

> Blow on the coal of the heart.
> The candles in churches are out.
> The lights have gone out in the sky.
> Blow on the coal of the heart
> And we'll see by and by . . .

For all the arid intellectualism of Satan, the environmental conditioning of psychology, the amorality of communism, and the dogmas of the contemporary Church, it is in the mystery of Job's non-empirical faith that the modern dramatist finds the most valid pointer to the meaning of life.

[2]*Christian Century* (April, 1959), p. 419.

And unlike the writers of earlier decades, he does not turn his back on modern thought in a desperate attempt to shield his faith, but finds in his own dissatisfactions with current philosophies the confirmation of his belief in the parallel of human and divine love.[3]

This play epitomizes the new sensitivity among biblical playwrights of the mid-century. There has not suddenly appeared in our midst a Salvation Army of dramatists eager to lead an evangelical revival. Even those most earnest in their religious beliefs speak hesitantly from the midst of their own doubts and perplexities—perplexities which by their very awareness that religion offers no easy path to the intelligent believer are all the more persuasive. Where at the turn of the century the bastions of orthodox Christianity had been stormed by the rationalists, the mid-twentieth century has seen a regrouping of forces. The inhabitants of the citadel have grown restless under the cold dictatorship of science, and in their search for warmth are beginning to look back nostalgically, if not to the stringent pietism of the Victorian, then at least to the dignity of man in the biblical world. Evolution has depicted him as an advanced organism justifying himself in the survival pattern solely by biological procreation; psychology as a complex of subtly preconditioned responses; and even democracy has left him with little but the infrequent use of a ballot box. Appalled by such cosmic alienation, the mid-century writer is less inclined airily to dismiss as outmoded the biblical world-picture in which the welfare and morality of each individual is of vital concern to his Creator.

In an era proclaiming the death of God, it is unlikely that a sudden religious revival is imminent; but there are signs

[3] I have discussed here the published text, used in the productions at Yale and in Europe. During the Broadway production, MacLeish was persuaded by his producer, Elia Kazan, to introduce changes in the concluding section which merely confused audiences. The Broadway text appears in *Theatre Arts* (February, 1960), and is discussed in Burton M. Wheeler, "Theology and the Theatre," *JBR xxviii* (July, 1960), 334. The correspondence between MacLeish and Kazan on these changes can be found in *Esquire* (May, 1959).

that the cultural pendulum is slowly beginning to swing back. The existentialists are groping for meaning and for human contact in an otherwise empty world; the psychedelics have ostentatiously turned their backs on scientific progress in favour of mystical experience, taking love as their watchword in place of reason; Zen Buddhism and the myth of Sisyphus are no longer the absurd beliefs of ignorant forebears but are being seen anew as poetic projections of the human predicament. In each era biblical drama has responded to subtle fluctuations in the contemporary scene, and we may expect it to respond in our own generation to this growing respect for the mythic cycles of the past. The sudden lowering of biblical sanctity during the first half of this century produced an impressive list of dramatists interested in the Scriptures—Shaw, Yeats, D. H. Lawrence, Isaac Rosenberg, Laurence Housman, Bridie, Frost, Fry, MacLeish, and numerous others. Many of them exploited its themes with cynicism, some with deliberate iconoclasm. But by now the iconoclastic impulse has expended itself, the Bible remains below that degree of sacrosanctity which would preclude effective dramatization, and its archetypal themes await the modern playwright searching, like MacLeish, for the majesty of ancient walls in which to house his own spiritual problems.

VIII MacLeish's *J.B.*—Is It a Modern *Job?**

W. D. White

Department of Religion,
St. Andrews Presbyterian College
(Laurinburg, N.C.)

One of the most illuminating ways to get inside MacLeish's *J.B.*[1] is through comparing it with the ancient biblical model from which it draws, in some sense, its inspiration. Such an approach, however, must be used with great care; for the creative artist is by definition free to take his materials from whatever source he will, and to use them however he will to effect his own artistic purposes.

MacLeish himself, in justifying what he calls his "trespass on a monument," has said: "I have constructed a modern play inside the ancient majesty of the Book of Job . . . dealing with questions too large to handle but which will not down. . . . *J.B.* is not a reconstruction of the Book of Job . . . in which the discovery of the model is part of the adventure." He goes on to add that when J.B. and his family appear, it is not out of the Bible that they come; nevertheless, MacLeish tells us, the two broken-down actors whom we first glimpse in the play "believed, themselves, that the play is the Book of Job and that one of them is acting God and the other, Satan."[2] Obviously, MacLeish expects his audience to approach his *J.B.* with the biblical *Job* in mind. And whatever the author's expectation, it appears self-evident that from both a literary and a religious point of view any modern *Job* must invite comparison with its ancient source.

The specific question which engages us, then, is: "Is *J.B.*

*From *Mosaic: A Journal for the Comparative Study of Literature and Ideas*, Vol. 4, No. 1 (Fall, 1970): 13-20, published by the University of Manitoba Press, to whom acknowledgment is herewith made.

[1] In this essay, underlining will distinguish *Job* and *J.B.* from their respective leading characters.

[2] Archibald MacLeish, "About a Trespass on a Monument," *New York Times* (December 7, 1968) Section II, p. 5. [Reprinted below, pp. 373-78.]

a modern *Job?* If so, in what sense? If not, why not?" In the course of the discussion I shall try to show that *J.B.* is only in the most obvious sense, and therefore on a relatively superficial level, a modern *Job;* and that in its fundamental thrust, in the formulation of its basic problem, and in the suggested answer to its major questions, *J.B.* is far removed from its biblical model. It should be clear that these facts in themselves make no comment on the literary achievement of the poet; and I shall not, indeed, attempt to assess the poetic or literary value of *J.B.* I will suggest that insofar as it fails dramatically, this failure is not to be attributed primarily to any basic flaws of its structure or stagecraft, but rather must be explained in terms of its projected vision of the world—a worldview which, one might add, is a poetic statement of MacLeish's own vision.[3]

From the Book of Job MacLeish takes the major elements of his structure, the plot of events, and the personalities of the action. Throughout the play he employs, often happily, a considerable amount of biblical idiom, quoting at length passages from the Book of Job, and making many allusions direct and subtle to other biblical texts. The play therefore reflects in this sense "the ancient majesty of the Book of Job" upon which it is to this extent modeled. But at this point the similarities cease, for MacLeish has exercised great liberties in the use of his source.

A mere cursory analysis of the structure reveals, for example, that by far the greater part of the play is based upon materials presented originally in the prose Prologue and Epilogue of the Book of Job. These biblical elements are developed and expanded, reordered and interpreted, modernized and redirected in such a way that they become the fundamental stuff of the play, taking up over eighty percent of the entire text. Of the total of eleven scenes, only Scene IX specifically draws upon structural elements that appear in the poetic part of the biblical *Job,* while Scenes I and X

---

[3] For an illuminating prose statement of this view, see MacLeish's discussion of his play in "About a Trespass on a Monument," above reference.

represent purely imaginative creations that have no immediate source in the Bible. As a sheer structural question, one cannot but be surprised that in MacLeish's use of his source, his center of gravity lies so strongly in the prose parts of the Book of Job, and so little in the poetry itself. I take it that this is a significant fact for our observation.

Other considerations, not yet however the most crucial, but of some significance, must also be made with reference to MacLeish's free use of his source. *J.B.* is structured as a play within a play. In the Prologue, two erstwhile actors, Mr. Zuss and Nickles, now reduced to selling popcorn and balloons in the circus, assume the roles of God and Satan respectively; throughout the rest of the play, from their elevated position above the world of J.B. the hero, these two omniscient onlookers set the scene, comment on the story, and through their dialogue drive the movement forward. This is a significant departure from the biblical situation in which the Prologue in heaven does little more than set a frame of reference for the unfolding of the main interest, the poetry itself. One of the dramatic results of this change is that in MacLeish's play Nickles becomes the protagonist rather than J.B. One might even say that Nickles and Sarah (J.B.'s wife) replace J.B. and God as protagonists.

Another significant change in the movement is effected by drawing out to great lengths the reports of the disasters that strike Job. Whereas in the biblical Prologue these announcements come in direct, rapid-fire, highly-stylized sequence, in MacLeish they are extended through indirect, enigmatic dialogue to form the basic matter for some eight scenes of the play. This centering of interest in the calamities themselves, in conjunction with the preempting of J.B.'s part by Nickles, tends to shift the center of interest in MacLeish's play from the personal problem of Job to the wider context of mankind in general, with particular reference to the tragic implications of modern warfare for society at large.

This means further, that J.B. the man is *not* Job the man: J.B. bears little relation to his biblical prototype, whom MacLeish casually refers to as "That ancient owner of camels and oxen and sheep."[4] Samuel Terrien is correct when he so brilliantly shows that J.B. is not the defiant Job of the biblical poetry; but I suggest that he is less correct when he identifies J.B. with the patient Job of the Prologue.[5] J.B. is submissive, to be sure, but he lacks the moral stature and personal integrity of the Job of the biblical Prologue. MacLeish himself describes J.B. as a "vastly successful business man" who, having everything, "believes as a matter of course that (he has) a *right* to have everything."[6] While J.B. is no doubt more than one critic calls him, "half literary creature, half solution to the ills of the world,"[7] he nevertheless lacks human presence. He reveals no depth or passion, no dramatic or religious movement. Or if there is any movement at all, it is into that state of consciousness captured in the medieval concept of sloth—which (as Dorothy Sayers put it) does not mean "lack of hustle"[8]—but rather the slow sapping of all the faculties, by indifference; and the sensation that life is pointless and meaningless and not-worthwhile; that *sloth* of body and mind which issues in emptiness of heart, which dissipates energy and purpose, and leaves a common grayness over all. At best J.B. is a kind of "atomic-age Everyman," as is suggested by Mr. Zuss's statement: "Oh, there's always Somene playing Job"; to which Nickles adds:

"Thousands—
Millions and millions of mankind,
Burned, crushed, broken, mutilated,
Slaughtered—" (p. 12)

"Job is everywhere . . .
His children dead, his work for nothing . . .

[4] MacLeish, "About a Trespass," p. 5.
[5] Samuel Terrien, *Christian Century* (Jan. 7, 1959), p. 9.
[6] MacLeish, "About a Trespass," p. 5.
[7] Irving Feldman, *Commentary* (August, 1958), p. 183.
[8] Dorothy Sayers, *Unpopular Opinions* (New York: 1947), p. 6.

Counting his losses, scraping his boils . . .
Discussing himself with his friends and physicians." (p. 13)

Plaintive and puzzled, finally beaten into sheer submission, impotent before the cold indifference of a subhuman universe, J.B. is such a dramatic character as to cause one critic to quip: "The author's J.B. is so fatuous that most readers will be tempted to applaud Satan for wiping the turkey-stuffed grin off his face."[9]

But this down-grading of the hero is not yet the most crucial way in which *J.B.* must be differentiated from its biblical source. To center our attention unduly on the personality of J.B. would be to fall into the kind of humanistic reductionism which so frequently characterizes dramatic criticism dominated by the popular understanding of the Aristotelian conception of the tragic hero. To be properly understood, the tragic hero must himself be seen in relation to the wider frame of reference, the "divine background," so to speak, against which he is set. It is at this point that the most crucial difference between the biblical *Job* and MacLeish's *J.B.* becomes clear. Both literatures concern themselves in some sense with human suffering, with man's existence, with the inexplicable mysteries of the universe; but the presuppositions operative in the respective treatments of these concerns set a great gulf between the Book of Job and *J.B.* The frame of reference dramatically realized is in the one case radically different from the other.

Wherein does this difference lie? It lies fundamentally in the overarching, pervasive and penetrating God-consciousness of the biblical book, an element totally missing in MacLeish's *J.B.* In the Book of Job, as a sheer question of dramatic realization, God as Creator is a *"given"* element and the reality of this *"given"* is never questioned. Another dramatically realized *"given* is the tragedy of Job himself, of his own person caught in his situation. Job's

[9] Feldman, p. 184.

problem, then, is to bring these two fundamental *"givens"* into some structured relationship; to fit his situation into that given reality of a Creator God, who is essentially good, and to interpret his situation meaningfully in the light of this existing reality. Hence he rages against God, protests his innocence from personal moral guilt, laments the day of his birth, demands a hearing, thrusts himself toward death, and declares that even against God he will hold fast to his integrity. And all this, not simply as a sheer act of *hybris*, but as a basically realistic appraisal of his situation, as is shown by the frame of reference (the Prologue) in which the poetry is cast. Job's struggle is fundamentally an attempt to understand how a Creator God who is good—the God who is dramatically realized as a fundamental *given* in the poem—how such a God relates himself to such a man as Job in such a situation as his; and conversely, how such a man as Job in such a situation responds to the givenness of his tragedy and the givenness of such a God. Whatever problems we see as integral to the Book of Job and whatever (if any) emerge, these problems and these answers must be formulated in the context not merely of Job's situation in itself, one of the givens of the literature, but in the context of Job's situation as this relates to the Creator God, that other dramatically realized given. The relational category is therefore here crucial.

When we turn to MacLeish's *J.B.* we see something vastly different. The problem of J.B. is not formulated in the way that Job's problem is; for in the play there is but one dramatically realized given, the reality of J.B. himself in his own situation, whether happy (as at the first) or pathetic (as in the later scenes, and even in the end). There is no God-consciousness in the play; the reality of God is never dramatically actualized. And this alters basically the biblical source material; this redefines the problems in the drama and the possible answers given to these problems. The only reality which J.B. must face and deal with is his own historical and immediate situation. Since this is the only actuality projected, whatever meaning or happiness or tragedy is to be found there must be found in J.B. himself and in his human situation; no meaning can be seen in this given that is derived outside of, or from beyond itself. There is a fundamental difference between the issues that can be raised in a literature that moves only on this one plane of reality, the human situation as such, and those issues of a literature that includes the dimensions of the human situation, the Creator God, and how these relate meaningfully.[10]

That the play is limited to the level of the human situation can be demonstrated in the text itself. Not that there is no attempt to elicit a dramatic realization of God-consciousness: there is a considerable amount of verbalizing concerning God, and there are structural, idiomatic, and histrionic turns designed to project God-consciousness. But all these fail, for in reality they have nothing to do with God. These fail, for they are in fact only extensions of the human situation, projections of human emotion, and externalized human conceptions named with the name of God.

This attempt to incorporate God-consciousness can be seen first in the presentation of Mr. Zuss (God) and Nickles (Satan). From the outset, and throughout the play, Nickles is given more and better lines than Zuss, who is at best an expression of the three biblical friends' (Bildad, Eliphaz, and Zophar) *conception* of God. The mask which Zuss wears for God is a "huge, white, blank, beautiful, expressionless mask" (p. 16) bearing a look of "cold complacence" (p. 20). Mr. Zuss's understanding of God is neatly summarized in these lines:

> "God will teach him!
> God will show him what God *is*—
> Enormous pattern of the steep of stars,
> Minute perfection of the frozen crystal.

[10] This raises at least by implication, the question of whether MacLeish's play has within its self-definitions the possibility of authentic tragedy, or whether we merely see before us a pitiful spectacle that elicits a certain pathos.

> Inimitable architecture of the slow,
> Cold, silent, ignorant sea-snail:
> The unimaginable will of stone:
> Infinite mind in midge of matter." (p. 47-48)

Furthermore, the God of J.B. is no-God, a pseudo, a false God. The God of J.B. is of his own making, created in his own image. J.B. sees only the "shell of a deity, a God without presence";[11] for his God is but a verbalization of his conception of God, and a verbalization at that that MacLeish never brings to life as dramatic reality. As MacLeish himself puts it, since J.B. "believes in his life," he believes in "God's goodness to Him."[12] Yes, to be sure! J.B. affirms: "I believe in it [the world]. I trust in it. I trust my luck—my life—our life—God's goodness to me" (p. 38). And here, in a nutshell, is J.B.'s God; it is his world, his luck, his life, the goodness of it all. In his prosperity he can say "Of course God's just. He'll never change. A man can count on Him. Look at the world, the order of it, the *certainty* of day's return . . ." (p. 39). Then when disaster strikes, J.B.'s comfortable conception of God emerges as a dogma, to which he holds tenaciously, because it is necessary for him to believe in order to protect his demand for justice in the universe. "God would not punish without cause." "God is just." "HE knows the guilt is mine. He must know. Has he not punished it?" (p. 109). "I have no choice but to be guilty" (p. 110). And when Sarah admonishes him to curse God and die, he replies, after a long silence:

> "God is good or we are nothing—
> Mayflies that leave their husks behind—
> Our tiny lives ridiculous—a suffering
> Not even sad that Someone Somewhere
> Laughs at as we laugh at apes.
> We have no choice but to be guilty.
> God is unthinkable if we are innocent." (p. 111)

These passages show clearly that the God easily identified in J.B.'s happiness with the sheer goodness of his life, is

[11] Feldman, p. 184.
[12] MacLeish, "About a Trespass."

J.B.'s own creation; for in the crises of his life, he protests, not his innocence, as the biblical Job, but his guilt. He must be guilty; otherwise, his idea of God cannot stand; and since his idea of God is the only dramatically realized God in the play, the puncturing of his idea means the abolition of God. Whereas in the Bible, Job protests his innocence despite his belief in God, in MacLeish, J.B. protests his guilt in order to protect his belief in God. The biblical Job has to define himself and the meaning of his situation finally with reference to the given reality of the Creator God; hence his struggle with God. But J.B. has to struggle in his situation to sustain a definition of God which is finally but a projection of something within himself, an extension of his own necessity to believe that human life meets justice and knows ultimate meaning.

In a similar way, Sarah's God is but a projection of her sense of guilt; to her, all life's blessings come pregnant with doom, for "God doesn't give all this for nothing." Her God, therefore, is the creation of her sense of guilt and experience of anxiety; it is then no mystery that when tragedy befalls, she cries out "He kills—He is our enemy." The three comforters further develop the no-God thrust of the play; for each of them represents some modern problem of the tribe or market place. Zophar, a caricature of the churchman, identifies the Imago Dei with man's guilt, and J.B.'s response to him is: "Yours is the cruelest comfort of them all, / Making the Creator of the Universe the Miscreator of mankind" (p. 126); Eliphaz, the modern medicine man, is a caricature of the idolatry of scientism and psychologism; and Bildad, as a thinly-disguised Marxist, can offer only the panaceas of utopian historicism. Once again, the only gods that are dramatically realized in the play are the gods created in the images of the men who entertain them.

And what is the issue of all this? When J.B. encounters the Voice in the Wind, he learns to *see;* but he sees precisely what Nickles sees through the mask of Satan. These eyes, Nickles says,

> "See the world. They do. They see it.
> From going to and fro in the earth,
> From walking up and down, they see it.
> I know what Hell is now—to SEE—
> Consciousness of consciousness . . ." (p. 22)

For J.B., to see reality is to abhor self and to suffer, with no escape. J.B.'s final religious insight, revealed in the not-dramatically-convincing closing scene where Sarah has returned to him, is expressed in the words: "He [God] does not love. He IS" (p. 152). To which Sarah replies, "But we do. That's the wonder." As they cling to each other in the rising darkness Sarah continues climactically, "Then blow on the coal of the heart, my darling."

> "Blow on the coal of the heart.
> The candles in churches are out.
> The lights have gone out in the sky.
> Blow on the coal of the heart . . ." (p. 152)

MacLeish's *J.B.* tells us that "It is in man's love that God exists and triumphs: in man's love that life is beautiful; in man's love that the world's injustice is resolved." [13] Whatever problems are raised in *J.B.* are problems limited by the definitions of the human situation itself; and whatever answers can be adduced from *J.B.* must likewise be found in the human situation itself; for in *J.B.* there is no God-consciousness, there is no reality beyond the human situation. The only light let into the picture is the light that comes from human love, without ever raising the more fundamental question of what light love itself must be set in.

J.B. does not suggest the possibility, although perhaps MacLeish intends to, that the human situation might be illuminated through the interpersonal categories of God and Man in an I/Thou relationship; for that matter, neither the Book of Job nor *J.B.* takes into account the possibility of

[13] Tom Driver, quoting MacLeish, *Christian Century* (June 11, 1958), p. 693.

dealing with human suffering through the positive power of love of God and love of man. It is a long cry indeed from the affirmations of the ancient Job—or those of the modern *J.B.*—to the twentieth century Christian affirmation such as that of Georges Bernanos: "I feel that such distress, distress that has forgotten its name, that has ceased to reason or to hope—that lays its tortured head at random—will awaken one day on the shoulder of Jesus Christ." [14]

[14] Georges Bernanos, *The Diary of A County Priest* (New York: 1954), p. 41.

IX Teaching *Job* and *J.B.**

Ruth D. Hallman
Department of English,
Walter E. Stebbins High School,
Dayton, Ohio

Our study of the *Book of Job* and Archibald MacLeish's *J.B.*
is the unit I always enjoy teaching most, for it offers so
many possible approaches. In fact, one of the chief
difficulties is in deciding which topics to omit, since there is
never enough time to include all of them. I will suggest just
a few of the approaches which I have found particularly
rewarding.

The *Book of Job* is obviously the starting point, and I find
that an outline of the overall structure of the book is helpful
to the students. Most students are already acquainted with
the Job of the prologue and the epilogue. But it is the Job of
the poem to whom they respond, and this Job *few* of them
know. They can identify with this man who cries out, "I
wish I were dead! Why was I ever born?" This Job ceases to
be an unbelievable religious fanatic or a stereotype of the
impossibly humble and devout. He's a man asking the
questions they have pondered, insisting on answers which
do not deny their experiences of life.

Both MacLeish and the Joban poet make use of the
framed tale, even though the frames are as different as the
ways the two writers employ them. A discussion of this
device makes a good starting point for comparison of the
two works. If the Bible you are using does not *show* the
poetic structure, you may need to call attention to the fact
that the folk-myth frame for the *Book of Job* is in prose,
whereas the rest of the book is poetry. (With some classes,
you may want to examine the characteristics of Hebrew

*From *English Journal*, 61 (May, 1972): 658-62. Copyright © 1972 by
the National Council of Teachers of English. Reprinted by permission of
the publisher and the author.

poetry. *Twentieth Century Interpretations of the Book of Job* from Prentice-Hall has an excellent essay on the poetic structure of the book.)[1] As you consider the prose frame for Job, you will certainly want to question why MacLeish devotes two-thirds of his play to incidents which occur in those first two introductory chapters of the Biblical story. Job's misfortunes are related in concise, almost cryptic announcements. What does MacLeish accomplish with his individually realized messengers and the sordid details of the disasters which descend on his protagonist? Is this difference related to a difference in purpose of the two writers?

Students will note that the circus-carnival frame is a much more integral part of MacLeish's drama. They will probably point out that, despite the frequent references to his frame, MacLeish concludes his drama without a "frame closure." The poet of *Job*, on the other hand, returns to his prose-tale frame at the end. Many students object to *Job's deus ex machina* ending until they consider that it may suggest the idea, which MacLeish has stated more explicitly, that man is willing to take up his life again, risk it all again and yet again, despite repeated losses and sufferings. Is this to imply that the two poets arrive at the same conclusion, merely following different routes? Not at all; for a more important question in the two works seems to be WHY the protagonist is willing to go on, and here the two writers part company.

A consideration of the imagery in these works can occupy as much time as is available, for it opens up so many related areas. Let's take just one short passage from each as an example. In the opening scene of *J.B.*, Nickles' song contains imagery which is to be repeated with variations a number of times throughout the play:

---

[1] Edward J. Kissane, "The Metrical Structure of Job," in Paul S. Sanders, ed., *Twentieth Century Interpretations of the Book of Job* (Englewood Cliffs, N. J.: Prentice-Hall, Inc., 1968), pp. 78-85.

> I would not sleep here if I could
> Except for the little green leaves in the wood
> And the wind on the water.

The suggestion of the unending cycle of life, nature's constant renewal of herself—her re-creation—is evident in the "little green leaves." The class will have no difficulty in finding echoes of that imagery when J.B. questions whether we "owe for the greening of the leaves" and when Sarah sings her "Under the grass tree,/Under the green tree" song, or when, in the final scene, she brings in the forsythia which she has found growing in the ashes. (If students are not familiar with the myth of the phoenix, surely you will want to tell them of it so that they can see the significance of the allusion in that new-life-from-ashes image.) The students will find many more examples of the "green leaves" imagery once you have started them on the way. The final line of our quotation is perhaps even more significant, and understanding its significance requires turning to the first chapter of Genesis. There, the first act of creation is recorded as "the Spirit of God moving over the face of the deep." But the Hebrew word for *Spirit* is *ruach,* which is also the word for *wind.* So the "wind on the water" suggests the act of creation itself. And when Sarah comes back in the final scene, she speaks of having left Job with the hope of finding "a way away"; she says she "thought the door opened into closing water"—certainly an allusion to the original watery chaos, a wish for "uncreation." There are other references to both wind and water whose meaning you will want to explore together.

For a different kind of insight, let's take our example of the imagery in *Job* from the sixth verse of Chapter 7:

> My days are swifter than a weaver's shuttle,
> and come to their end without hope.

Here we have an opportunity to point out both the Hebrew delight in word play and the problems facing a translator. The Hebrew word for *hope* is a word very similar to their word for *thread,* so in the original the poet could carry through his metaphor without any loss of meaning, but the translator must choose between abandoning the metaphor and losing the literal meaning. In this chapter, too, we find Job using the Spirit/wind dualism in yet a third meaning of that Hebrew word as he cries out "my life is a *breath*" and again "my days are a *breath,*" reminding us again not only of the original creative act of the "wind on the water" but also of Yahweh breathing into man the breath of life. Surely any discussion of the translator's problem will lead to a consideration of the controversial 13:15, where the King James version renders the verse in the familiar form of "Though he slay me, yet will I trust in him," but recent scholarship indicates that a more exact translation of the original is "Behold, he will slay me; I have no hope." A comparison of several translations, including the New English Bible, is a fruitful activity.

No doubt we will continue to examine imagery even though we direct our attention to other elements of these works. As we turn to the comforters, for example, students invariably ask why MacLeish specifically directs that Zophar be lighting the stub of a cigar; Eliphaz, a broken pipe; and Bildad, a crumpled cigarette. The condition of their smoking materials may suggest the "disrepair" of their philosophical theories, but students want to know whether it matters who is smoking what. I doubt that it does, but I'm glad that it occurs to them to ask the question. One of them may yet find a significance there which I have overlooked. A comparison of the comforters in the two works invites the conclusion that there was a greater consensus in Job's day than in ours regarding the relationship between guilt and suffering. The overlapping arguments propounded by Job's comforters and the difficulty in distinguishing them by any specific point of view are in clear contrast with the disparate personalities and schools of thought represented by their counterparts in *J.B.* Students enjoy trying to provide an additional comforter for

J.B. The boy who wrote this one was especially pleased with the name he had chosen for his comforter and pointed out its significance as a Latin word, just in case I should fail to notice it.

(Job sits alone on the floor, rocking slowly back and forth. Mort, the garbageman, dressed in his grey work suit enters at the left carrying a garbage bag.)

Mort: Say ho! Is anybody home?

J.B.: [Stops rocking] Eh?

Mort: Oh . . . there ya are. [Mort pulls out a folded piece of paper and reads] "J.B., 428 Runnyhill Lane," right?
I'm Mort . . . your trashman.
[J.B.'s face doesn't register at all]
Y'know—Mort. I dump yer trash once a week.

J.B.: Please leave me. Can't you see I've nothing to give?

Mort: Look—I don't make housecalls for a joke.
Yer payment's due. Cough it up.
Sum total: five fifty.

J.B.: Please, please leave me be.
Can't you see
My life has been ruined and diseased?
My house, my car, my family,
My pension, pride and Christianity—
All soured and spoiled.
So soured I haven't anything to give,
Not even trash.

Mort: [Face lighting up]
Yea . . . sorta noticed yer face looked creepy.
But ya just can't expect things at all,
Without trash.
That, ya see, is where it all goes to:
Trash.

J.B.: [As J.B. begins his speech, Mort begins rummaging through his garbage bag]
But I've worked well and strongly
All my life.

I've slaved and made myself a friend
To everyone I've met.
And yet my children—
My five children—gone.
A just God can't allow it!
They couldn't have done
A crime so heinous that they should be slaughtered!
They can't be thrown
On top of a pile like . . .
[Mort pulls a tomato out of his sack]
Like that tomato!

Mort: See this tomato here.
Looks pretty nice; never had a bad thought in its life.
[Mort turns the tomato around]
Look at this rotten spot:
Disease . . . or a worm . . . or some such stuff.
[Throws it in his sack]
No good.
Yer no different than this tomato—
'Cept you hope God'll reward you if yer lucky.

J.B.: [Under his breath] To hell with the rewards.
My skin hurts now!
My chest hurts now!
My misery cries out for help.
My suffering and all I've been through
Cries out: Why?
I have a right to know! It's my life!

It's my life he's puppeteering
And my strings are too tight!
I look for help and you tell me it's a
Cruel and unjust universe.

Mort: Now, wait a minute, Mac—
Everybody and everything gets its chance.
There's no place for injustice:
Everyone gets a life;
Everyone gets it taken away.
Y'have just as good a chance as anybody.

An' as fer God lovin' ya . . .
Well, the way I look at it he's sorta
The Big Trashman.

369

> Everything too old, rotten, or helpless
> He pushes off to the side.
> Anything less than that he leaves alone:
> It might just turn out to be useful
> For Him in the long run.
>
> If things didn't die
> There'd be an awful lot of crap floatin' around in the
>   universe.
> So just because yer turning to trash
> Doan mean the Lord doan love ya.
> I, myself, love every piece of rotten junk
> I collect, and I'm sure God—

J.B.: —O GOD! YOU CALL THIS COMFORT!
> Get out! Your talk of turning God into a chimney sweep
> Doesn't help at all!
> It doesn't help my sores! In fact it makes them worse!
> Get out . . . you're full of . . . garbage!
>   —Mark Cassidy, 12th grade,
>   W. E. Stebbins High School

There are at least three books which will enhance the teaching of this unit. *The Voice Out of the Whirlwind* (Chandler Press, 1960) provides, in addition to the King James version of the *Book of Job*, relevant passages from elsewhere in the Bible; reproductions of five of William Blake's illustrations for the *Book of Job;* critical essays on both *Job* and *J.B.;* the "Prologue in Heaven" from Goethe's *Faust*, where we find a parallel with the opening scene in *Job;* and other interesting materials, including Robert Frost's delightful "Masque of Reason," which students enjoy doing as Reader's Theater.

Besides the Chandler Press book, I find two versions of *J.B.* indispensable. The reading copy from Houghton-Mifflin (1956) serves as our basic text, but the acting version from Samuel French (1958) presents some extremely interesting variations in the dialog. We compare some of the more significant variations, especially the last scene where the acting version gives J.B. a final speech not included in the other. Instead of ending with Sarah's "We'll know. We'll know," MacLeish has J.B. respond, "We can never *know*. . . . We *are* and that is all our answer. We are and what we are can suffer. But . . . what suffers loves." Most students prefer this latter ending, and I challenge them to defend their choice on the basis of both literary and dramatic values. The opening line of the acting version is worth noting, too. Here MacLeish injects the circus-carnival imagery into the dialog immediately as he has a roustabout announce, in cryptic carnival jargon, that trouble is brewing. For the uninitiated, that opening "Hey—Rube!" may have to be explained. If you have time to discuss the specialized jargons of various fields of work, you can take it from there. The acting version also includes a foreword from MacLeish in which he discusses his purpose in the drama and comments on its relevance. You will find here, also, a photograph of one stage setting for the production of *J.B.*

Although a recording of *J.B.* is available, with Christopher Plummer and Raymond Massey playing the roles of Nickles and Zuss (RCA Victor LD6075), I seldom use it in the classroom because the students enjoy their own performances much more. They occasionally want to listen to parts of it on their own, however, in order to decide how best to read a line. I do find the Herbert Marshall recording of *Job* (Caedmon TC 1076) extremely helpful after we have discussed the major ideas of the book.

We have only begun to explore the possibilities for study offered by these two works. Students debate heatedly why Job is satisfied after God speaks to him and which writer has the more satisfying ending. They are seldom agreed on the question of whether Job's God is more real to him than J.B.'s is to his modern counterpart. They enjoy exploring the symbols MacLeish uses, especially the circus setting with its balloons and popcorn, and the names Zuss and Nickles. They appreciate the imagery Job employs as he complains of being used for God's target practice. They discuss the court of law imagery as he yearns to plead his case before Yahweh. They are intrigued by the implication of man's creating God in his own image when Yahweh rebukes Job for wanting to set the terms of God's justice and yet wanting God to be omnipotent and they note MacLeish alluding to the same problem in Nickles' song. We read Gerard Manley Hopkins' sonnet and hear the echoes of Job in his "Thou art indeed just, Lord, if I contend/With thee; but, sir, so what I plead is just." This leads, of course, to the passage in Jeremiah which actually served as a basis for Hopkins' sonnet, and we find there the strong parallels to Job's cries of despair.

There really is nowhere to stop, but after you have introduced students to the possibilities, they will continue exploring for themselves long after you have moved on to other material.

X About a Trespass on a Monument*

Archibald MacLeish
Dramatist and Critic

If the invitation to write this piece means that the drama
editor of *The New York Times* regards my play as crying
out, like Job's boils, for justification, I can only agree. A
man may be forgiven for dramatizing an incident from the
Bible and even for modernizing it in the process. But what I
have done is not so easy to excuse. I have constructed a
modern play inside the ancient majesty of the Book of Job
much as the Bedouins, thirty years ago, used to build within
the towering ruins of Palmyra their shacks of gasoline tins
roofed with fallen stones.

The Bedouins had the justification of necessity and I can
think of nothing better for myself. When you are dealing
with questions too large for you, which, nevertheless, will
not leave you alone, you are obliged to house them
somewhere—and an old wall helps. Which is perhaps why
so many modern plays have proved on critical examination
to be reconstructions of the myths of Greece. That appeal to
precedent, however, is of little use to me, for my "J.B." is
not a reconstruction of the Book of Job—not, at least, a
reconstruction of the kind presently familiar in which the
discovery of the model is part of the adventure. My play is
put in motion by two broken-down actors who believe,
themselves, that the play is the Book of Job and that one of
them is acting God and the other, Satan. When J.B. and his
family appear, however, it is not out of the Bible that they
come.

But justification is still necessary and necessity is still the
only justification I can plead. I badly needed an ancient
structure on which to build the contemporary play that has

*From *The New York Times* (December 7, 1958), Section II, pp. 5, 7. ©
1958 by The New York Times Company. Reprinted by permission.

haunted me for five years past, and the structure of the poem of Job is the only one I know of which our modern history will fit. Job's search, like ours, was for the meaning of his afflictions—the loss of his children, the loss of everything he possessed, the loss of his wife's kindness, who turned upon him in his agony with those ineradicable words, surely the most dreadful ever spoken by wife to husband: "Curse God and die!" There is no reason for all this: no reason the mind, at least, could grasp. Job was, by witness of God himself and twice repeated, "a perfect and an upright man" and his destruction was, by the same unquestionable authority, "without cause." As for ourselves, there can be very few of us who are perfect, but the enormous, nameless disasters that have befallen whole cities, entire peoples, in two great wars and many small ones, have destroyed the innocent together with the guilty—and with no "cause" our minds can grasp.

Questions of Guilt

We attribute these sufferings, except when it is we ourselves who have inflicted them, to the malevolence of our enemies, but even so we are appalled by all this anguish. Hiroshima, in its terrible retrospect, appals us. And we attempt—millions of us, the psychiatrists say—to justify the inexplicable misery of the world by taking the guilt upon ourselves, as Job attempted to take it: "Show me my guilt, O God." We even listen, as Job did, to the Comforters—though our Comforters are not like his. Where Job's Comforters undertook to persuade him, against the evidence of his own inner conviction, that he WAS guilty, ours attempt to persuade us that we are not—that we cannot be—that, for psychological reasons, or because everything is determined in advance by economic necessity anyway, or because we were damned before we started, guilt is impossible. Our Comforters are, if anything, less comfortable than Job's for they drive us from the last refuge in which our minds can hide from the enormous silence. If we cannot even be guilty then there are no reasons.

There are those, I know—because I have heard them—who will object that Job's story bears no true relationship to our own because God has changed in the interval. The God of Job is God the Creator of the Universe, and science, they say, now knows that there is no such Creator—that the events of time progress by an automatism of their own—that the watch winds itself and ticks by its own juggling. The modern God of the scientific age, that is to say, does not control events: not, at least, events in the world of here and now.

Question of Faith

I have no wish, and certainly no competence, to argue the questions of faith that underlie that attitude. But two things may be said from the merely human position. The first relates to the statement that science knows now there is no Creator. Does it? Einstein has told us that he was following, in his plumbings and probings of the universe, the track of an Intelligence far beyond the reaches of his own. The second thing to be said is this: that there has been nothing in human history that has brought mankind closer to the immanence of an infinite creativity than the revelation that the minutest particles of inert matter contain an almost immeasurable power. To me, a man committed to no creed, and more uncertain than I should be of certain ultimate beliefs, the God of Job seems closer to this generation than he has to any other in centuries.

J.B. Himself

My hero, called J.B. after the current fashion in business address, bears little relation, perhaps, to that ancient owner of camels and oxen and sheep. He is not a particularly devout man. But he is, at the beginning of the play, prosperous, powerful, possessed of a lovely wife, fine children—everything the heart of man can desire—and he is aware, as he could hardly help being, that God has made "an hedge about him and about his house and about all that he hath on every side." Not that the name of God is often in his mouth. He is one of those vastly successful American business men—not as numerous now as they were before the Great Depression—who, having everything, believe as a matter of course that they have a right to have everything. They do not believe this out of vulgarity. They are not Babbitts: on the contrary, they are most often men of exuberance, of high animal spirits, of force and warmth. They believe it because they possess in large measure that characteristically American courage that has so often amused Asian and European visitors, the courage to believe in themselves. Which means to believe in their lives. Which means, if their tongues can shape the words, to believe in God's goodness to them. They are not hypocritical. They do not think that they deserve more at God's hands than others. They merely think that they have more—and that they have a right to have it.

Such a man is no better prepared than Job for the sudden and inexplicable loss of everything. And such a man must ask, as our time does ask, Job's repeated question. Job wants justice of the universe. He needs to know the reason for his wretchedness. And it is in those repeated cries of his that we hear most clearly our own voices. For our age is an age haunted and driven by the need to know. Not only is our science full of it but our arts also. And it is here, or so it seems to me, that our story and the story of Job come closest to each other. Job is not answered in the Bible by the voice out of the whirling wind. He is silenced by it—silenced by some thirty or forty of the greatest lines in all literature—silenced by the might and majesty and magnificence of the creation. He is brought, not to know, but to *see*. As we also have been brought.

Troublesome Chapter

And what follows that *seeing* which cannot know? What follows is a chapter of the Book of Job the theologians have tried again and again to explain away. Job is given all he had before twice over—all but his children who are the same in number but more beautiful. And that is not all. Not only is Job *given* his life again: Job *accepts* his life again. The man who was once highest and happiest and has now been brought lowest and made most miserable, the man who has suffered every loss, every agony, and for no reason, moral or intelligible, the mind can grasp; the man who has cried out to God for death, begged over and over to die, regretted the womb that bore him, yearned never to have been, never to have breathed the air or seen the light—*this* man accepts his life again, accepts to live his life again, take back his wife again, beget new children mortal as those others, risk himself upon the very hazards on which, before, his hopes were wrecked. And why? Because his sufferings have been justified? They have not been justified. God has merely lifted into the blazing fire of the imagination his own power and Job's impotence; his own immeasurable knowledge and Job's poor, trembling, ridiculous ignorance. Job accepts to live his life again in spite of all he knows of life, in spite of all he knows now of himself, because he is a man.

Our own demand for justice and for reasons comes to the same unanswering answer. A few days before he died, the greatest of modern poets, and the most modern of great poets, William Butler Yeats, wrote to a friend that he had found what, all his life, he had been looking for. But when, in that letter, he went on to spell his answer out in words, it was not an answer made of words; it was an answer made of life: "When I try to put it all into a phrase I say, 'Man can embody truth but he cannot know it.'" Which means, to me at least, that man can *live* his truth, his deepest truth, but cannot speak it. It is for this reason that love becomes the ultimate human answer to the ultimate human question. Love, in reason's terms, answers nothing. We say that

Amor vincit omnia but in truth love conquers nothing—
certainly not death—certainly not chance. What love does is
to affirm. It affirms the worth of life in spite of life. It
affirms the wonder and the beauty of the human creature,
mortal and insignificant though he be. It answers life with
life and so justifies that bravely tolling line of Shakespeare's
that declares that love "bears it out even to the edge of
doom." Love does: and for us no less than for the ancient
man who took back his life again after all that wretchedness. J.B., like Job, covers his mouth with his hand;
acquiesces in the vast indifference of the universe as all men
must who truly face it: takes back his life again. In love. To
live.

I suppose, if I am really to justify my trespass, I must go
on to say that, though human beings have taken back their
lives over and over, generation after generation since time
began, they have, perhaps, never done so with such
desperate courage as in these past, strange years. Men, our
own contemporaries, have already sat as Job did on an
earth reduced to ash-heap, picking in agony at the cinders
of the bombscorched skin, asking Job's eternal question.
We know that they have sat there. We know that we may
sit there too. But we also know something more. We know
that even men like these can learn, in Yeats' words, to "live
it all again."

Index to Biblical Texts
Alluded to or Discussed

Genesis

2........21, 24-29, 30-35, 89, 95-97, 118-33, 169, 186-87, 190, 226, 239-48, 265, 269-71, 273, 283, 311n

3........24-29, 30, 33, 89, 103-17, 118-33, 169, 186-87, 218, 226, 239-48, 265, 269-71, 283, 315n

4........19, 22, 31, 137-47, 148-53, 255, 310n, 312n, 320-26

5........99, 314n

9........283

11........89, 97, 185, 208-9, 217

12........265, 266

15–35........265, 267-68

16........37, 252, 318n

19........173, 226, 227

21........36, 38-39, 252

22........34, 90n, 198-204, 320-26

28........218, 219, 280

30........318n

32........219, 281, 318n

37........33-34

37–50........89, 253

41........315n

48........332

Exodus

General........38, 89, 190-91, 219, 224-25, 282

1........89

2........31

3........69, 253

4........31

20........89, 311n, 318n, 327

26........155

32........251, 273

Numbers

4........206

Deuteronomy

4........224-25

Joshua

3........281

6........280, 282

Judges

7........282

14–16........255, 258-59, 279

I Samuel

General........71-78, 257-59

1........208

9........83

16........74-75, 282, 283

17........75, 314

18........33, 67, 76

28........82

II Samuel
11........19-20
12........199
13–18........320-26
15........315n
18........65, 249-50

I Kings
3........135-36, 276
10........233
16–22........39-61

II Kings
2........34, 92-94, 109-10,
    113, 265, 266, 281, 283
4........92
5........94
6........93
8........94

I Chronicles
16........206

Esther
General........252

Job
General........48, 90n,
        344-78
1........39
3........75
5........209
9........214
30........208
41........219
42........96, 214

Psalms
1........209
2........317n
8........276, 277

19........318n
23........68, 218
55........305
59........309n
73........316n
74........219
90........233, 310n
104........219
109........80
121........278
137........188-89, 191, 206,
        214, 230, 283
144........310n

Proverbs
9........225
12........226
18........180

Ecclesiastes
9........278
12........276, 314n

Song of Solomon
General........331

Isaiah
1........22
9........69
14........313n
27........219
32........283
40........68, 69, 283
42........69
52........230
53........33, 208
55........225-26

Jeremiah
General........55-62
2........58

7........56
13........312n
20........56
31........62

Daniel
3........283, 320-26
4........318n
5........20
6........283
7–9........46
12........281

Hosea
5........333
11........305
12........333

Joel
2........283

Amos
7........283

Jonah
General........53-62
1........283
2........315n
3........315n

Malachi
3........318n

Matthew
2........47, 235-38
3........38, 107, 111, 116
4........293, 317n
5........21, 68, 70, 219, 222,
    277, 311n, 317n, 319n
6........49, 68, 215-16, 276
7........21, 67, 68, 181, 191,
    218, 283, 300

8........313n, 318n
9........216-17, 219, 280,
    283
10........305
11........283, 314n
12........308n, 315n
13........20, 187-88
14........216-17, 219, 280,
    283
16........275, 277
18........68, 222
19........278, 314n
25........48, 70, 216, 256
26........69, 70, 179, 183,
    228, 286-93, 313n
27........155-57, 168, 210-
    12, 217, 282, 283, 284-86,
    308n, 309n

Mark
1........114, 115
3........164
5........30, 180, 315n
6........263-64
7........215
8........166, 215
9........222, 314n
14........179, 183, 286-93
15........168, 210-12, 284-86

Luke
1........20, 111, 305
2........20, 21, 297-307
3........305
4........283
5........281
6........30, 113, 316n
7........215, 219
8........30, 191, 215
10........199, 215, 218, 274,
    275

13........181
14........283
15........67, 283, 314n
16........281, 283, 315n, 317n
17........283
18........105, 318n
22........179, 183, 286-93, 207
23........68, 205, 210-12, 283, 284-86

John
1........114
2........260-62, 283
3........111-12, 208, 220
5........180, 230, 280
7........22, 318n
8........215, 299
9........214-15
10........300
11........186-87, 293
12........22, 186-87, 208, 283
13........22, 179, 274
14........22, 276, 283
15........180, 204, 237
16........166
17........313n
18........286-93
19........283
20........206, 283

Additional references, of a more general nature, to the Gospels

Crucifixion........30, 69, 158-60, 167, 212-13, 219, 230-34, 236, 237, 265, 268-69, 284-86

Jesus........34, 68, 90, 161-78, 180, 204-9, 223
Judas........35, 179-85, 219-20

Acts
1........34-35
2........20, 69
5........34, 283
16........281
17........34

Romans
2........318n
3........315n
7........315n
11........69, 213-14
12........106, 273
13........315n

I Corinthians
3........310
15........14

Galatians
1........106
6........218

Philippians
2........315n

Thessalonians
2........32

Hebrews
13........69

James
2........33, 315n
5........314

II Peter
1 301

I John
3 . . . . 299, 314n
14 66

Revelation
1 . . . . 256, 283
3 181
5 283

6 . . . . 46, 236, 283
7 . . . . 281, 283
8 282
9 22
13 46
14 . . . . 281, 283
15 281
17 22
20 191
21 . . . . 20, 191, 283
22 281